KICK THE
TYRES

LIGHT THE
FIRES

KICK THE TYRES

LIGHT THE FIRES

One man's vision for Britain's future
and how we can make it work

TORQUIL NORMAN

Copyright © Torquil Norman, 2010

The right of Torquil Norman to be identified as the author of this book has been asserted in accordance with the Copyright, Designs and Patents Act 1988.

First published in 2010 by
Infinite Ideas Limited
36 St Giles
Oxford
OX1 3LD
United Kingdom
www.infideas.com

A CIP catalogue record for this book is available from the British Library

ISBN 978–1–906821–53–1

Brand and product names are trademarks or registered trademarks of their respective owners.

Cover designed by Red Giant Projects
Text designed and typeset by Nicki Averill
Printed in Great Britain

Contents

Acknowledgements

I have many people to thank for helping me to write this book, including, particularly, my children. My daughter Lulu, a gifted writer, helped me on endless occasions with editing my early (often subsequently aborted) texts and of course the version that survived. She and my son Casey have been through my biographical section and made valuable corrections and editing as well as giving ideas for stories and episodes that I might include.

My son Jesse has helped me at all stages and made valuable suggestions on the structure and layout of the book – but I must emphasise not on its contents. As a prospective Conservative candidate for Hereford I suspect he may disagree with some of my conclusions but he has been good enough to allow me to hang myself on my own.

I am deeply grateful to all my children and to Iga Downing for their help and encouragement.

My nephew Alexander, himself a distinguished writer and biographer of the Dalai Lama, made valuable suggestions on the concept of the book and its structure. He also urged me to keep going when things looked a bit bleak.

Matthew Elliott, the distinguished Chief Executive of the Tax Payers' Alliance not only helped with early research on tax and other figures – kindly undertaken by Matt Sinclair – but also encouraged me to continue with the book when on several occasions I was doubtful about going forward. He gave me several valuable introductions and other helpful suggestions regarding layout and contents. Without his interest I might easily have packed the project in.

David Martin, who I contacted when I read his Centre for Policy Studies book *Benefit Simplification* has been generosity itself. I had been struggling for months trying to master the benefit system (failing miserably), and when his book appeared like a heaven-sent life raft to a drowning man, I was in touch with him at once. As well as benefit simplification he kindly helped me work out my general ideas for income tax simplification and a higher threshold. He also encouraged me to continue when I was doubtful about going on.

I must also thank Rupert Darwall, who had written a most constructive paper on reform of the tax credit system and whose ideas I have adopted. I too had been anxious to find a way of changing the system to encourage those in work and to bring about a reduction of the high marginal tax rates involved.

I thank Baroness Frances d'Souza for her encouragement after reading an early draft and her kind introduction to Chris Mullin MP who generously read my section on parliamentary reform and gave me some valuable advice and comments. I take it as a huge act of kindness by both of them. Nevertheless, for their protection, I should add that the opinions expressed throughout the book are my own, or adopted by me.

I am hugely grateful to Aly Boyt who has been a friend for most of our lives. His mother was my wife Anne's best friend from her days at the Slade. He has been a huge help in reviewing my work on prisons and particularly on the drug problem in this country and he gave me valuable advice on references and sources of information. He may not agree with everything I have said but where we differ he is probably right.

I must thank Katy Emck, also a family friend who runs Fine Cell Work, a charity working with prisoners and who gave me some valuable insights into prison life and its reform.

Patrick Barbour, who has for years supported many research organisations and think tanks to carry forward his ideas for reform of many aspects of our society, was extremely kind and helpful with encouragement and ideas for how to proceed with this book.

I am very grateful, also, to Lorraine Faissal a long time colleague at the Roundhouse who helped me with suggestions regarding young people and research on various aspects of prison, particularly relating to women prisoners, and to Marcus Davey, Roundhouse Chief Executive for his helpful suggestions.

I must also thank Ian and David Robinson and their colleagues at City Links in Newham for allowing me to look round their impressive organisation which provides a wide range of services to their local community (and further afield). They are a wonderful example of how to bring real help to inner city people of all ages and needs.

Mark Wolfson, an old friend and long serving Member of Parliament and also a previous Head of Youth Services at the Industrial Society, kindly read an early draft of my book and made many helpful comments as well as giving encouragement, on the slimmest of grounds, for continuing.

I would like to thank a number of researchers who helped me at the beginning: Jonathan McClory, who researched the activities of the entire membership of the UK Parliament and also did valuable research for me on the US system of Select Committees as well as other work, Philippa Ingram, who gave me encouragement when I sorely needed it, made a number of important editing suggestions and helped in several discussions. And also Abi Senthilkumaran and Kes Adamson who helped with research in the early stages, when I was still feeling my way.

Finally I would like to thank, most warmly, my old friend Bobby Monks for his early good advice and encouragement, when I finally found the good sense to try and follow it.

Introduction

My motivation for writing this book grew over the eleven years that I worked on the Roundhouse project. I bought the building in 1996 as a charitable enterprise with the idea of turning it into a major facility for encouraging young people to realise their potential – especially those often failed by this country's education system, with few academic qualifications, but with huge, untapped creative talent. The Roundhouse would provide the necessary equipment (recording studios, media suites and so on), and all the support they needed. At the same time the building would be restored as an even finer performance space than it had been in its heyday, which would contribute towards funding the work with young people.

It took many years to raise the necessary funds, buy the adjacent car park from the Police Estates Division, redesign the building and build, restore and equip it. During the latter six years or so, in spite of the Roundhouse still being undeveloped, we started to work with young people on all kinds of projects, so that we might all gain experience for the longed-for day when we had the fully equipped suite of studios and media facilities that we dreamed of.

During these years I had the real pleasure of meeting and mixing with large numbers of young people from all backgrounds – often very deprived and disadvantaged – who never ceased to inspire me with their good sense, skills and ability. They came from all nationalities (Haverstock school next door, for example, has around 100 first languages), but they all loved being at the Roundhouse because we never tried to tell them what to do, to 'educate' them, or to over-organise them. They were there because they wanted to be there in order to work on creative projects, many of which had to do with music – a medium that the Roundhouse through its history understood well – after all, the ghosts of Jimi Hendrix, Jim Morrison, the Ramones and hundreds of others were everywhere.

Our job was to encourage, even inspire, them and to increase their level of skills and above all their confidence. We soon established a terrific team of people of similar ages to help and support them.

Though my background – well off and very English – could not have been more different from those of these young people, we made firm friends. My life, though privileged, has not been a sheltered one, and the varied and fascinating influences and experiences I have had, as well as a few hard lessons learnt, had given me much to think about through the years and had no doubt influenced me as old age approaches, to 'give something back', in the time-honoured phrase. I should stress that the enduring influence and love of my late wife Anne was key in all this.

Alas, during the period when the new incarnation of the Roundhouse was formed and built, Anne became tragically ill with Alzheimer's disease at the young age of fifty–seven and died in 2007 at the age of seventy. All of us miss her terribly.

I am very aware that I have had enormous privileges and much luck throughout my life from the timing of my birth onwards. I have not tried in this text to disguise the self–indulgent way I lived and the reader will find a rather heavy emphasis on flying in this section, as well as other pleasurable pursuits. I make no apology for what may come across as sheer hedonism at times. I never had much money in my early life but I spent what I had. It is because I made what money I now have rather late in my life, that it never seemed particularly important. It was wonderful to have it but we managed fine for many years when we didn't. Anne taught me to understand that friends and family and creativity are the most important and precious things. (She was much better at living that way than I have been so far.) It had seemed particularly apt to both of us that the first money involved in starting the project was made in the toy industry.

I believe, however, it is reasonable to say that I forged or grew up with a fairly independent cast of mind, which has stayed with me to this day, and which will, I hope, become clear throughout this book. No doubt as with most people, such characteristics are generally formed in the early years of life, and I think that lack of home life, independence and the need to survive my youth and early childhood has stood me in good stead, and also informed many of my views.

The autobiographical section should make clear that I have no formal qualifications for writing the book that follows, but perhaps some knowledge of my background will give the reader an idea of *why* I am writing it and the ideals that inspire it. ★ The views expressed are entirely my own with much research work thrown in.

★ *My purpose in writing this book was to suggest a way of transforming our country's future.*

I added an autobiographical section to give readers an idea of my background. I am told that there is too much about flying in it, but found it impossible to leave out.

The book proper starts on page 77, so do please go straight there if you prefer to read the main book first.

Part 1

How time flies
A glimpse of my life – so far

Chapter 1
Childhood

The last of three sons, I was lucky enough to be born in London at I think a perfect moment in our history – almost to the day, as it turned out. It was in April 1933, a few weeks after Hitler burnt down the Reichstag. I was too young, therefore, to go to war myself, unlike my extraordinary dad, Henry Nigel St Valery Norman (known as Nigel). He had joined up for the Royal Artillery in 1917 through lying about his age and joined up again in 1939 when he was given the job of helping to start the Airborne forces as Commanding Officer of the Airborne Forces Experimental Establishment at Ringway. He later went on to become Lord Tedder's Chief Operations officer in North Africa in 1942 with the rank of Air Commodore.

Alas, in 1943 on his way back to North Africa from England, where he had been helping to plan the invasion of Sicily, he was killed when his aircraft had an engine failure at night and crashed in the West Country soon after take-off.

At the age of five my father had flown me to Austria in his Leopard Moth to spend a year with friends of the family in the mountains at Leogang, since I had contracted a form of TB. Clear mountain air was apparently the only known cure at that time. Georg von Seifertitz, the head of the family, was no friend of the Nazis and was arrested by the police while I was there, but happily, was later released. However, after nearly a year there I was sent home just before the Anschluss.

My mother Patricia, who like many others thought the war would be much shorter than it turned out, decided to evacuate my brother Desmond and me to cousins in the USA. So a few months later we took ship with my aunt Sheila and her two children to New York. Our eldest brother Mark was considered old enough to stay at home and go to Winchester College. I remember that bombs fell on Liverpool the night before we embarked and the ceiling in my hotel bedroom came down in the night.

Our cousin Edith Eustace was a grand old lady who lived in a beautiful antebellum house called Oaklands near Leesburg, Virginia. Her son-in-law David Finley helped build and was the first Director of the Washington National Gallery.

Desmond was sent to school at Portsmouth Priory, which left me with my old aunt Edith. She could not have been kinder, but there was at least seventy years difference in our ages so I suspect I was a considerable nuisance around the house. As a result my closest friends became her warm-hearted, voluptuous black cook Beulah and the other staff who looked after the house; I spent most of my time in the kitchen.

I was sent to the local high school. This would have been perfect, except that my only way of getting there was to be driven by Aunt Edith's chauffeur in her huge Cadillac. The two things that I remember best were the joy of raising and lowering the huge window between the back where I was sitting and the driver, and insisting that he dropped me about three blocks from the school so that I didn't have the embarrassment of turning up there every day in such grand circumstances.

Meanwhile my father's mother, another grand old lady named Menie Muriel FitzGerald had moved to Tucson, Arizona, where she had built a one-storey house to live out the rest of the war. I suspect her views on the war were gloomier than my mum's since she had built the walls of the house extra thick so that they would support a second storey into which she thought the rest of our family might have to move when we lost the war. She suffered seriously from asthma and Arizona was certainly the perfect climate for her.

Inevitably, I suppose, the two old ladies discussed my future and in 1942 at the age of nine I moved to Tucson to live with my grandmother Menie. She was a quite remarkable lady who in her youth had been one of the great liberal authors of the Victorian era as well as being a great traveller. She had thought nothing of hiking through the Himalayas with 100 bearers and her Mannlicher Schoenauer rifle. This, she proudly explained to me, was the finest rifle in the world as it had a rotary magazine, which meant it never jammed. (My two brothers and I were delighted when, a few years ago, she came second in a Booker sponsored prize awarded for the best 100 year old book with her novel *Gallia* and we each received a posthumous present from her of just over £300.) Menie even owned a closed Chevrolet coupé with a rumble seat that opened outside at the back. This became my favourite travelling position.

In every way Menie was a formidable old lady and although we worked out a way of living together, I am sure I was the very last thing she wanted around during the last few years of her life. Of course I was sent off to the local boarding school in the desert, inappropriately named Greenfields (there wasn't a blade of grass in sight), which kept me out of the house during term time at least. During my first year there we went to California together with her companion Martha for the summer holidays. But the following year I was sent to a kind of military boot camp where I recall constantly being in trouble and spending a lot of time marching round the baseball diamond in full kit under the blazing sun.

I should add that for a lot of the time spent with Menie, I was madly in love with her companion Martha, who was a very cosy kind of person. Hugs with Martha have stayed with me all my life! Alas, she betrayed me terribly when she agreed to marry an older man, Ed Vidler, and was kind but firm in rejecting my own advances.

My memories of Arizona are nearly all wonderful. School was a blast. I learnt to ride very well (western style) and even to rope the back legs of young steers and hog tie them. We went for two or three day expeditions into the desert to camp, grilling T-bone steaks over a log fire and sleeping out.

My grandmother arranged for a naturalist student (named Johnny Henderson, I think), from the University to take me out on field trips and we soon became close friends. He was studying snakes at the time and we would catch rattlesnakes and press their fangs into jam jars covered with greaseproof paper to squirt out their venom. We even found water moccasins and gila monsters. Menie gave me a copy of the *Field Guide to Western Birds* and I was soon able to identify everything that moved, as well as all the cacti. This was a wonderful education for an eleven-year-old.

I also spent a summer holiday (I don't remember which) at a sailing camp on Cape May in New England. What I do remember clearly is being put on the Santa Fe express to Chicago with a label round my neck for identification by the people meeting me.

I had a very good school friend, Dicky Peters, with whom I hung about in the evenings and at weekends. It is fair to say that we got up to quite a bit of mischief, mostly stealing comics from the stands in front of the local supermarket and using pea shooters to target sunbathers at the Arizona Inn round the corner. Although we would set off for the local Catholic Church on Sundays we very rarely arrived.

The bad memories were mainly to do with the time the headmistress confiscated our chromium pea shooters and converted them into towel rails, and the all too frequent occasions when I was prevented from shopping in town on Saturday mornings due to some minor misdemeanour.

The other bad memory (in May 1943) was learning from the headmistress about my father's death.

When my grandmother Menie died in March 1945, another friend of the family came out to Arizona to help me and Martha bury her and then returned me to cousin Edith in Virginia before I embarked on the ship home. I remember having my twelfth birthday on the ship and seeing flames at night as some unlucky ships in the same convoy were torpedoed in what must have been one of the last such episodes of the war, which was to end just over three weeks later.

We arrived safely in Liverpool and I was reunited with my mother and my two brothers and introduced to my new stepfather – a lovely man named Bobby Perkins. Almost immediately I was sent off to prep school, Oakley Hall, in Cirencester. The school said (I think as a joke) that they would have trouble getting me into any public school except Eton. But luckily that is where my mother wanted to send me to join Desmond, who had come home from America three years earlier.

So I scraped into Eton at a slightly older age than was normal, but luckily caught up my lost year while there, as my schooling in Tucson must have been better than it appeared.

Luckily, with a little time, my mother and I hit it off wonderfully well as we got to know each other again and established a real feeling of family. She was a wonderful, tall, strong, funny Irish Catholic from County Down in the north, with principles of steel.

My stepfather Bobby was also a very kind and helpful man as well as being an experienced pilot. In the thirties he used to fly into Germany in his Gipsy Moth (a single engined bi-plane) looking at airfields that were being used by the illegal German Air Force for training. He once met Hitler, and on another occasion smuggled home a vile book of anti-Jewish drawings and Nazi propaganda for use in schools, that he found at the Nuremberg book fair. On his death, via my neighbour David Cohen, I donated it to Yad Vasham in Jerusalem where it is still on display. During the war he combined being a junior air minister in Churchill's government with a job as a sergeant pilot, flying Tiger Moths, teaching RAF pilots to fly. During his early service he carried out anti-submarine sorties over the Bristol channel carrying Mills bombs in a kind of basket arrangement. The idea was to throw one at any submarine that showed itself on the surface. He was much involved with teaching Polish pilots and after the war when we lived in Grosvenor Gardens in Victoria he would take me to the Polish Flying Club in a basement around the corner to eat steaks. He said they were either whale meat or horse but I enjoyed them just the same.

I loved my time at Eton mostly due to having the most captivating and inspiring housemaster, Hubert Hartley, who with his extraordinary wife Grizel looked after everyone in the house with great care and affection. Even then they were legends of Eton life.

In spite of the food shortages the post-war period entailed, we were acknowledged as having the best food in Eton thanks to Grizel and Hubert spending their own slender resources to keep fifty of us fed. I do remember, however, that we did from time to time eat the most appalling junket-like substance, made, rumour had it, with fish bones. One of my friends was most upset to find his watch-strap in the stew.

What almost literally saved our lives was that my close friend Reggie Norton, with whom I messed, was from Gibraltar and regularly received food parcels from his family (happily, his uncle was the agent for Nestlé chocolates). They also contained Spanish delicacies, including the most powerful red garlic chorizo sausages in the world. Whenever we cooked them in the passage kitchens we were almost thrown out of the house by our school mates who couldn't stand the smell; we had to delve into our scarce supplies of chocolate to pacify them.

Both Hubert and Grizel had been close friends of my father and I was extraordinarily lucky to have been accepted into their House where my brother Desmond was already in residence. Both Des and I opted for rowing, rather than cricket, in the summer months. Hubert had rowed in the winning British crew during the 1919 Peace Regatta, and was a highly distinguished oarsman. We gained a lot from him and both turned out to be good enough for the Eton eight – Des about three years ahead of me. In fact because of living on the good food of Arizona during the war I had added several inches to my height and found myself in the eight for the long period of three years. Through seniority I also attained the dizzy heights of becoming Captain of the Boats. This in turn contributed to my becoming President of the Eton Society (Pop). Never again would I wield so much influence over my fellow human beings.

There were so many stories about Hubert that it would take a huge volume to cover even part of them. He was famous, for example, for being a bit absent-minded when coaching us from his bicycle. Occasionally while looking at the river with his megaphone in his hand he would run over a loving couple in the grass. Of course he would come flying off his bike but never failed to doff his hat and apologise politely as he stood up, dusted himself down and bicycled on. What the couples thought of this we never found out, but we often heard loud cries of distress.

Hubert said that I had outgrown my strength during my first year in the crew at age fifteen. He said there was only one way of building me up and invited me over to his side of the house after dinner in the evenings where he would give me a bottle of Guinness, or sometimes a half bottle of champagne. Needless to say I had no reluctance in telling him how much better I felt as a result of this novel approach to training.

Even now I often think of one thing Hubert said to me in the house one evening on one of his regular rounds. He asked what I had been doing that afternoon. I said I had gone up to the running track to practice high jumping but the rain had been so heavy that I came back. He said, characteristically clearing his throat, "I think that was very wet of you!" It seemed like a good thought to carry through life.

Hubert and I left his house on the same day (he was retiring and I was graduating) at the end of the summer half in 1951. In order to give him a good send off my fellow librarians (prefects) and I organised that everybody in the house should put their names down for every conceivable school competition and activity that existed. Since we were doing it for Hubert everyone agreed to have go. I also coached the whole house in attempting to win the prize for the best army corps section, and in spite of one of our younger members (who must remain nameless) being totally incapable of keeping step, we won the cup. He had been out of step throughout but during the march past he was so perfectly out of step that no one noticed and he had the sense to keep his arms going with the rest of us.

Someone (I suspect Reggie, who was an excellent boxer) put my name down for the heavyweight competition. I was too afraid of the shame in removing it, so there was nothing for it but to take a few lessons and have a go. I guess I was fairly fit from rowing so wound up with the cup, but also a broken finger. In fact between us all we won more cups than I have ever seen and probably set a record. Certainly Hubert was amazed. There was nothing like enough room in the Library to hold them all.

As a leaving present for Hubert the old boys from the house (one of whom I think knew the manufacturer) and the present members clubbed together to buy Hubert and Grizel an Eton blue Hillman Minx. They were very pleased, but unfortunately Hubert drove it into a ditch fairly soon after he got it and it had to be replaced. But after that it remained with Hubert and Grizel for many years and we saw it often when we visited them in Dorney where they lived.

Chapter 2
National Service

I had been flying with Desmond for several years before I was old enough to get my licence, which I finally did when I reached the age of eighteen, the summer after joining the Fleet Air Arm and going solo. I was lucky enough to have been accepted into the Fleet Air Arm as a pilot for my National Service, in spite of my height which at 6' 7" was 3" taller than the maximum allowed for fitting into military aircraft. This required a certain amount of fibbing during the joining process and I was almost exposed by the Commander (Air) at our induction parade, who accused me of lying when I said I was 6' 2 ½". He exclaimed: "Rubbish, I am 6' 2" and you are at least 4" taller than I am. Chief Petty Officer take this man away and measure him!" So I was marched off but bent my knees during the measuring process. The Chief said 6' 2 ½" and I never heard anything more about it.

In 1952 I rashly blew part of my father's inheritance on a 1933 de Havilland Leopard Moth, similar to the one in which he flew me to Austria, in what I am sure was part of a lifelong effort to be worthy of him. I asked Hubert if he would like to fly down to Gibraltar with me to visit Reggie. At the time I had about forty hours' civilian flying experience and had never flown abroad. To my astonishment he said he would love to, as my father had been the first person to take him over 100 mph in a motor car. I can't think of any other sane man who would have flown with me, but Hubert didn't bat an eyelid.

So we took off from Croydon, but after a few minutes the engine started running rough as we flew south. Somewhat alarmed, I decided to divert to Shoreham where Rollasons looked over the engine and found at least one broken plug lead. With the engine running smoothly again we set off for France in glorious sunshine. I can't remember where we spent the night but the following day we stopped for lunch at Perpignan, where a delightful restaurant had set out its umbrellas on the grass along the edge of the airfield. So we taxied over and parked right next to it and had a delicious lunch.

We paid the bill and left to get into the aircraft when my inexperience led to something approaching disaster. I started the engine and ran it up briefly to check the magnetos when something made me turn round and to my horror I saw we had churned up a huge cloud of dust with the propeller. This engulfed the other diners and several of the umbrellas had been blown down, and people were standing up everywhere shaking their fists. I am ashamed to say that I didn't pause for a second but headed for the runway and took off at once. I don't know how much Hubert took in about all this but our next stop was in Spain and by a miracle we heard no more about it. We certainly avoided Perpignan on the way home.

We made it without further incident to Gibraltar, where Reggie and his family were delighted to welcome us. I recall one further incident on the way home, I think at Oporto, when the control tower sent a fire engine to block the runway as apparently we hadn't paid our landing fee or had overlooked some other formality. We had already started our take-off run when the fire engine appeared and I am glad to say that we got airborne and flew over the fire engine with about five feet to spare. I suppose the best way to learn anything is through experience and in those days communication was far less efficient than it is today! When we got home to Croydon, Hubert declared that he had enjoyed every moment of the flight, particularly the bit at Oporto. I was amazed.

My time in the Fleet Air Arm consisted of almost undiluted pleasure. I was part of a course of, I think, twenty three who had passed a day-long aptitude course at RAF Hornchurch attended by hundreds of aspiring applicants. The course had involved some written work and then a series of tests in which one member of each team took command of the rest of us to solve some idiotic problem. This was usually connected with crossing an imaginary river in the gymnasium with the help of a couple of planks, some pieces of rope and an oil drum.

Somehow these tests were adequate to enable the Navy to select a small minority for flying training. The group selected contained young men from a wide range of backgrounds and I must say it was a very successful exercise in social mixing. Among us were three or four public schoolboys, perhaps half a dozen grammar school boys and the rest from all kinds of educational backgrounds. The one thing that we all had in common was a burning desire to fly.

I started my naval career as an Upper Yardman in bell-bottoms, first at Lee-on-Solent with our time spent learning parade drills and the like, then a further period sleeping in hammocks on the upper deck of HMS Indefatigable in Devonport Harbour. I recall that I had to write to the 4th Sea Lord ("Dear Sir… I have the honour to be your humble servant etc.") for permission to let a 15" grommet into my hammock as I was too tall to fit into the standard issue. He sent me a letter back with the words "Permission granted". During this period I remember polishing the brass on the 'flats' outside the Admiral's quarters but not much else.

From Devonport we were sent for three months to a small air station at Donibristle just across the Firth from Edinburgh for ground school, which was hard work and involved learning everything about aerodynamics, meteorology, navigation, air law and so on. What made it bearable were the evening ferry trips across to Edinburgh to sample the local beer and other delicacies. The weekends were spent, as far as I was concerned, learning how to fly a Tiger Moth at Scone airport in Perth or playing golf, as a close friend of mine from Eton, Nick Wadham, also on the flying course, was a scratch golfer. I tried his patience terribly, but somehow he put up with it.

I remember Nick and Dru Montagu, another Eton friend and scratch golfer, on the flying course ahead of us (he was a cousin of my future wife, Anne) and I used to go to Gleneagles at weekends to play golf but had to stop – at least for a while – when it was discovered that the room numbers we had supplied for payment of the green fees were fictitious.

Having Nick around made the whole experience even more enjoyable. He had a wicked sense of humour and was something of a practical joker and so, with a few others, we did get up to a certain amount of mischief. Two episodes stand out in my mind: the first was when we hatched a plot to take down a large iron road sign which had the words 'Dollar' pointing in one direction and 'Sterling' in the other. After too good a dinner one evening, four of us drove up to the corner where this road sign was displayed, parked the car very close to it and set about trying to get it down with a large monkey wrench. One of us noticed that there was a police station two or three hundred yards up the road, so we hit on the idea of jacking up the car, taking the spare tyre out and, when a policeman was sighted, set to work changing the wheel. The sign proved unbelievably difficult to dislodge and the process of getting it down was very noisy. But it suddenly gave way and fell to the ground with an enormous clang. It was much heavier than we had imagined.

We got the wheel and the sign into the boot in a matter of seconds and returned to base. By a miracle it was never traced back to us and I remember years later puzzling how to get rid of it as it was taking up a lot of space in the London flat that Desmond and I shared while I was at Cambridge and he was working in London. Obviously we couldn't just hand it back to the police, so I am ashamed to say, we just abandoned it at the side of the road on the way to Gloucestershire.

The second episode nearly brought at least one promising career in naval aviation (mine!) to an abrupt halt. Perhaps because of my height I had been deputised to raise the standard at our passing out parade from Donibristle. I cannot recall whose idea it was, but one of us conceived the notion, after a fairly alcoholic dinner on the night before the parade, of raising all the ropes on the flagpole up to the top of the pole, in such a way that there was nothing within about ten feet of the ground. A senior admiral had come down to take the parade and during the ceremony the flag party – myself and two others holding the flag – marched up to the pole. Of course we were unable to find anything on which to attach the flag.

Consternation broke out among the assembled naval officers and the commanding officer stepped forward and instructed whoever had carried out this stupid prank to step forward. Of course nobody moved and so the net result was that all the midshipmen were confined to their quarters until somebody owned up. After some discussion it became clear that the three of us who had perpetrated this horror had no option but to confess. The result was several parades, a good deal of work around the station and a brutal reprimand, with the promise that this would remain on our records for the rest of our (promised to be short) naval careers.

After Donibristle we moved to the RAF station at Syerston, where the RAF took over our flying training. This was a most rewarding period of intensive flying, punctuated by one terrible incident.

Initial training was in an awful aircraft called a Percival Prentice. It had three seats but the third was strapped off with a note saying it was not to be used, as spinning was forbidden if occupied. This meant that if there was weight in the back, the aircraft would not lower its nose during a spin and would therefore spin into the ground. It was also an extremely heavy aeroplane powered by a six cylinder Gypsy Queen engine. In the event of a stop and go landing, the aircraft would barely climb with the flaps down and if the flaps were raised it would sink alarmingly.

I suppose this is what made it a good aircraft for training pilots. Luckily, because of the hours I had already accumulated in the Tiger Moth at Scone I was able to go solo in just a few hours and soon moved on to a far superior aircraft, the T6 Harvard. The Harvard was a powerful American aircraft with a 600 hp radial engine, two seats and a retractable undercarriage. This was the advanced trainer that was to take us up to 'wings' standard. In it we learnt aerobatics, night flying, formation flying and everything else to make us competent operational pilots. Like all American aircraft it was very roomy and I for one found this a great help.

It was at this stage that we had to decide with the help of our instructors whether we would go forward as fighter pilots or as pilots of non-fighter aircraft or helicopters. Most of us were anxious to become fighter pilots but some preferred a slightly more sedentary – but no less difficult – form of flying. Our instructors were helpful in advising which to go for. I was lucky enough to join the fighter section.

Towards the end of our time in Harvards, Nick and I went with the rest of the squadron to Carlisle as part of our training. On the day before we were scheduled to return to Syerston we decided that we would do our training session together and in the course of it fly over to beat up the house of a girlfriend of Nick's who lived in a valley about fifteen miles north of Carlisle. We started our engines and while checking the instruments I discovered that my generator was unserviceable and consequently my battery was not charging. I radioed Nick to say that I thought I should conserve the battery power for the return flight to Syerston the following day and asked if it would be okay for him to do the trip on his own. Of course he replied that it would be fine, so I wished him a good flight, shut down my engine and returned to the mess.

About an hour later we heard the dreadful news that an aircraft had crashed near the top of a mountain in the area where Nick was flying and it was soon confirmed that Nick had been killed. Of course this was shattering news to me and all his friends (he had hundreds) and to his family. I think his father was no longer alive, but his mother Connie was a good friend of my mother's and I went straight down to London to break the news to her. What seemed to have happened was that Nick had flown up the valley below cloud and low over the house where his girlfriend lived and then pulled up to fly over the mountain, but entered cloud and hit the mountain just a hundred or so feet from the top, where the aircraft caught fire. Nick must have died instantly on impact.

I suppose one has to accept with flying that very occasionally there will be accidents and people will be killed. All pilots know this and accept the risks. I have had several friends over the years who have had fatal accidents of different kinds. My father and Nick were the closest to me. I can never forget them, but thank heavens, memories usually filter out the sadness and concentrate on the good times.

My graduation ceremony at Syerston, where we received our wings, got off to an unusual start. Just before the ceremony was due to begin, a two seat twin jet Mk 7 Gloucester Meteor landed with a considerable racket and my two brothers Mark and Desmond got out, dressed immaculately in city suits with bowler hats and the regulation 601 Squadron red socks, to attend the ceremony. Our commanding officer was somewhat taken aback – probably by the suits and red socks – but he smiled and waved them to a couple of chairs.

My next posting was to Lossiemouth on the Moray Firth, the air station where the Navy took over our operational training. This was extremely exciting, particularly for those who had opted to become fighter pilots. It was here that I had the fantastic opportunity of flying ex-Second World War naval Spitfires designated Supermarine Seafire 17's. These aircraft had the larger Griffon engines which were considerably more powerful than the earlier Merlin engines fitted to RAF Spitfires. They handled and flew beautifully. At the time we had no idea of how extraordinarily lucky we were. Today I don't know a single pilot who wouldn't give his right arm and leg to fly a Spitfire of any kind. But we took it all very much for granted.

I remember my first flight well. In the Navy each aircraft was looked after by its own pilot's mate and my aircraft's mate was named Ledbetter. He showed me around the aircraft, pointing out the various features, and I couldn't help noticing a largish pool of oil on the tarmac under the engine. So I asked him about it and he said not to worry; he was keeping an eye on it. In some alarm I asked if it wouldn't be better, rather than keeping an eye on it, to do something about stopping it, and after some discussion he agreed this wasn't a bad idea. So my first flight was delayed to the following day.

Because of my height I found the Seafire cockpit very snug and difficult to move around in. In fact it was over a week before I discovered it had an artificial horizon which was hidden from my view by the gun sight. But wild horses couldn't have prevented me flying it and I had been carefully briefed. There were two obvious things to look out for during take -off, the first being an alarming tendency, because of the Griffon engine's huge torque when the throttle was opened, for the aircraft to swing hard right. So it was important to open the throttle gently and at the same time keep the plane straight by applying left rudder. The second thing was the fact that you couldn't see over the nose while taxiing or during take-off, and the inclination was to push the nose too far forward, which had the effect of knocking the tips of the propeller off on the ground. We soon learnt to take off with the aircraft in a climbing attitude and only one member of the course actually clipped his propeller blades.

There followed three months of pure joy, learning how to fly to operational standards, which included aerobatics, formation flying, tail chases, air to air combat, low flying and everything else associated with learning how best to operate and fly this phenomenal and highly manoeuvrable aeroplane. A few members of the course dropped out for operational reasons, and I think two were tragically killed. One, I remember, hit the sea when it was glassy smooth on his way home one evening.

I myself only had one serious episode, which occurred one day when returning to Lossiemouth after an exercise. About two miles from landing, my engine started to run rough and the oil pressure began to fluctuate wildly, eventually settling at almost nothing. I called for an emergency straight in approach and the engine kept running just long enough for me to reach the field and land. I pulled up on the runway, at which point the engine stopped. The aircraft was towed to the hangar and when we opened the cowling I found that one piston had burst through the side of the crankcase, leaving a great hole and oil all over the place. I was amazed that it had continued to run even for two or three minutes on eleven cylinders.

After three months of pure heaven (albeit a rather tiring heaven) at Lossiemouth, life grew even better. We moved on to Culdrose, another glorious air station on the coast near the tip of Cornwall. Here we were introduced to yet another even faster and more powerful World War II aircraft, the Hawker Sea Fury. The Sea Fury was a lighter naval version of the RAF Tempest; the main differences were that it had folding wings and a large hook, which stuck out below the tail.

It was roomier than the Seafire and far more powerful. The Bristol Centaurus radial engine was silky smooth and produced nearly 3000 bhp. The top speed was said to be 435 mph and at one stage it held the world air speed record. It was far heavier than the Seafire and because it didn't have the same tendency to float over the deck when landing, it was infinitely superior for deck landings.

We spent the next few months practising air to air firing with live ammunition against a banner, air to ground dive bombing with 16 lb rockets, formation flying and above all, deck landings. Initially these were dummy deck landings on the airfield and then actual deck landings at sea. Meanwhile, incredibly, at weekends I was allowed to take a Sea Fury home to Gloucestershire, landing at Aston Down about six miles from where we lived.

Deck landings in those days were not at all easy and took a great deal of practice to carry out successfully. On the airfield, they rigged up a section at the end of the runway the size of an aircraft carrier, with arrester wires and barriers and a position for the batsman, exactly as it would be on HMS Illustrious where later on it would be for real.

The problem with this practice arrangement was that it was so easy. It was impossible to blank out the sight of the airfield on both sides of the make-believe flight deck. So training this way and with the batsman's help, we became very proficient at this kind of deck landing. The essential thing was to learn to stop looking at your instruments and concentrate with total focus on the batsman. His job was to manage your speed, height and attitude through a few simple signals transmitted via the bats in his hands. Height and attitude were easy for the batsman to manage but he was also fantastically good at estimating your speed. He did this by gauging the position of your horizontal tail plane as it appeared behind the wings and was uncannily accurate to within one or two knots – which was just as well since you couldn't afford to take your eyes off him for even a split second without causing total disaster.

When we transferred to HMS Illustrious itself, it was an entirely different matter. First of all the carrier appeared to be about the size of a postage stamp from just a few hundred yards away. The few yards on which you were supposed to land was of course at the stern of the carrier, and in front of this were two wire barriers and, as often as not, a collection of parked aircraft. This area looked minuscule and one's first reaction on seeing it was that the whole business was utterly impossible. The situation didn't look any easier when you noticed that the stern of the carrier could be going up and down by anything up to 15 feet. It was the batsman's job to make sure that you arrived pointing in the right direction, at the right speed and about 10 feet above the deck just as it was starting to go down. If you hit it on the way up you would be bounced over the barriers and into the parked aircraft at about 100 mph.

The other difficulty, of course, was that when you were flying slowly on the approach to the carrier, the carrier itself was completely blocked from view by the huge engine sticking up about 12 feet in front of your head. The only thing you could see, and only if you were perfectly positioned, was the batsman himself on his platform on the extreme left-hand edge of the carrier's stern. (This was in the years before some bright spark invented the angled deck which simplified the whole process radically.)

The idea was that the batsman would position you exactly over the end of the carrier, at which point he would signal the cut and you would close the throttle instantly. The nose of the aeroplane would drop and you had a split second as you saw the carrier and the deck in front of you to kick the aeroplane straight with the rudder pedals and simultaneously pull the stick hard back into your lap to bring the tail down onto the deck. At which point you arrived like a ton of bricks and the aeroplane stopped in about 50 feet, hung up on an arrester wire.

So the first time we flew off from Culdrose to find HMS Illustrious somewhere in the Bay of Biscay was a memorable occasion to say the least. It was also probably the first time that I had experienced total numbing fear. We were due to stay on the carrier for a week to practise deck landings. Illustrious had been involved with great distinction in the war against Japan and the island – the part of the carrier which stuck up on the side of the flight deck – had been badly dented by a kamikaze pilot. It had also been damaged below the waterline. Instead of repairing it, it was considered easier simply to close down the watertight doors on the lowest deck, which meant that the ship was carrying a good deal of water around with it all the time.

For us it meant that in very light winds it couldn't maintain sufficient wind speed over the deck for us to be travelling slowly enough at the time of landing, or fast enough into the wind at take-off. We needed something like 30 knots over the deck for our landing speed over the carrier to be reasonable. When new, the carrier was designed to do 25 knots, but I think Illustrious in her then condition struggled to get to 20 knots.

Most of us arrived safely but one or two sensibly decided that discretion was the better part of valour and decided that deck landings were not for them. There were several incidents among the rest of us, two of which were serious and resulted in the loss of two good Sea Furies.

The first occurred to my dear friend David Cockburn who managed to get himself into the terrible position of being low and slow on the approach (something we had been taught to avoid like the plague) and when he tried to open the throttle to correct this, the torque of the engine was so enormous that the aircraft simply flipped over onto its back and plunged into the water about 100 feet behind the carrier. David told me afterwards that he managed to undo his straps and get out of the aircraft just at the very moment it got dark and he thought everything was all over for him. Thank heavens he came out of it with no damage at all to himself.

The second episode involved me. As I was being boosted off the deck by the catapult I heard a loud bang behind me at the tail of the aeroplane and subsequent inspection on a fly-by established that the hook had fallen down while I was still on the catapult. We later found out that the heavy spring (which pressed the hook onto the deck so that it could catch the arrester wires during the landing) had broken, meaning that the hook simply popped up when it hit the deck and avoided catching any of the wires.

The result of this was that on landing, my aircraft bounced into the air, caught one wheel on the barrier, cartwheeled over with the engine hitting the deck, and caught fire. The aircraft eventually slid backwards up the deck – luckily the right way up. I had never been much good at getting out of the aircraft during practices but I must say on that occasion I broke all records.

As I was running to the side of the carrier, because the aircraft was on fire and I thought it was going to blow up at any moment, the flight deck officer (whose name, Normand, was similar to mine) passed me, running towards the aircraft. When he reached it he jumped in and turned off the fuel and electrics. In my haste and fear this had never even occurred to me, to my eternal shame. Eventually the foam extinguishers put out the fire and the aircraft was bulldozed over the side. I managed to keep the offending arrester hook and a photograph, taken by an army officer who was our guest for the day, as a reminder, but the drinks were certainly on me that night.

I didn't feel a bit shaken by the episode at the time and was laughing about it while the Surgeon Commander took my arm and walked me around the deck. Apparently it is standard practice on such occasions for the spare aircraft to be wheeled out and the pilot who had the accident to then complete a further deck landing to demonstrate that he hadn't lost his nerve.

Sure enough our rattly old spare aircraft was brought up on the lift and I was strapped in. By this time it was starting to get dark, the wind seemed to be getting up and I felt the deck heave underneath me as I was hooked on to the catapult. But in no time I was airborne and being instructed to make my approach back to the carrier. If I was frightened on my first deck landing it was as nothing compared to the way I felt this time. I was so tense I could hardly control the aeroplane at all, and how I managed to get it back on deck in one piece I shall never understand.

The irony of it was that all this occurred on Friday the thirteenth! I have never been able to work out whether this was an unlucky or a lucky day for me. I rather think the latter, as I am still alive to write this.

Along with others on the flying course, I volunteered to join our Sea Fury Squadron aboard HMS Ocean, which was stationed off Korea. My mother was concerned about this decision. I didn't want to worry her and explained that this is what I had been trained for and was paid to do, and eventually she agreed, albeit reluctantly. Of course I now understand she had been thinking about my father, her husband, and didn't want to lose another member of the family. Of course being young and a keen pilot, I was excited as well as a little daunted by the prospect of fighting in Korea. During training we had heard quite a bit on the grapevine about conditions there. One of our pilots had been credited with shooting down a Chinese Mig 15 which was quite an achievement, given the 200 mph speed disadvantage.

As it turned out the Korean War ended about three weeks before I was due to go out and almost immediately I received a telegram from my mum saying, "Bad luck. Please report to Trinity College Cambridge on X date in October". At the time I was very disappointed, but now of course, I consider it a great stroke of luck and the timing of my birth had paid off again.

Chapter 3
University and the Royal Auxiliary Air Force

From the first time I'd heard of it, and encouraged by my two brothers who were already members, I had wanted to join them in 601 Squadron. As soon as I could, I applied to be transferred from the naval air reserve to 601 (County of London) Squadron, Royal Auxiliary Air Force, based at that time at North Weald. The Auxiliary squadrons were operational squadrons that flew only at weekends and during a two week summer period, which, excepting one year, we always spent in Malta training with the US Air Force. 601 Squadron had a very distinguished war record, having fought throughout the Battle of Britain, then at El Alamein in North Africa, at Malta and in Italy in support of the invasion forces. Because of 601's history of flying to the rescue of Malta during the war (it was one of very few RAF squadrons to have been winched onto a US aircraft carrier, the USS Wasp, in the Clyde, and to have flown off it to Malta when it passed Gibraltar) we were treated like kings when we arrived for our summer camp and royally entertained by many of the local families.

I only remember one incident where one of our aircraft was damaged and this involved my brother Desmond, a superb pilot and one who (rightly) believed in flying aircraft to their limits. He was among the very few people who actually enjoyed doing an outside loop (called a bunt) in a Meteor. Apparently he performed one on this training flight at Malta and somehow pushed the aircraft to its limiting speed. In the extreme heat, the cockpit canopy exploded above his head, leaving Desmond exposed to the elements (but thank heavens protected by the front windscreen) at something like 500 miles an hour. If the ejector seat had accidentally operated, as it so easily might have (it was operated by pulling a flap over one's eyes from behind one's head), I think the worst would have happened. When the canopy left it took a chunk out of his starboard wing and also the elevator. Desmond somehow flew it back to Takali in one piece, arriving back at the mess slightly shaken, his eyes bloodshot and red. Happily there were no further consequences: Des was flying again the next day and his eyes recovered naturally over the next week or so.

We were known as the millionaires' squadron because of our very distinguished members from before the war. Apparently when the Auxiliary Air Force was set up, Lord Edward Grosvenor, the first Commanding Officer of 601, interviewed potential members from among his friends, in White's Club, which was clearly the way things were done in those days. My father, Nigel Norman, had also been CO in the late 1930s.

But there were precious few millionaires in it when I joined. In fact most of us were utterly skint, with overdrafts that were continually being stretched by wild Saturday nights out in London. I won't dwell on the excesses of youth except to say that most evenings started at the Antelope pub near Sloane Square, moved on to Bentley's in Swallow Street for a dozen or so West Mersey Essex green oysters – the most delicious I have ever tasted – and wound up all too often at the Bag of Nails in Swallow Street, where the girls had become good friends of the entire squadron – occasionally even platonic friends. Richard, a fine man and friend of ours, who opened the oysters at Bentleys, had (I think) nine sons, all of whom were in the RAF, and when we were awarded our Squadron banner by Prince Philip (still our Honorary Air Commodore) in a parade at Buckingham Palace, we invited him and his whole family along. He was as proud as any of us.

I can't imagine a more convivial group of people to be with than the pilots and ground crew of 601 Squadron. It was also amazing to be in the same squadron as my brothers Mark and Desmond (I think, too, it may have been unique in the annals of the Royal Air Force to have three brothers flying simultaneously in an operational fighter squadron).

At the time of my joining, 601 was equipped with Meteor IV twin jet fighter aircraft from the end of the war, but soon after we were upgraded to the more powerful Meteor VIIIs. We also had one two-seat Meteor VII. I remember turning up as the squadron new boy and being introduced to everyone, after which the commanding officer Chris McCarthy-Jones sent me straight out for an hour's dual in the two seater (I had never flown a jet aircraft before). He then showed me over the single seat Meteor IV. He asked how tall I was and then told me he'd got some bad news. When I enquired what it was, he said that I couldn't use the ejector seat as if I did I would lose both legs from 4" above the knee. I asked him how I would get out of the aircraft if I needed to and the answer was: "You eject the canopy, turn the aircraft on its back, undo your straps, put your foot on the stick and push hard. You'll come out like a cork!" So I resolved, of course, never to use the ejector seat and in fact during the nearly four years I was in 601 I was lucky not to have had to think of it at all.

A phrase used by RAF jet pilots came back to me and inspired the name of this book. "Kick the tyres, light the fires, the last one up's a sissy" (or words to that effect) was a frequent description of one's feeling when, dismally hung over after a late night and contemplating foul weather, the time came to take to the air. The procedure was to clamber into the cockpit, strap yourself in (if necessary with help from the ground crew), switch on the oxygen to emergency high flow, start the engines (again with help) and as the aircraft started to move forward, one's head miraculously cleared and all was well with the world again. Roughly what the country needs at the moment!

Most weekends, then, I would leave university at Cambridge and go down to North Weald to fly. We did everything required of an operational squadron, including air to air gunnery practice with one of us towing the banner, exercises with regular RAF squadrons, formation flying and the rest. Towing was interesting as the attacking aircraft was using live ammunition and hits were counted on the banner after landing according to the colour of the bullet holes (from the paint applied when the ammunition was loaded). If the towing pilot could hear the sound of gunfire it meant that the attacking aircraft was pointing more or less straight at him, which led to some interesting radio exchanges!

We were all completely devastated in March 1957 when the government – in the form of Duncan Sandys – decided to close down the auxiliary air force as an economy measure. From a personal point of view I could understand their reasoning. The auxiliary air force was undoubtedly the finest flying club ever created and to be able to fly those aircraft every week with a group of close friends at her Majesty's expense was undoubtedly an extravagance. But from a national perspective, to have a number of highly trained, highly motivated squadrons available to support regular squadrons in times of trouble must in fact have been a very economical way of strengthening our armed forces. I notice that one or two auxiliary squadrons have since been reformed and have served with distinction in Iraq and Afghanistan – but not in the air.

I would like to explain my close relationship – even dependence – on my brother Desmond, who was undoubtedly one of nature's great creations. He was like the father I never had, as well as an older brother, fellow hell-raiser and a huge part of my life. He was nearly four years older than me and so naturally taught me many things. He introduced me to motorbikes (he was fanatical about them, owning a 1938 International Norton, a Tiger 100, and a Square Four Aerial among many others) and to flying, since his love of motorbikes was matched only by his love of aircraft. We had many memorable flights together, including a run to Barcelona to see the Spanish Grand Prix in his Miles Gemini and quite a few trips to Toussus-le-Noble in Paris, on a couple of occasions taking along our bank manager Frank Payne. Frank was a real friend and also allowed us ridiculously high overdrafts. On one occasion I asked Des about the cost of taking him and he replied that it would probably cost around £200, but it was worth thousands! The problem arose when Frank retired and was replaced by a young, new broom kind of manager. It took us years of hard graft and misery to get our overdrafts back to within reasonable limits.

Des was, in his way, one of the funniest men alive. His sense of humour was the dry, deadpan kind and utterly hilarious. It is impossible to reproduce but a flavour of it was exemplified in a flying trip to Rheims. We had flown down there to join a group of French and other pilots on a tour of the Champagne country laid on by Moët et Chandon. I was flying the Leopard Moth with a couple of my children and Des the Tiger Moth with his stepdaughter. We got up in the morning and went to the airfield to find a huge long table set out in the sunshine in front of the club house on which were about fifty glasses and several wine buckets of iced Champagne. So everyone had a few glasses and we set off for Epernay. When we arrived, there was another table of Champagne and we had a few more glasses. Although the glasses were fairly small I asked Des how he was managing with all the Champagne (he was flying my Tiger Moth!) and I think it is not unjust to say that he was quite fond of a tipple – usually whisky. He paused a moment and replied, "Absolutely fine – I am exercising iron discipline." I asked him what this meant and he said, "I am limiting myself to five glasses at every stop." He then added, rather sheepishly, "But I am afraid I haven't been very successful at keeping to my resolution!" Luckily there was only one more stop but general flying discipline on that trip became rather ragged, evidenced by the French and British pilots taking off simultaneously in opposite directions and a German pilot in a Great Lakes biplane, with my son Casey in the front seat, flying under some high tension wires.

Des had an extraordinary career in aviation, beginning with the wooden aircraft he used to build as a boy, for which our mum sewed linen for the wings. He would then run down the hill trying to take off. On one occasion he asked her to tow him across the field for a glider take-off in our old Standard, which resulted in a broken spring and a furious mother. He did his national service in the RAF and then went to the de Havilland Technical School where he met John Britten. Together they formed Britten Norman and designed and built one of the first hovercraft (the Cushioncraft) and an amazing succession of aircraft, including the Islander, the Trislander, the Fieldmaster (a crop sprayer), The Firecracker (a candidate for the RAF turbo trainer) and the Freelance (a touring aeroplane) of which some bits still remain (my nephew Alexander is rebuilding one to flying condition). Des's and John's accomplishment was almost unique in modern times in the British aviation industry.

Des and John, with an Australian friend Jim McMahon, also designed and built the first and best rotary atomizer for use in crop spraying, and even started a company called Crop Culture with which they went all over the world to spray crops, often in Tiger Moths. They also flew several Tiger Moths across Africa to India and back, by filling the huge hopper that normally carried the chemicals, with petrol (for the long legs across the desert). I remember one Farnborough airshow when Des and John had five of their aircraft performing; truly an amazing record for such a small team. Tragically, John died at a very young age, leaving Des to continue with the design and building of aircraft. He was much loved by everyone in the aircraft industry and whenever I fly anywhere in the world I am always asked if I am related to Desmond. He died about five years ago and I miss him terribly.

The other person who filled the role of stand-in father to me in my youth – and wonderfully well he did it – was our beloved woodman Ben Legg. He was a dear, small, funny man who had married my grandmother's dairy maid Doris before the Second World War. They both lived in a little cottage near our house.

Ben used to take me out to do the round of his snares, picking up rabbits. We would spend time together in the woods that he looked after beautifully. He taught me a lot about nature and was a famous character to everyone for miles around. He had a wealth of funny stories that he told in his inimitable way. He was famous for them. He was a regular visitor on his bicycle to the local pub in Colesbourne, where he was friends with everyone. He and my wife Anne loved each other dearly and he made her laugh to the point of tears. He was a terrific friend to all our children who loved him in exactly the same way.

His father had been a famous poacher and Ben used to tell us of the occasions when he was very young and his father used to wheel him into Cirencester in his pram. The real purpose was to deliver to Charlie Barnett the local fishmonger (and famous English cricketer) a load of rabbits and pheasants that he had stashed under the pram mattress.

Ben taught me to shoot and to fish and to catch crayfish in the river. He used to rear pheasants in the woods for my whole family, brothers, stepfather, uncles and so on, to come down and shoot, and was in constant trouble with the local hunt. Ben wouldn't allow them near the woods during the shooting season and if a fox was so foolish as to approach his young birds it was instantly despatched.

On one occasion our neighbour was shooting young pheasants which had jumped over the wall into his field just outside the woods. He laid down his gun to go and retrieve a wounded bird, and Ben, in his fury at losing what he considered to be one of *his* birds, picked up the twelve bore and broke it in two pieces on the wall. This of course was a terrible thing to do as the gun even in those days was very valuable. Of course our family had a whip round to pay for the repairs but Ben was taken to court and although we gave all kinds of character support he was found guilty and fined and bound over to keep the peace.

The *Daily Express* somehow picked up the story and a photographer came down and took a picture of Ben, outside his cottage, holding an old antique musket, which was widely publicised. Ben got loads of letters from friends all over the country. One friend in Wales wrote to the effect that he always suspected Ben would be had up by the law for some offence connected with pheasants, but never in his wildest dreams had he ever conceived that it would be for defending them!

Ben lived until the age of about eighty when he developed cancer and quite quickly died. Doris was so distraught that she died in the local nursing home about three months later. They were both dear friends to Anne and me, and Ben taught me so much about how to behave and the importance of nature from the age of five onwards, with gaps of course during my time in Austria and during the war. He was a perfect gentleman.

At Cambridge I studied economics for one year and then law. I had the great good fortune, very soon after arriving there, to meet a lovely American man, Bobby Monks and his equally lovely wife Millicent, who have become two of my dearest friends. Bobby was a Fiske scholar from Harvard and went on to become a distinguished lawyer, administrator of US Government pension funds and then a writer and powerful advocate of reforms to improve standards of corporate governance. Our children and grandchildren are also close friends, and the friendship has given a precious dimension to all our lives.

At Bobby's suggestion, and also because I discovered that my grandfather Henry Norman had been there, I decided to apply for a year at Harvard between my last two years at Cambridge. My then CO at 601 Squadron, Peter Vanneck had also spent a year there and suggested that the best way to apply was to telephone the Dean of Admissions on the transatlantic wire and explain the connection with my grandfather, since Harvard greatly respected family ties of this kind. The Dean was friendliness itself and told me that there was a long-standing link between Trinity College, Cambridge and Winthrop House at Harvard for an exchange student. It hadn't, apparently, been taken up in years and he couldn't see any reason why I should not apply. So I applied at once, even though no money was involved and Britain was still subject to severe exchange controls.

I had a marvellous year at Harvard and made some terrific friends. Bobby, who by this time was at the Harvard Law School, had been in both the Harvard and Cambridge boat race crews and so we often rowed together, recreationally, in a pair on the Charles River. We would spend weekends either at Harvard playing touch football and going to Saturday football games, or in Maine, where Millicent's father lived and where she and Bobby had a house. I studied a great deal of American history and also enrolled in law courses, which expanded and contributed to my law degree at Cambridge.

That summer I worked at various jobs in Canada including laying a pipeline, logging and even driving a heavy truck for the aluminium smelter at Kitimat. I wound up at Prince Rupert near the Alaska pan handle, where I had a great job helping to survey an airfield site which was on an island about a two hour boat ride to and fro each day from the mainland. I started as an axe man but moved on to operating the transit (theodolite). The pay was fairly good but of course the four hour boat journey was included, so the hours were long, which led to a hefty pay packet at the end of each week. The gang I worked with were fairly rough types, one of whom was a German who explained that he had designed dozens of Luftwaffe airfields on the Russian front and another was, I think, a Lithuanian, who had been conscripted to work on them. Needless to say there were quite a few arguments amongst us on the trip out, but it was a good deal quieter on the trip home, about ten hours later after a hard day's work.

To get out to the west coast I had answered an ad in the local newspaper in Boston for someone to fly a Piper Tri-Pacer to California. I signed up for it but found it extremely uncomfortable as the bottom edge of the dashboard pressed sharply into my legs. I finally landed in California having picked up a fellow traveller en route and also having been cleaned out at the tables in Reno. I then hitchhiked to Seattle where I had to wait a few days for the passport I had left behind in Boston to arrive.

In the course of making my way north I hitched a ride on a freight train (something I had always dreamed of doing since childhood, having watched too many westerns) on the outskirts of Vancouver, heading for Williams Lake. I hung about the freight yards until I found a train that looked like it was about to pull out. It was all going well until some time in the evening the train stopped suddenly in the middle of nowhere, shunted mine and several other wagons onto a siding, and then steamed on. I had a very cold, uncomfortable and rather frightening night listening to whatever beasts were in the forests around me. When morning finally dawned I hiked a couple of miles across the valley to the road and was very pleased to get a lift in a passing car.

Near Williams Lake I spent a week with two friends from Harvard, twin brothers named (as I recall) Benny and Roddy Dane. Benny and Roddy had a lodge and a large ranch where they indulged in the mad sport of hunting grizzly bears — with bows and arrows! I had been invited to join them. The fourth member of the party was an experienced hunter named Dave who watched over everything with a powerful rifle. I was simply an unarmed spectator.

At the start we marked out a huge triangle about ten miles long on each side and Dave shot a wild horse in open country at each point of the triangle. When three horses had been shot we went back to the first and set up camp in a sheltered position downwind. During the three days it had taken us to do this, the first horse had blown up like a balloon, which is apparently when it is at its most appetising for grizzlies. However, after three days of lying out in the sun and being bitten to death by black flies and mosquitoes there was no bear to be seen, and since I was running out of time I had to say goodbye and leave them to it, not without, I admit, a strong sense of relief. I heard later that a few days afterwards they had shot at least one grizzly bear and the hunt had been highly successful.

The system of drinking in Canada in those days was a little strange. In Williams Lake, for example, there were only two beer parlours in town and the queues outside them lengthened rapidly in the evenings. Once inside, two beers were put down in front of each of us, which we paid for and when those were finished, two more. After drinking the second pair we were thrown out and had to start queuing again at the other beer parlour. The town gradually filled up with drunken loggers and Indians, The lucky ones among us made it back to camp and the unlucky ones were thrown into jail for the night.

When the time came to head south I answered another ad, this time in the Prince Rupert paper and agreed to drive a woman and her two young children in their car from Prince Rupert to Vancouver, where her husband was a fisherman on a halibut boat. This turned out to be very trying since the children wouldn't keep quiet for a moment and the woman couldn't control or entertain them at all. I began by stopping the car when the racket became unbearable, leading to all kinds of trouble with their mother. Eventually I hit on the idea of going fast if they were quiet but slowing down as the noise level increased until they would suddenly notice that the car was merely crawling along this huge highway and being overtaken by all and sundry. They would then quieten down and finally some kind of peace was established.

I returned to Cambridge to complete my final year. What with flying (I still had my Leopard Moth), rowing and generally enjoying myself, the time flew by. I guess the logging must have toughened me up because I managed to scrape into the Cambridge rowing crew and we notched up a fine victory over Oxford in the Boat Race that year. I am pleased to say I have since attended both our fortieth and (recently) our fiftieth anniversaries, with the entire crew present, and we are keeping our fingers crossed that we will all make it to the sixtieth!... As if! Our crew was made up of a very fine bunch of men including my particular friend and room-mate Jim Meadows, a tall southerner who went to Yale and whose father after the race donated our own oars to each of us, which was a very generous gesture. Jim lives in Nashville and we are still firm friends.

During this last year I met a furniture manufacturer in Cambridge, I forget his name, who owned a de Havilland Rapide with eight seats, which he very kindly lent to me, in an act of reckless generosity, so that I might take some friends down to the 24 hour motor race at Le Mans. We left with four women and three other men and arrived at Le Mans in good time for the race but in lousy weather.

We had agreed that the women would sleep in the tent that we had brought for them and the men would sleep in the plane, which I must say because of the rather steep angle was extremely uncomfortable. We pitched the tent in the shelter behind the starboard engine. The women asked us to wake them in the morning but as it was pouring with rain at that time, we were rather reluctant to go outside for this purpose. We had deliberately not tied the guy ropes too securely, so agreed that the best way to wake them was to start the starboard engine. The engine roared into life and the tent shuddered briefly and then went flying off down the field in the slipstream, leaving the four girls, semi naked and utterly exposed to the elements. I have never seen such fury in four otherwise rational human beings. One of them, when she failed to open the locked door to the plane, actually tried to push her hand through the fabric so finally we had to open the door and let them in to avoid serious damage to the aircraft. In the end peace broke out and we all enjoyed the huge fun-fair and the motor racing, only marred by one terrible tragedy.

It was the year (1955) when Pierre Levegh, driving a Mercedes, blew a tyre as he was passing the crowded grandstand. The car flew off the track killing Levegh and eighty-two spectators and wounding one hundred more. Although we were standing only about 200 yards from the accident the crowds were so thick that we only heard the details of it later on the news. On the Sunday afternoon we flew back to Croydon to drop everyone off, and to prepare for the upcoming Trinity May Ball.

I had persuaded a good friend named Charlie Dean to help us to organise the ball. He was a neighbour of ours in Gloucestershire, having retired from his work as a most distinguished butler to some of the grandest families in Britain. My mother and stepfather had an arrangement with him to come and help at table whenever Bobby had distinguished guests for dinner, as he often did as a result of his political work. Charlie was not only a terrific butler but also a lovely man and a close friend to all of us. He also had a wicked sense of humour. When I asked if he would help us with the May Ball he agreed with alacrity and oversaw the buying of suitable provisions from Fortnum and Mason's. I remember his asking if he should include some Château d'Yquem and I said why not throw in a couple of cases. I only mention this to demonstrate how different the 1950s were to the present time. Today twenty-four bottles of d'Yquem would cost thousands of pounds, but in those days I don't think we considered them a particular luxury and they were nothing like as expensive, more on a par with any other decent wine. We piled all the food and drink into the Rapide, and Charlie and I flew up to Cambridge together. The flight took far longer than it should have done as Charlie was constantly asking me to divert over some large house or other where he had spent time as head butler. He adored the flying and having toured every corner of Hertfordshire and Essex at about 500 feet, we eventually arrived in time to prepare for the May Ball dinner.

I had not been a very diligent student during my last year because of all these extracurricular activities, although I had attended most of my lectures. So I was relying rather too heavily on my uncle's advice about attending university: "It's not the work you do that's important – you can do that in a few weeks – but everything else." But in fact I was relying even more on my friend and neighbour Francis Francis Jr., an active member of the Cambridge Footlights who was also studying law and had a brilliant set of notes, which he kindly loaned to me in exchange for regular coffees or snacks on our way to and from the library. I asked him what grade he was expecting and he replied "a first" as though it was inevitable. In fact we both got seconds and I shall always be grateful to him because, without his help, I know I wouldn't have done as well. Of course he was very disappointed, while I was over the moon.

Chapter 4
And so to work

Because of the time I had spent in America I wanted to go back to work there, and having read a biography of JP Morgan and studied the period of America's great industrial past – the Carnegies, Rockefellers, Vanderbilts, Henry Ford and so on – I decided to try and get a job at JP Morgan & Co, the celebrated New York bankers. Through a family friend I got a letter of introduction and was accepted.

So I spent four and a half highly formative years at 23 Wall Street, starting in the mailroom and working my way through all the bank's departments until I reached the Foreign Department. Under a very nice man, Sidney Butler, I helped to maintain JP Morgan's contacts with foreign branches and correspondents and our overseas customers, which included spending time at Morgan Grenfell in London and Rothschild's in Paris among others. There were overseas loans, letters of credit, other financing deals and so on and I found it all extremely interesting.

For the first three years I shared a flat and then a small house with an English friend, Nigel Pemberton, and for the last eighteen months I rented a very nice apartment near Madison Avenue. The only problem was that I had to walk up four storeys to reach it. My landlady, a friendly German woman called Lotte, said that I looked exactly like her dear friend Sir John Foster and seemed convinced I was his illegitimate son. When I met Sir John later we were able to clear up this little misunderstanding.

I had sold my Leopard Moth before arriving in New York but I felt utterly lost without an aeroplane. So I found a beautiful second-hand four seat Cessna 180 tail dragger and kept it at Teterboro in New Jersey. This made all the difference to my life. It meant weekends flying out to Long Island to visit girlfriends or flying down to Virginia to play golf and over to the Canadian lakes in summertime.

I used to fly down past Leesburg to Harpers Ferry, over the Blue Mountains and then let down to 300 feet with the flaps down and cruise down the winding Shenandoah River looking at all the glorious houses on the hills above. The journey home on Sunday night, usually with a friend, was always easy. The huge mast at the end of the Teterboro runway was WINS radio New York whose slogan was something like, "You give us 22 minutes and we'll give you the world". I could pick up this station on my radio compass from about 300 miles away so I'd simply sit back and watch the lights of the towns pass by, listening to the latest news or chatting with whoever I was fortunate enough to have with me.

Later I swapped the Cessna for a series of Piper Comanches. I would buy the sales demonstrators from my brother Desmond's agent, Alex Muller, who sold the Britten Norman Islanders. With long-range wingtip tanks the Comanche has a range of well over 1000 miles. So, whenever we had a holiday, my friend Norbert Leroy (who worked in the bank and owned a Beechcraft Bonanza) and I would fly down to the West Indies for a few days. I remember on a couple of occasions we flew to Cuba, where Norbert had a girlfriend called Mercedes. This was in the days of Batista when Havana, and Cuba as a whole were wide open as far as foreigners were concerned, and full of the American mafia. On our first approach to landing there, I was surprised to see a train puffing straight across the middle of the runway. Luckily we passed just behind it. I assume it has been re-routed since then.

I also used to go to St Barts, long before it was developed into the sophisticated tourist resort it is today. I stayed with my friend Remy de Haenen who had built a beautiful, if rudimentary, little hotel on a rock called Eden Roc on the east side of the island, next to the airstrip. The airstrip itself is or was something of a challenge as the approach was through a pass in the hills onto a fairly short strip, which stretched downhill to the beach. Any mistakes and it was easy to wind up in the sea.

When I first met Remy he was flying an old Chance Vought L13, a high wing five seater in a rather battered condition. He was also the Member of Parliament to the Assembly in Guadaloupe. We became good friends after I had stayed with him and his wife Giselle (a gorgeous red-headed Creole woman) at the hotel a few times. When the L13 finally gave up the ghost after sustaining damage in a hurricane, I bought him a second-hand Helio Courier, which he collected from Venezuela.

The deal was that I would take ownership from him of a plot of land on the beach next to Eden Roc, with a view of perhaps one day building a house on it. The Helio Courier was well-known for being a short take-off and landing aircraft but it was useless at St Bart's because it had such a high aspect ratio wing that it floated forever on landing and was very difficult to get down onto the ground – especially with this particular downhill runway and an onshore breeze. A few years later Remy swapped it for a twin engined Cessna 310, which is much faster but at least it came down like a dose of salts.

The Comanche was OK unless it was full or over-full as we often ran it, when the speeds had to be exactly right. There was a windmill at the end of the grass on a small hill. If, as occasionally happened, we were going too fast down the runway it was possible to turn hard right up the hill and park beside the windmill – which made all the difference. When I stayed with Remy I did a lot of the shopping for the hotel: vegetables from St Kitts, meat from Antigua and delicacies or cheese from Guadaloupe, which had a direct Air France flight from Paris.

Sadly Remy sold my plot when he ran into difficulties with Giselle and the bank. We remained friends but I sometimes dream of the beach house that might have been.

There was a lot of feuding between Remy and two others in St Barts, Ledée and Gréaux, about the airfield, as Remy possessed the only French commercial flying licence on the island and the other two were flying commercially in French territory on US licences, which Remy considered illegal. Remy kept attempting to stop them and Gréaux, who lived in a house in the middle of the airfield, used to run the sheep out onto the runway when we were landing; it was something of a miracle we never hit one. On one occasion Remy assaulted Gréaux and the magistrate Bernard who presided at the court hearings (and was an old friend of Remy's) phoned to say that he couldn't stay with us (as he usually would for the court sessions) because Remy was up before him on a charge. He came by while he was there and everything turned out OK.

In New York, I used to get telegrams from Remy, who looked upon me as a partner in Eden Roc, which always amused the JP Morgan mailroom. On one occasion the telegram read: "Giselle has run off with an Air France pilot, would you please authorise her immediate replacement?" and on another "There are two B25s (Mitchell bombers) for sale in Arizona. Please buy them for us. They will be invaluable for the lobster trade between Venezuela and Florida. And by the way, please don't remove the armament".

(Remy was endlessly involved with local politics mostly concerning the regime in the Dominican Republic of which he thoroughly disapproved.) Needless to say I wasn't very helpful in either of these requests although I did 'authorise' a new cook for him, which he would have got anyway.

So life in New York was full of fun and interest and a great deal of flying. We all speculated wildly on the stock market and because I had access to some of the bank's research I managed to make a bit of money. I also discovered that Comanches in England had a higher market value than in the USA and I found that by putting a plastic ferry tank in the back and flying across to England I could sell my Comanche at what seemed a huge profit (somewhere between £500 to £1,000). I did this twice. My first trip involved landing at Kennedy (a most frightening experience since the airport was completely unprepared for light aircraft), then on to Bermuda and from Bermuda to Santa Maria in the Azores and then on to Gatwick. My second was on my final trip home with Anne Montagu, who later became my wife.

Everything seemed more easy-going in those days compared to what goes on today. I imported one of the first Minis to America, which caused quite a stir on the New York streets and the bumpers certainly weren't much use in protecting it from the local system of parking. A large black man in an open fuchsia-coloured Lincoln came alongside one day when I was stuck in traffic in the theatre district, and since my Mini was right hand drive he was able to lean over and look down at me, and said: "Say son – what's that gonna be when it grows up!"

My father and his life have always exerted a powerful influence on my own, even though I had seen him and known him so little. Because of my father's work in training the Airborne Forces I had always had a strong desire to parachute. He had done one jump because he felt he couldn't ask others to parachute if he hadn't done it himself. Unfortunately he had a bad hip and therefore decided to do his jump over Lake Windermere. He survived, but only just, as he became tangled in the cords after landing and nearly drowned. So in around June 1959 when I heard of a parachuting school in Orange, Massachusetts, I decided to fly up and investigate. The owner and manager of the school was a Belgian named Jacques Istel who was a world class parachutist. He had brought together a fine group of instructors and of course I joined up immediately. Jacques and I and my brother Desmond, when he came over, became firm friends and Jacques and I still keep in touch.

I would spend quite a few weekends parachuting, as the whole process of free-falling, group jumps, baton passing and so on, was exciting stuff and the group of people I was with were huge fun. I held the record at one point for taking the fewest jumps (I think it was eleven or twelve) to complete my first baton pass, but it only lasted a few days as a young man about ten years my junior managed it in less than ten.

Because the airfield at Orange had no lights, Jacques and I worked out a system whereby I would phone him before taking off from Teterboro and he would position himself on the downwind end of the runway around the time I was due to arrive. I had worked out how to find the field by flying east from (I think) Greenfield, along a main highway for a set number of miles and then when I came across a dark patch of ground to the left of the road I would orbit it and Jacques would switch on his car lights. I would come down behind the car and the lights would illuminate the runway and he would drive behind me, keeping it lit as I landed.

The first time we tried this, I asked him to position himself at the upwind end of the runway but then nearly piled into him because it was impossible to judge one's height (or distance) when flying in the dark towards a light with no other reference point; it was a miracle I got the aircraft onto the ground in time to stop. After a few tries the other way round we had it down to a fine art.

After a few visits to Orange I heard that a very pretty English girl had arrived. She had come up one weekend with a girlfriend and stayed on at the bunkhouse – known as the Inn at Orange – but she was never there when I came up. I later found out that this was because she had come to America with her cousin Gemma to get over an affair with an Englishman and didn't want to see another one for some time. So, having heard about me, she stayed away at weekends. Needless to say I was intrigued by this and somehow arranged to see her one weekend.

Her name was Anne and she was without doubt the most beautiful woman I had ever seen. She was very zany, very funny, very left wing in her politics and extremely independent. She was also a highly gifted and dedicated painter. I fell in love with her instantly, but it took thousands of miles of flying, months of parachuting, many nights spent dancing and generally having a wonderful time together, to persuade her to marry me. I even followed her out to California at Christmas where Jacques had a winter parachuting school at Hemet outside Los Angeles. Anne flew out with the team of instructors in the Norseman and Jacques and I flew out in my Comanche a few days later.

When they were about halfway across the country, Anne opened the Norseman's door to throw something out and the door promptly flew off its hinges and landed in a field. Luckily one of the others grabbed Anne so she didn't follow it and they plotted the field where it had fallen. They landed, reaffixed the door and set off again for Hemet. Anne, who had taken a job as a chambermaid in a local hotel, used her spare time sign-writing and painting and we spent about ten days together parachuting and joining in all the fun. Jacques kindly agreed to fly the Comanche back to Teterboro for me and I took an airliner back as I had a few weeks' work still to do before finishing up my job at JP Morgan.

I had accepted a job from Kenneth Keith, the chairman of a very up and coming London merchant bank, Philip Hill Higginson Erlangers (named after all the banks that made it up, but which later became Hill Samuel after merging yet again with M. Samuel & Co.) and I was looking forward to getting home and seeing family and friends.

There was an amusing incident when Anne saw me off at LA airport. I refused to check my parachute into the hold with the other luggage but insisted on having it as cabin baggage. The truth was, I couldn't afford a penny of excess baggage. It so happened that the airline I was flying with had been the victim of a major disaster the week before when one of their aircraft ran into another and crashed onto the streets of Brooklyn, killing hundreds of passengers. So almost without thinking I explained to the girl at check-in that I always felt safer travelling with my parachute. She tried to explain that it was against the rules and I enquired whether it was one of their aircraft that had crashed the week before over Brooklyn and she had to admit it was! We had a long discussion while a queue of impatient passengers formed behind me. I was explaining it was only a legitimate piece of safety equipment and could I please speak to her supervisor who eventually arrived. In the end I was forced to ask what the press would say about an airline (with their record) refusing such a request. They eventually let me on with it. Much to the other passengers' consternation, Anne checked the rip cord pins in the departure lounge and asked me to phone her if I needed to be picked up anywhere.

I settled down in the front row of the tourist class and hung the parachute on the hook in front of me (being rather tall my feet often travelled first class). The stewardess came up and asked if she might hang up my coat. I explained that it wasn't a coat but a parachute and after another short discussion agreed to let her and her companion stow it in the locker at the rear of the cabin on the understanding that if I called for it they would swiftly bring it back. There was an anxious moment when she began by grabbing hold of the ripcord handle, which would have caused a disaster as, being spring loaded, the parachute would have burst open filling the entire cabin with huge quantities of nylon. Eventually, however, the two of them gingerly carried it back and everyone relaxed.

I suppose it was pure mischief (or more likely lack of a proper upbringing) that made me press the call button when we were about half an hour out of New York and the fasten seat belt sign came on with the pilot's announcement of turbulence. When a pale stewardess approached I asked her to bring my parachute. With considerable trepidation she did so, with all the reading lights suddenly switching on as she walked up the aisle. But at least there was no excess baggage charge.

When Anne got back to New York we decided to do a final flight around the States together, before flying down to the West Indies and St Barts and then setting off back to England in the Comanche. We stopped all over the place and had tremendous fun. I remember landing for lunch at a ranch in the middle of the desert in, I guess, New Mexico where we noticed an airstrip very close to the main house as well as a swimming pool. It turned out to be a hotel. Anne had still not agreed to marry me but she wore a curtain ring that night on her ring finger so that we could fib a bit about being married. It was still necessary in those days, but just the sight of it kept me hopeful.

I remember we went to visit a cousin of Anne's in Los Angeles and because I was trying everything to impress her, we hired a stretch limo and spent two nights at the Bel Air Hotel. It was one of my happiest memories, we had a roaring fire in the room and a stream ran through the garden outside. I remember spending most of the evening laughing and even went to the lengths of betting Anne that I could tear the Los Angeles telephone directory in half. I nearly, but not quite, got her to say that she would agree to marry me if I could. Of course there is a knack for everything and I knew how to do it. I think she must have suspected this as she wouldn't take the bet.

About a week later, on the way to St Barts, we flew into Antigua to hear a steel band, Brute Force that had become a great favourite of mine from earlier visits. We had a glorious evening dancing to steel band music and when walking home rather full of rum and high spirits, she finally said YES.

So full of joy (and some trepidation at meeting her family for the first time) we flew back to Fort Lauderdale, fitted a huge long-range fuel tank, picked up life jackets and a dinghy, installed an HF Radio with a 30' trailing aerial and set off for Bermuda.

When I used to fly to the Piper factory at Lockhaven I met a great Piper pilot, Max Conrad, who was famous as the flying grandfather (he was in his fifties) and he performed the most amazing long distance flights. I remember one he did non-stop from Casablanca to Los Angeles (in a 250 hp Comanche like mine) in just under fifty-nine hours. He told me that the secret of staying awake was to eat very little before a long flight and virtually nothing en route.

On the few longish distance flights that I have made I have found this advice works perfectly. So in summer 1961 Anne and I flew direct from Bermuda to Lisbon which took twenty-one hours and we had no inclination to fall asleep. The HF radio packed up, the weather was lousy – loads of thunderstorms and icing and we couldn't find the weather ship that was promised somewhere in the middle. But we reached Lisbon with plenty of petrol left, though not much oil, which after filling up in Bermuda I had forgotten about altogether.

We eventually wound up at Southampton aerodrome (near my mother's house at Downton in Wiltshire) where the customs officer, who arrived on a bicycle dressed in white, direct from a cricket match, impounded the aeroplane because he simply didn't believe we had come from the USA via Bermuda and Lisbon.

I introduced Anne to my mother and stepfather and they became great and lifelong friends. (Mum said she was the most intelligent woman she had ever met – implying, no doubt, that the previous girlfriends I had brought down weren't!) Anne soon met my two brothers Mark and Desmond and it was good to be home and with Anne among family.

So what with one year in Austria, five years in the US, a year at prep school, five years at Eton, two years in the Fleet Air Arm, three at Cambridge followed by a junior year at Harvard and then going to work for five years for JP Morgan in New York, I could hardly be said to have experienced any home life at all since the age of five.

I hold Hitler responsible for all of this disruption.

I won't discuss my family at length in this book because this is not intended as a proper autobiography – just a sketch, really, to give a flavour of my chequered past. But I must make very clear that living with Anne changed my life completely. She was beautiful not only physically but inwardly. She always thought the best of people and I never heard her say a nasty word about anyone. She wasn't in the least materialistic, to the point of being totally bohemian. Anne hardly ever bought clothes or jewels or in fact anything else. She didn't even like me buying them for her. She was wonderfully funny and laughed easily. She loved all children and of course particularly our own, and felt sorry and concerned for anyone who was not as well off as we were, in whatever way and would spend much of her time helping others.

Our honeymoon was a bit unusual in that I had managed to book us into the Colombe d'Or in St Paul de Vence. This is a magical place and particularly special for painters since the original owner had accepted wonderful paintings from the artists themselves when they were too short of funds to pay their food bills. These paintings were all over the walls including a fabulous Leger mural. It was a beautiful place to stay with a large swimming pool and a marvellous terrace where we ate under parasols looking across the mountains towards the Mediterranean. We arrived after a night in Paris with Anne suffering from a terrible cold, which kept her in bed for two or three days – not the ideal way to start your honeymoon. I went down to the pool in the morning for a swim to find none other than Simone Signoret in sole occupation. She picked up a football from the side and asked would I play water polo with her. Needless to say I was too tongue-tied to refuse and so for the next few mornings we had a regular water polo session. The first time that Anne, miserable with her cold looked out of her window and surveyed the scene below, her mood was not exactly improved, but since she so admired Signoret and her husband Yves Montand who was with her, she came round in the end. Simone would call up to our room at about 11 am every day, shouting "TORKILLE – FOOTBALL!"

Better still, on 14th July, Yves himself organised a private firework display that was breathtaking. He had a helper François, with whom he planted the arrangement of rockets and starbursts on the hillside below the terrace. When it grew dark, Yves started shouting orders to François, who was to light the fuses, at the top of his voice (with quite a few *merde* and other expletives thrown in). About every fifth rocket came flying through at close to table height and the starbursts were all over the place. It was a miracle nobody was burnt but the entire audience was so high that we wouldn't have noticed anyway. This certainly put an end to Anne's cold and we had an enchanted night surrounded by the stars of the French film industry, some of whom were great heroes of ours. When the honeymoon was over, I felt fortunate that Anne still wanted to come home with me.

In London, after several moves and with help from Anne who sold a painting, we settled on buying a big family house in Avenue Road, St Johns Wood, which had quite a large garden. By this time we had four children, Jesse, Casey, Lulu and Caspar with Amy soon to arrive. Eventually I built a swimming pool in the garden because I was always leaving the house very early and an early morning swim was my favourite form of exercise. Of course it was wonderful for the children as they grew up, and every Monday Anne opened the pool to all the children from the local area and nearby housing estates and we made lots of friends and a terrific racket. Our children still remember those wild afternoons in the pool.

Anne's politics were very left wing, in reaction to her father who was a very right-wing Member of Parliament. Her approach to bringing up our children (we had five under the age of seven) was very loving and warm but utterly without discipline. This was the one area where she and I had differences of opinion and occasionally argued quite strongly. However her egalitarian principles, kindness and wonderfully generous, open, approach to other people was a perfect example to our children. One they have all followed.

When she dressed up she looked absolutely stunning but most of the time at her studio she was in her painting clothes – workman's trousers and layers of woollens - and her hands were covered in paint, as were her clothes and often her face. I will never forget one evening when the doorbell rang and a policeman was there at the door with Anne, whom he had arrested in Regent's park as a vagrant and – what upset her more – under the impression that she was a man, since her face and hands were covered with paint and her hair and was under a kind of tight cap. We all teased about this for years afterwards.

As our children grew up they were extremely unruly and, of course, did an enormous amount of crayoning, drawing and painting. In fact it was almost impossible to stay in a hotel with them on holiday because their first instinct would be to crayon all over their bedroom walls. Luckily I had made a little money with a friend in the British Virgin Islands and came up with a solution.

I bought a 30' Bedford chassis and delivered it to Plaxtons the coach builders in Scarborough. They kindly built a body on it to my design which, when equipped, meant that we could sleep nine people in it, with a motor scooter in the boot and a small sailing dinghy on a vast roof rack. I think we had the first, the best and undoubtedly the biggest camper van in the business.

I knocked down the prefabricated garage beside the house in Avenue Road so that we could park our beautiful red, white and blue bus alongside the house with the front well clear of the pavement. A few people used to complain but I think we felt we had raised the tone of the road considerably. Heaven knows what Camden Council would say these days.

The bus proved to be one of the best things I have ever done for our family. The kids loved it and it gave us endless opportunities to be together and learn how to live with each other at close quarters – not always easy with five and often seven children (we usually invited a friend or two, which made the kids more civilised) between the ages of four and eleven. We used it for years and went all over Scotland, Spain, Austria, and France and to visit friends or relatives in the English countryside.

It was laid out in three separate spaces. At the front next to the driver's seat there were three facing seats. Behind the driver there were four seats which could be facing either forwards or backwards. When they were in the backwards position they were part of a large table with seats around two other sides. The table could itself be raised or lowered according to whether it was being used as a table or to sleep on. The cushions from the back of the seats could be put onto the table to make a complete mattress for a double bed. (This was where the children's friends usually slept.) Behind the table was a narrow kitchen which had a large sink, a gas cooker, cupboards, shelves and a refrigerator.

A door in the wall led into the kids' bedroom, where there were five bunks – two along each wall and one along the side of the bus between them. Underneath that bed there was a chemical loo on computer rails which slid in and out when needed. Each bed had its own bedside light as well as a cup holder. In the rear section was a large double bed for Anne and me, with a hanging cupboard, two drawers and a basin. The rear window opened on hydraulic struts, and there were steps in the side of the bus which made direct access easy.

It is hard to describe how many ways the bus proved to be popular. Driving along at night with all the kids sitting up in their pyjamas and drinking hot chocolate was a kind of sublime experience. We had some wonderful tapes including all of Bob Dylan, Irish ballads, the Ink Spots, Little Richard, Fats Waller and many others. It wasn't long before we knew most of the words by heart. As they started to feel dozy, Anne would lift them off into their bunks where they would instantly fall asleep. Usually I would then keep driving for two or three hours until we came across a beach or another nice place to stop, and then I would tiptoe back usually around midnight and crawl in beside Anne.

The problem was, of course, that one of the children would wake up with the sun at about four or five in the morning saying "Daddy, look at the beach, can we go fishing?" So I'd wearily drag myself out of bed, get all the fishing gear from the boot and off we'd go.

Depending on the place, we might get the dinghy off the roof and go sailing. We often spent the night in the car park of a convenient 'Routier' restaurant, and we became world experts on every twenty franc menu in France. When we had found somewhere nice to stay, near a cliff, beach or some other isolated spot, we would use the scooter to go to the local shops. If we had an *au pair* with us Anne and I would go out to dinner in the nearest village. I remember the great chess match between Bobby Fischer and Spassky, which we listened to on television in some bar in Austria and our own games of chess (of a rather humbler variety).

One of my great pleasures in the evenings after supper was to sit on the floor between all the bunks and make up weird and wonderful stories to get the children off to sleep. These became very popular and my problem was to ensure that the two heroes (often two mad ants named Horace and Abigail) had ever wilder and more exciting adventures.

When we caught fish Anne insisted on our cleaning them and then cooking them, which was okay with ordinary fish. But, for example, with razor clams it was quite a business. Incidentally, razor clams were among the most popular things to catch since they were so easy – you just poured salt into their holes and they slid up out of the sand (presuming the tide had come in) so that they were easily pulled out. The children thought it was pure magic. But razor clams were nothing like as popular as fish to eat. We also had shrimping nets of a size that the children found easy to use and these were very popular.

In Spain, particularly, we used to go off the road onto dirt tracks to find good places to camp near rivers and we had the most hair-raising adventures trying to get the bus round corners which were too tight for it, on roads that had a way of disappearing under the wheels. Somehow we survived all these but looking back, I am not sure how.

The bus of course solved all our problems connected with crayoning on hotel walls and exorbitant hotel bills and, as I mentioned, had the huge benefit of our learning to live with and devising ways to deal with each other's foibles. Anne was endlessly creative at finding things for the children to do.

I had left JP Morgan a few months after they had merged with the Guaranty Trust (having been there nearly five years) at which time the bank changed its name to Morgan Guaranty. The whole business of merging was very disruptive, and it was one of the things that had encouraged me to come back to England.

After about four years with Philip Hill Higginson Erlangers, the same thing happened when they merged with M. Samuel & Co, becoming Hill Samuel.

I think by then I'd reached the conclusion that I wasn't really cut out to be a banker. I had enjoyed travelling to every part of the country talking to old and new customers, particularly on the occasions when I could use the bank's aeroplane. The bank owned a beautiful de Havilland Dove which was flown by a pilot called Ken Souter. Ken was a lovely man and his job was to pick up Kenneth Keith, the Chairman, from his farm in Norfolk on Monday mornings and deliver him home again on Friday afternoons. Most of the rest of the time he was grossly underemployed. When I discovered this I programmed a huge number of meetings with our customers all over the country as part of an effort to build our banking business. Ken allowed me to fly the aeroplane most of the time we were together and we became close friends. It was a sad loss to me when I heard, after I had left the bank, that Ken had been tragically killed one evening in lousy weather flying back into Luton. I believe he was on his own, possibly coming back from Norfolk.

Although I enjoyed the travelling and the customers, I had begun to feel that I wanted to be doing something in industry myself, and was afraid after the merger with Samuel that I was simply going to turn into a banker (not in those days a term of abuse). I didn't enjoy the lunches and the concentration on making money, and didn't like the fact that we rarely lent money to the people who really needed it. I was more attracted to the venture capital business, which was in its infancy then, and of course is very different today.

During my travels I had come across an extraordinary man by the name of Ken Bates. He had just sold his ready mixed concrete business in Lancashire to one of his major competitors (or rather its assets, as he would never let them see his decidedly dicey balance sheet). The year he sold it there was a freezing cold winter, which made it difficult to mix concrete and move it around. Ken's (typical) reaction was to buy a new Rolls Royce and visit his creditors who were somehow comforted by his obvious affluence. When I met him he was being paid for the assets and was busy applying for (and usually being granted) planning permission for many of the small batching plants he had put up without it.

I'm well aware that Ken has, over the years, become fairly controversial in some quarters but from the first day I met him we became close friends and I'm pleased to say that we still are today. I could write a book about the things we did together but I think there are already several more or less truthful accounts of his life.

In all the years I have known him I cannot remember us ever having a cross word. We didn't agree about everything but we always managed to talk our problems through and come up with a result we could live with. Ken's mind works so fast that he got the point in seconds so we didn't spend loads of time going over the same ground again and again. His energy was phenomenal and the one trait of his to which I objected strongly (without ever managing to modify it) was his habit of calling me at any hour of the night or early morning excitedly to discuss his latest idea.

He is an enormously generous man as many of his friends will testify; for example, years later, he gave a very generous gift to the Roundhouse when I became deeply involved in that project. He had one element in his personality, however, that used to cause me unease. If someone attacked him in the press his reflex was to respond in kind, which led to him making not a few enemies and certainly affected his standing with the media. I tried to dissuade him from some of these reactions and occasionally he agreed.

We were strange partners: me with my privileged background, a fairly unreconstructed public schoolboy with some financial knowledge and contacts but inexperienced in the ways of industry and the world, and Ken, a working man who had met his father for the first time when he was twenty-one and made his money entirely through his own efforts and hard graft. But he taught me a lot and I hope I may have been some help to him.

Anyway, we formed a company 'Batehill', half owned by Ken and the other half by Philip Hill, whom I represented, with a nice, helpful man called Stanley Newsome, a background partner who was always available to help.

Over several years (during which my main job was as a banker with Philip Hill) we built up a small group of about seven or eight companies in a wide range of different industries that were not strong enough to borrow money, but were willing for Batehill to inject capital into them for either a controlling stake or one where Batehill had an option to take control should certain situations arise. It was an early form of venture capital company, which was a seedling compared to the gigantic companies of this kind that have grown up in the years since.

Whenever a new company came into the group, Ken and I would visit them and decide with management the policy for growth. Ken would then take over the main responsibility for seeing that this was carried out successfully. Interestingly, most of them succeeded and became large companies, but a few failed or nearly failed and then Ken and I would work out what to do.

We did one major advertising effort as we became successful, taking a four page insert in the Financial Times. The front page showed a huge pair of roller skates under which were the words "Batehill Ltd. Putting Skates on Businesses: that's what we do". We got literally hundreds of replies and it took ages to sift through them and find those that might be worthy prospects. In a way we had invented a kind of miniature Dragons' Den.

Separately, I started a company for Philip Hill named London Bridge Finance, with a man named Malcolm Hamlyn (whose basic idea it had been), which developed a totally new form of factoring corporate invoices. This meant that a company could sell its invoices to us for cash without its customers having any idea that they were doing this. A brilliant lawyer – a senior partner at Slaughter and May, Alastair Mallinson, helped us with the enormous legal complications of drawing up the agreements to put such transactions into effect. For Philip Hill it was a way of bringing in small companies as future banking customers.

I found my time at Philip Hill enormously stimulating and interesting but decided, at the time of their merger, that the time had come to leave.

I accepted a job at an interesting company, Minerals Separation Ltd. (Minsep), as general manager. The company had a huge subsidiary, Foseco, started in Germany before the war by Eric Weiss, which supplied chemicals to the steel and foundry industry. Minsep itself was a very rich investment company that, as well as owning Foseco, had built up a portfolio of smallish diversified companies and wanted to do more in that field.

Minsep was run by an extraordinary old man, by then around eighty, named John Buchanan, whom I had met several times during my years as a banker, and we got on very well. He had extremely left-wing views for someone in his position, a great sense of humour and very clear ideas about how Minerals Separation should be run. I liked him enormously and was excited at the opportunity he gave me of running the small group of companies that existed within Minsep. Minsep also bought out Batehill from Hill Samuel, which expanded the group. As part of this deal I had taken a stake in Berwick's Toy Company, the largest company in Batehill. My duties had nothing at all to do with Foseco.

I won't spend much space on my work at Minsep except to say that things didn't work out the way I had hoped. My first job was to go around each of the companies it owned, meet the management and try to gain an idea of their strengths and weaknesses. They turned out to be a fairly mixed bunch. Under the previous regime they were allowed almost total freedom to do whatever they liked with their businesses and the reporting procedures were various and inadequate. I formed a view that two or three of them had no future at all and were being run as private companies for the benefit of the management and not the shareholders. Some of the others were fairly marginal, and two or three had real possibilities. So when I completed my review I discussed this with the chairman and in principle he allowed me to get on and do the things I felt were necessary. For a start we needed a proper reporting system on broadly similar lines for everyone, so that we could understand on a monthly basis how the companies were performing. This I started to implement with considerable wailing and gnashing of teeth on the part of most of the companies involved.

Another factor was that Ken was still running Batehill and it became clear that he and John Buchanan would never see eye to eye. In fact I think they cordially disliked each other.

A further factor was that on a visit to Tortola in the British Virgin Islands, Ken came across what he felt was a tremendous opportunity. From his hotel room he would watch a small dredger at work all day dredging sand out of the harbour, and he noticed that because it had to stop work at night to avoid noise disturbance, most of the sand found its way back into the harbour during the dark hours.

He telephoned me in the middle of the night to describe this and suggested that we make an offer to the American man who ran the dredger to include taking over the dredging rights. He pointed out to me that the waterfront was a huge mangrove swamp, which restricted the expansion of Roadtown, the capital. A large expanse of land could be reclaimed from the sea and a brand new harbour constructed. It would enable Roadtown to expand from its narrow base along the hills in such a way that the main road could become dual carriageway, thereby solving the constant traffic jam that made movement in the town almost impossible.

Since under our arrangement with Minsep, Ken and I ran Batehill independently, I suggested that he pursued it further. The whole scheme was typical of Ken's approach to business opportunities.

When Ken got back from holiday it became clear that the amount of money required to hire a professional Dutch dredging company, not to mention all the additional costs, would be far beyond Batehill's modest resources. So I asked Ken to write a note on it all and arranged a meeting for him and me to see John Buchanan. It proved a very uncomfortable meeting because John and Ken so clearly had no confidence in each other, and I felt like piggy in the middle. The upshot was that Minsep declined to have anything to do with the Virgin Islands scheme, but Ken was totally determined to find a way of doing it.

At about this time, I think, Buchanan and Eric Weiss, his co-director and the founder of Foseco, were starting to feel that owning small troublesome companies (Minsep's principally but perhaps also Batehill's) was a mug's game. When the three of us discussed it they came to the conclusion that we should set about selling or closing down the companies that they owned and subsequently they decided to organise a reverse takeover of Minsep by Foseco. The group would then combine to become first, a major power in supplying the steel and foundry industry and secondly an investment house with a large portfolio of stocks, shares and cash (which had formerly been Minsep).

So I started the difficult task of divesting ourselves, by selling, closing down or otherwise getting rid of the Minsep portfolio of small companies and at the same time trying to figure out with Ken what to do with Batehill and how to get the Virgin Islands project off the ground.

The details are unimportant but between us, over a period of a few months, we managed it. The plan involved us bringing in the Ionian Bank to take over Batehill. They agreed to do this on three conditions. First, that we sold all the Batehill companies except the largest, Berwick's Toy Company. Second, that Ken would have nothing to do with Batehill, that his shares in it would be sold to the Ionian Bank (and some to me). Third, that Ken would concentrate fully on the Virgin Islands opportunity, in which they would have no interest, but about which Ken (and I) were passionate.

I parted from Minsep, I thought on good terms, having worked myself out of a job, although inevitably I had considerable regrets, since the opportunities at Minsep had been enormous. On the other hand, running Berwick's Toy Company proved enormously appealing since I discovered I had a real interest in toys and in industry and, with five young children, a home-based research centre.

I have several fond memories of Minsep. First I had the largest, most beautiful office I have ever had, looking out over Hyde Park towards the Foreign Office. Secondly I very much enjoyed working with John Buchanan even though not as constructively as I had hoped. He couldn't have been more charming and encouraging (except of course over Batehill). The only drawback was that he became rather forgetful in his old age, mostly after lunch, at which he had a habit of drinking a significant quantity of Scotch malt whisky from the bottle on the table placed beside him. This encouraged me into the good habit of getting him to sign a contemporaneous note of everything we agreed. But he didn't enjoy the occasional disagreements that resulted, at which point he would say: "I never agreed to that!", only to have a cheeky subordinate about a third of his age handing over his signed note.

Finally, I remember the day he sent me to Henry Moore's studio to buy an enormous bronze sculpture entitled *Mother and Child*. When I reached the studio I discovered that it was one of, I think, ten identical sculptures. I rang John Buchanan to explain this and asked whether he really wanted to spend £10,000 on something of which there were nine duplicates. "Don't be stupid," he said, "go ahead and buy it", which, of course, I did. (It subsequently lived in the garden in front of my office window, to my and many others' great pleasure.) With hindsight I can say that the Henry Moore was a wonderful investment, but he would have made considerably more money had he backed Wickham's Cay, our Virgin Islands project.

Ken and I successfully sold off the other Batehill companies, in the main to their managements with some outside shareholders, and most of them prospered. Meanwhile we worked unbelievably hard to set up Wickham's Cay Ltd. and find the huge amount of money needed - something like £3 million, which was a huge sum in those days. After going out to the Virgin Islands together to look it all over thoroughly, we decided to check out the neighbouring island of Anegada, a huge low-lying island full of iguanas with a population of, I recall, about 150. Ken immediately took to the island and we included it in the project.

To cut a very long story short, by dint of hard work and selling everything we owned and with the help, too, of a local Manchester broker we raised about half the money we needed. We negotiated an overdraft facility with Barclay's DC&O. With the folly of youth, we were confident that we could raise the rest once the project was well underway.

We hired an ace Dutch dredging company with a huge dredger, cut down the mangroves, then dredged and lined with concrete the basic harbour, part of which was predesignated as a base for the local fishermen. Ken meanwhile moved his entire family, including his then wife Teresa and their children, to a large caravan based on a remote part of Anegada, powered by its own generator. There he supervised the building of a jetty, a ring road, a cold store and an airport, and moved forward with the provision of electricity for the local inhabitants.

But on the political front we had all kinds of trouble. In the UK, the Foreign Office became worried that the kind of insurrection that had recently taken place in Anguilla – where they had had to send in English bobbies to maintain order – would spread to Tortola, where locally there was a small but vociferous Communist Party. The party was run by a glamorous lady called Patsy Pickering who was once a hairdresser in Miami but had returned to her native Tortola. Patsy and her gang were real troublemakers.

In the Virgin Islands, we had negotiated with the local government a lease on Anegada which eventually wound up as 999 years. We also

Anne with our two eldest boys, Jesse and Casey in 1965.

With Anne at a Bluebird factory party in Merthyr Tydfil around 1994.

With the Big Yellow Teapot (our first toy) and friends.

Caspar at about four getting ready for his first
trip on our bus in 1971.

With a model of the Roundhouse in 1999 –
a toy approach to raising £30 million.

The second Patricia in Groningen before heading south.

One of the most beautiful aircraft ever built – en route to Oshkosh, August 1995.

The 1936 DH 90 Dragonfly at the time of purchase, St Louis 1990.

With Henry a year later after finally arriving.

Before and after – Sea Fury on board HMS Illustrious, 1953 (note the flattened propeller boss and broken engine caused by a cartwheel).

Our 1993 DH 85 Leopard Moth (Geoffrey de Havilland's favourite touring aeroplane, and mine), en route to Oshkosh, July 2000.

The view of Baffin Island in poor forced landing terrain, taken from the Dragonfly, August 1995.

A smile of relief after arriving safely at Oshkosh, August 2000.

With Iga in the 1939 DH82A Tiger Moth in South East Australia, January 2007 (shipped out in a container!).

negotiated the creation and development of 'Wickham's Cay', which was designed to produce something like eighty acres of flat land for the expansion of Roadtown as well as a grand new harbour.

At a public meeting which we arranged with the local government so that the general public could understand exactly what was planned for Wickham's Cay, Patsy turned up in her brand new Buick with about twenty young activists carrying banners saying among other things "Go home Ian Smith"(!) She had brought her own public address system which she set up in the hall in front of a worried row of local government ministers and began to lay into everyone in sight.

The atmosphere in the room was already dramatic since the only murder trial to have taken place in Tortola for decades had started in the same room that very day. I found myself addressing the assembled multitude, without the benefit of a microphone, with the details of what we were proposing and I remember winding up with something along the lines of, "if you think *you* are having difficulties with the project you should hear what the shareholders at home have to say!" The following day we did a series of radio interviews and when we finally left the island things had calmed down a little.

But back home, word of the meeting had reached the Foreign Office and Barclay's DC&O and Ken and I were summoned to a meeting first at the bank, and then at the Foreign Office. The bank said that they were concerned about the fact that we hadn't completed the fundraising and that they were considering calling in their overdraft facility with us. The Foreign Office said they were worried about the political storm that we were stirring up and were proposing to make an offer to buy us out of the project. I'm quite certain that the two institutions had been talking to each other. I believe that had Minsep been prepared to help us in the first place none of this would have happened and we could have completed the project as programmed. (We had already sold two or three plots at something like $US100,000 each, with others pending) and the basic dredging and concreting was nearly finished.

There was another meeting with the Foreign Office, at which they tabled an offer which involved paying off the bank and little else. Ken and I walked out. A couple of weeks later they called another meeting and in the meantime the bank had said that we ought to accept any reasonable offer as they would be calling in the overdraft.

The upshot was that, after talking it over, we couldn't see any alternative but to accept the improved offer from the Foreign Office, while feeling that the whole thing was a stitch up. I cannot ever remember feeling more bullied and abused and Ken was equally furious. We had worked extremely hard and one need only look at Tortola today to see that if we had been allowed to finish the programme we would have made an enormous fortune and the banks would have been extremely happy. Equally, we provided a platform for the local inhabitants to expand their capital town, improve their fishing harbour and allow dual carriageway circulation of traffic. It is no exaggeration to say that we gave them the springboard to become the highly prosperous island it is today.

I believe both the bank and the Government behaved in a totally unprincipled manner. The only good aspect of it all was that I used my share of the proceeds to buy our beautiful bus which gave us all untold pleasure.

Chapter 5
My beginnings in the toy industry

It was now around 1974 and my time at Berwick's Toy Company involved work that was both very interesting and highly satisfying. Being Chief Executive of even a small toy manufacturing business was a great challenge as well as hugely educational. The staff there were good fun and very helpful. Some of the products were incredibly old-fashioned and out of date, but that seemed to me the size of the opportunity. The factory itself was fairly rundown but the local men and women who worked there were terrific. Some injection moulding work was done there and there was a largish section of people sewing nurse, cowboy and indian outfits, but mostly the factory consisted of assembly and packaging.

The first job was to review the ranges, bring the quality up to date and modernise the packaging. We also had to find new lines to replace those that were showing their age. The process was fascinating and I found that designing and developing toys was work that I really enjoyed. It involved talking to professional toy inventors and going to toy fairs all over the world as well as working on the details of toy design, during a period when safety was beginning to be recognised as of paramount importance. In the course of several years of this work, I became a member, then Chairman and eventually President of the British Toy Manufacturers Association, as well as leader of the toy industry employers at the Toy Wages Council.

As well as strengthening Berwick's we bought Model Toys Ltd. in Shotts, Scotland. They were manufacturers of model toy figures that used a unique plastic overmoulding process invented by a great craftsman named Norman Tooth. The moulding process enabled, for example, one model figure to be built up in several stages so that the final figure had complete detail in several colours without the use of paint. Under the trademark Timpo and thanks, it must be said, to the continuous devaluation of sterling over several years, we developed substantial export markets in Germany and throughout

Europe, as well as in more distant world markets. The weakness of sterling enabled us to maintain the prices in local currency while at the same time substantially improving our own margins.

Building on the success of Berwick's and Timpo, we then bought Peter Pan Playthings, a leading manufacturer of games, outdoor toys and handicrafts. Part of the reason for buying Peter Pan was that it had a brilliant but completely mad management team. Bob Holden was the chief executive and among the sales people were two lunatic legends in the toy industry: Ken Simmonds and Eric Robinson (both alas, have recently died). They were all young and well-liked by both the UK customers and all the manufacturers around the world with whom they dealt as distributors. One of the outstanding privileges of my life was that they welcomed me into their midst and enabled me to get to know loads of people in the industry who are still my friends and together we formed a highly successful team in growing the business.

We also had an unbelievably wild and enjoyable time at international toy fairs which, looking back, I was fortunate to survive. I am simply not capable of describing our antics and escapades, partly because it would destroy any credibility that this short autobiography may hopefully have been establishing. But I can mention the occasion when Ken Simmonds announced to the whole industry that he was going to die on the 1st April one year. This was something everyone had thought was going to happen much earlier, in fact, as he was a prodigious smoker and drinker. April 1st arrived and Ken was still alive, but hundreds of telegrams flooded into the company from all over the world, the gist of most of them being "You stupid bastard! You've let us down again!"

Berwick's became a successful public company, still under the general umbrella of the Ionian Bank. I must mention here an illuminating episode that changed my life and that of the company and, incidentally, kept the entire toy industry amused for the whole summer of 1978.

Berwick Timpo, as it was by then called, had become a significant and profitable group and we had also taken over Harbutt's Plasticine. Bob Holden had left the group for family reasons and to take up a job in America (declaring he was fed up with Britain, the high taxes and the then Labour government).

Over time, the intrusion of the Ionian Bank became a political matter in the company and reached a point where I decided that I was not enjoying the job of group CEO and told the board of my intention to resign – which I did. But soon after doing so, three of the company's managing directors (all except one, with whom I had been having disagreements) said that they would like me to come back, as I was the person they reported to, and that they felt we had a strong future together. I spent some time thinking about it and consulted a friend at Charterhouse, the merchant bank.

As a result of that meeting, I asked the three directors to come down to London and make statements to the bank of their intention to support me and their reasons, which they duly did.

So after a period of reflection, I decided that Berwick Timpo had a real future and that I would still like to be part of it. So in discussion with Charterhouse, we approached the board with a view to making certain changes and, failing their agreement to do so, calling an Extraordinary General Meeting, also mentioning the support of the three company managing directors and some of the shareholders to whom we had spoken.

As a result of this approach, the chairman, who was an Ionian Bank appointee, interviewed the managing directors at some length on several occasions and by dint of giving them new contracts, new cars and more money they all changed their minds and decided to support the board.

I suppose I shouldn't have been surprised by this, or hurt, but since friends were involved, I was. Since then I guess I have gained a better understanding of the fallibilities of human nature. So after thinking about it all again, talking to the merchant bank and to further shareholders, my attitude became one of "what the hell, I believe in the cause, let's go ahead with the Extraordinary General Meeting". So, with the help of the bank, we drafted five resolutions, called the EGM and put them to the shareholders. In the meantime I spent the couple of months before the meeting talking to as many shareholders as possible, giving them the background to the dispute and seeking their support. All the public to-ing and fro-ing proved highly entertaining for the rest of the toy industry.

As a diversion (put up to it, I was later told, by the chairman) the fourth managing director took out a libel writ against me because the *Daily Telegraph* had published an interview with me in which I said that I had no confidence in him. During the interview I had also gone on to say that no doubt he had no confidence in me – but they didn't publish that part. The *Telegraph* initially agreed to cover my costs, but when my lawyer proposed that the two actions, against me and the *Telegraph* should (for economy reasons) be combined, the *Telegraph* for some bizarre reason refused and demanded that the cases be heard separately. The thought of going through the court action twice was too much to contemplate so we went ahead and combined the actions. At this point the *Telegraph* ceased supporting my costs.

They would not listen to rhyme or reason and my only satisfaction from the whole thing came when I sent the *Telegraph's* chairman a copy of the large notice, which I had taken off one of their news stands, which read "The *Daily Telegraph*: the Newspaper you can Trust", suggesting that he might at least change their slogan!

When it came to the EGM, despite all my efforts and the efforts of my advisers we won two of the least important resolutions and lost the three main resolutions by about 1% of the vote. As a result I was clearly out of a job. Two years later I won the libel action but, because of the *Telegraph's* action, was still forced to pay substantial costs.

Chapter 6
Bluebird Toys

I must say that after the EGM I felt a huge sense of relief that it was all over. I suddenly realised that I could do anything I wanted in life. I spent a month or two walking around the streets, and the garden, trying to work out what I really wanted to do. It came as quite a surprise to me that, at the end of it all, the only thing I had come up with was an idea for a new toy – the Big Yellow Teapot.

So just for fun I did some rough drawings and took them to a friend with a view to making a model. It took a surprisingly long time to work out all the details but I was very excited by the result. The thought of licensing this beautiful thing to another company was too awful to contemplate so I decided that I would start a small company of my own to make it. Of course you can't start a company with one product so I spent the next few months developing half a dozen more ideas to make up a small range of products. Among them were a beautiful traditional sweet shop and a new design of lunchbox. At that time, Margaret Thatcher had hugely increased the price of school lunches and so more and more children were taking their lunch into school in plastic bags. I thought they would much prefer something with a great character like Superman on it than a plastic bag. I also designed a flask with a wide lid so that they could take soup or fruit salad in their packed lunches.

The country at that time (1979) was entering a recession and I had a strong desire that all our products should be made in Britain. I had thought hard about an English name and finally came up with Bluebird. I found it was owned by the Mettoy company, for the model which they made of Malcolm Campbell's Bluebird record-breaking car. They kindly agreed to sell me the name for a few hundred pounds for use by the company but not of course for products that competed with their car. The other reason I liked Bluebird as a name was because, by changing the dot on the letter 'i' into the picture of a tiny bluebird, the reader had a double impact:

the name and image simultaneously. Perhaps that was nonsense but it was in my mind at the time.

I had to raise capital to start the company and calculated that we needed in total around £500,000. I sold our house in London, since most of our children had grown up and left home, and bought a smaller one in Gloucester Crescent, where Anne and I lived until a few years ago. The extraordinary boom in property prices at that time meant that I could pay off a huge overdraft, buy the new house, and capitalise half the new company.

I went to see an old friend of mine, Bobby Nicolle (he had also been on that flight to Le Mans), who at the time worked for another merchant bank, Kleinwort's. I took with me some of the models from our proposed first range including the Big Yellow Teapot. Bobby brought into the meeting a colleague, Harry Conroy, who ran a number of investment trusts aimed at small companies. As luck would have it, while we were discussing the venture, the tea lady came in and offered us a cup of tea. She caught sight of the big yellow teapot sitting on the table and said "Ooh, isn't that lovely!" I explained that it was only a model which we were thinking of putting into production. She immediately asked if she could have the first one off the production line. I said of course, if it was ever made. Harry said he thought it would be, and sure enough Kleinwort's agreed to put up the other half of the capital. Now that's how banking used to be done! And the tea lady got her teapot.

I am delighted to say that Bluebird Toys made the Kleinwort trusts a great deal of money and I remember many years later Bobby told me that in one trust it was their largest holding.

Bluebird was a dream come true. Tom Charnock, who was works director at Peter Pan joined us as well as David Laxton, who had helped us as a subcontractor with our tooling and injection moulding in the Berwick Timpo days. David became my principal partner and was the pillar on which the quality of our products and the integrity of the whole operational side depended. Even now he works with my son Casey in a highly successful toy design business, in which I play a small role.

We also assembled a salesforce made up of some great characters in the toy trade who were wonderful salesmen. After much searching, I found an empty factory on the outskirts of Swindon, which was very convenient as I had built a small country house for our family near Cirencester in Gloucestershire after Anne and I were married.

With David, Tom and the team we were building, Bluebird Toys was now up and running. I must say the complications of getting the new ranges just right as well as the packaging, TV commercials (which we mostly made in-house) and all the computer systems etc. was fairly demanding but we managed it all somehow and Bluebird even made a tiny profit in its first year.

Bluebird Toys turned out to be a fantastic company in all the ways that matter; it had its share of ups and downs, of course, but they were mainly ups. The toy fairs, both at home and all over the world were a combination of hard work and enormous fun. The toy industry globally is a surprisingly small community made up of manufacturers, trading companies, importers, wholesale and retail customers and inventors. Starting a small company, which was seen to be successful, was a huge privilege and it meant that our senior people and myself were welcome almost everywhere (There were, however, a few bars in almost every city where we were most definitely *not* welcome). But major toy inventors, such as Marvin Glass, were kind enough to deal with us and we acted as UK licensee for a number of oversees manufacturers.

My friend Joe Brewer, for example, insisted that I set up Bluebird's first range in his suite at the Majestic hotel in Harrogate, as we were too late in the year to book a proper toy fair stand. Joe was perhaps the foremost toy salesman in the industry at that time and taking Bluebird under his wing was an extraordinary gesture. All the customers came to see him and quite a few of them ordered all seven Bluebird products.

Joe and a group of friends from across the industry, most of whom were completely unhinged, would get together at every toy fair around the world for parties I wouldn't dream of describing. Somehow, in the middle of one of them, I was elected chairman of the World Table Walking Association – probably because I was the tallest and most likely to fall off – an association whose meetings nearly always ended in mayhem. We remain friends to this day.

In the early days we were proud to put a Union Jack on every Bluebird package with the inscription "All our toys are made in Great Britain". But after a few years it became clear that we would have to start making toys in China to remain competitive.

I will never forget the problems I had in persuading David Laxton to go out on his first visit to China to look over the tool-making and production facilities there. Very reluctantly, he eventually set off for

Hong Kong and we heard nothing for several days. Then suddenly a telegram arrived saying something like, "This place is amazing, we can get excellent tools here and the quality of production is terrific. Thanks for insisting that I come out".

So after that, every new product we developed, and some of our existing range, was costed for production both in our own UK factories and in China. A few years later we set up our own office in Hong Kong, which eventually employed around eighty people, and we sourced products from both Hong Kong and all over south China. David came to love his trips to China, where he was (and still is) welcomed with open arms by the local manufacturers. The reason he was so popular was that he always kept his word, was meticulously careful when products were costed, and was fair in every detail of our relationships. Of course they also liked the volumes that we were able to give them as Bluebird grew.

Among Bluebird's successful products were the Big Yellow Teapot, Manta Force, the À la Cart Kitchen, Mighty Max, and above all Polly Pocket. History repeated itself when we took over Peter Pan Playthings, which had itself absorbed Harbutt's Plasticine. Peter Pan produced some wonderful games including Frustration and Headache as well as Etch-a-Sketch and all kinds of craft items, chemistry sets and other educational toys.

We licensed Polly Pocket to Mattel as sales agent for most of the world, but retained all the manufacturing rights (it was made in China) and the sales rights for Great Britain. At one point Polly Pocket was Mattel's second largest toy range for girls (although far behind the legendary Barbie).

After a few years we became a public company, moving onto the main London Stock Exchange. But as time went by I was beginning to feel that I had accomplished all I could and was showing signs of my advancing years. So eventually I decided in 1994 that I would start to work my way out of Bluebird, retiring as Chief Executive in 1995 and as Chairman in 1996, at the age of sixty-three.

Chapter 7
'Retirement'

Some years before I retired, my wife Anne had given me a Tiger Moth aeroplane for my birthday (a most amazing, typically generous and loving present) and I had begun to fly again. My great friend, the writer Al Alvarez, and I used to go out to Panshanger and fly the Tiger at weekends. In due course with Vic Norman (no relation) and subsequently Nick Mason (of Pink Floyd fame), I bought a half share in a World War I aerodrome near our house at Rendcomb in Gloucestershire. This led to my building up a small collection of de Havilland aircraft – not for the pleasure of collecting, but in order to fly them. One of these was a de Havilland Dragonfly (I think there are only two extant worldwide), a plane I had loved since seeing one on the apron at Heston as a child. Mine had suffered a bad crash in St Louis in the States.

I noticed an article in a flying magazine showing a photo of the wreck, and as I was due to visit Chicago on toy business, I diverted to St Louis and looked it over. It was pretty badly damaged (it had swung off the runway on take-off and flown flat out into an eight foot ditch) but I negotiated a price with the owner. Then I had it shipped to Cliff Lovell in England, one of the country's finest aircraft restorers (who, by coincidence, had rebuilt it once before for Martin Barraclough and Tony Haigh-Thomas, who had brought it in from South Africa). I was relieved that Cliff would agree to undertake again the painful and detailed work of rebuilding such a complicated machine, and gratefully passed over to him the three year job.

The completion of the Dragonfly and my leaving the toy industry happened at about the same time and I hit upon the idea of marking my change of working life by flying the Dragonfly from Gloucestershire to Oshkosh in Wisconsin for the great air show which they hold there every August. I asked my friend Henry Labouchere, who kindly looked after my aircraft from an engineering point of view but who is also a superb pilot, if he would like to come with me. Without any hesitation he agreed, but I think his wife Gilly and their two daughters did have some serious reservations. From my point of view I had gained a pilot to share the flying, a great travelling companion, as well as a brilliant engineer to look after the old aeroplane.

We designed and fabricated a large steel auxiliary fuel tank, took out the rear seats to accommodate it, moved the third seat so that it was central (behind the pilot and co-pilot seats), installed extra radios including an HF radio and an inflatable dinghy – neither of which we ever used – and generally equipped the aircraft for a long journey. By the time we had finished, we had to apply for a new certificate of airworthiness on the basis of having increased the all-up weight by something like 1400 lbs above the normally permitted level. This was a bit alarming, since the two Gypsy major engines, rated at 143 hp each, were not sufficiently powerful, in our view, even at its normal all-up weight. It would just about maintain height in normal circumstances on one engine, as long as there were only two people on board, with little luggage and about half fuel. But certainly not with our huge overload.

Anyway Henry carefully checked over the engines and we set off in July 1995 from Gloucestershire heading for the famous Oshkosh airshow. There used to be a saying that flying consists of long periods of intense boredom punctuated by short periods of intense fear. We certainly had some periods of intense fear on that flight but not one second of boredom. Our first leg was from Lyneham, where we re-fuelled, and which had a long enough runway for us to get off the ground for the next leg to Stornoway. But we didn't make it to Stornoway that day as we hit a storm just opposite the island of Arran, which nearly turned the aeroplane on its back, forcing us to divert to Prestwick for the night.

The following morning Henry took over the helm to Stornoway and the weather was perfect with a glorious blue sky. Nothing could have been more beautiful than skimming along at about 500 feet beside all those glorious Western Isles. Henry was very happy flying the machine, pointing out where he used to spend his holidays as a child until, on the approach to Stornoway, I detected a note of concern in his voice. After a near perfect landing I asked him about it and he said that he had realised on the approach that he couldn't move the rudder pedals, due to the fact that we had neglected to take off the rudder lock before we left Prestwick. Neither of us had noticed this and of course we had put the lock on the previous night to stop the rudder banging about in the storm. It was a tribute both to the aircraft and to Henry's flying skills (as well as the fine weather) that he had managed such a perfect landing. But not much credit to either of us for forgetting to take off the rudder lock!

We parked the Dragonfly in a hangar alongside Bristow's air sea rescue helicopters and spent a comfortable night in the local hotel. We found a chandler who kindly sold us a couple of clips, which enabled us to connect our RAF lifejackets to our Royal Navy dinghies.

The main problem with flying old aircraft in those areas is the weather and how one negotiates it. The icing level in the summer is usually between four and six thousand feet, which is okay as long as you are over water but becomes dangerous when you are flying over mountains. And since our cruising speed at the weight we were carrying was about 90 knots, the leg from Stornoway to Reykjavik took about seven hours. There is nearly always bad weather somewhere on these long routes, virtually every day. The idea is that if you have to face bad weather it is best to do it somewhere in the middle of the leg and certainly not at your destination. So we often found ourselves at two or three hundred feet underneath a front in fairly heavy rain and then coming out of it in time to arrive at our destination in fine weather. Since we were flying so low, our VHF radios had very limited range, which meant that we had to ask passing airliners to forward our position to air traffic control based at one end or the other. This led to some fairly hilarious conversations, such as the one with an American Airline pilot who asked what on earth we were doing down there in that kind of aeroplane. We tried to explain that we were on a training flight from Gloucestershire but felt we might have taken a wrong turn. In any case the pilots were unfailingly courteous and of course we could hear them talking to each other in unguarded moments, too.

Thanks to our handheld GPSs we were able to find the gravel strip at Kulusuk, an island about halfway up the east coast of Greenland. The previous 200 miles had been absolutely wonderful, flying at about 100 feet above the pack ice, and looking at seals lying splayed in the sun. We were lucky enough to find two empty rooms in the 'Kulusuk Hilton'. This was a four room wooden shed with a large dining room attached, where an enormous Dane by the name of Fleming provided meals for the men working at the airfield and for any 'hotel' residents.

Our arrival at the end of July was not very well timed in one respect: the annual ship which delivered food to the island could only get through the ice in August and was due in about three weeks. The delicious dinner that Fleming produced, which consisted of frozen shrimps followed by a frozen steak with frozen vegetables, had been sitting in the deep freeze for over eleven months. Although I had no ill effects at all, Henry had a very uncomfortable night which of course was in broad daylight. The following day, Sunday, was a holiday for everyone, so Henry and I hired a couple of fishermen and their boats to take us for a run around round the bay through all the icebergs and to a fishing settlement a couple of miles down the coast.

To our huge delight the weather on Monday morning was gin clear with perfect sunshine and we decided to try and go over the ice cap direct to Sondestrom. This could only be done in perfect conditions as it meant dragging the Dragonfly up to 11,000 feet to get over the ice cap which, at its highest, was around 9,600 feet. At an initial climb rate of around 400 feet a minute, which rapidly fell off to almost nothing as we got higher, this was a considerable effort. However the approach to the ice was over fairly low mountains; we managed it with little difficulty after about an hour in the climb. The visibility in those latitudes is virtually unlimited. When we arrived on the Saturday we had seen Greenland from around 200 miles away as a black line on the horizon, and going across the ice cap in brilliant sunshine was indescribable. The only thing that was difficult was assessing our height above the ice since the light was so bright. But we saw the American Air Force observation station at Sea Bass from well over 100 miles away. And in no time at all (less than four hours) we were letting down at Sondestrom.

The weather clamped down and we were stuck there for a few days. But finally, after an abortive attempt to fly south, we headed west to Iqaluit via the very aptly named Cape Dyer which appeared all too suddenly out of the murk. After a night in Iqaluit we set off south for a very uncomfortable night at Kujuack and, badly misled by a gorgeous young woman in the control tower, took off the following day for what turned out to be a nightmare run to Sept Isles on the north bank of the St Lawrence.

The controller had explained that the weather was flyable if we started out to the west and then paralleled our route for the first three hundred miles returning eastwards as we approached the St Lawrence. In fact the cloud got lower and lower until we had no option but to climb to a safe altitude above the mountains and fly on our rudimentary instruments, an art in which I am only a moderate performer at the best of times. Henry was sitting behind me with the map and the GPS and I cannot imagine an act of greater courage than trusting his life to me in such circumstances. The problem was that the icing level was around 5,000 feet and the mountain tops (assuming we were where we thought we were) around 4,500 feet. The engines seemed to be running smoothly but every now and then one would give a hiccup, which we assumed was it coping with a bit of ice, at which time I would descend a couple of hundred feet, hoping that the mountains and our altimeter were behaving themselves. Henry, as calm as can be, was reading off our speed and position on the map. In short we had been extremely stupid and should never have set off in the first place.

But eventually we popped out of cloud into a lovely evening and knew that in no time we would be on land and tasting the lobster at Chez Omer in Sept Isles, which we'd been assured by Dru was the best in North America. The airfield had three runways and none of them were remotely into wind, but I pulled off a survivable landing in about 20 knots of cross wind and we went into town, only to find out from Omer that he was fresh out of lobster!

After that we headed down to Portland in Maine to spend a few days basking in Bobby and Millicent Monks's kind hospitality, and then headed west for Oshkosh. All was going smoothly for the first day, but as luck would have it we were cruising in fine weather over Ohio on the next day, when to my silent alarm I noticed that the oil pressure on the starboard engine was ever so slowly going down. When it reached the safety level I asked Henry if he had noticed it. He said he had and we agreed rapidly to land at the nearest airfield. Henry told me that this was Tiffin, about five miles ahead. So we transmitted on their local frequency to warn them of a straight-in landing and arrived a few minutes later with the oil pressure gauge reading zero. On stepping out of the aircraft onto the apron we both breathed huge sighs of relief.

Brad and his wife Kim Newman plus Kim's dad Dwight, a wonderful family who owned the field, gave us a warm welcome. When we explained the problem they could not have been more helpful. Henry checked the engine over and could find nothing wrong. We flew to the neighbouring airfield at Bowling Green, where they had some space for us and Henry and I (but mostly Henry) took the engine to pieces all over the hangar floor. Again we found nothing wrong and put it back together again. An air test showed the oil pressure going down again and since we had by then mostly missed the Oshkosh show we flew over in a friend's aircraft for the last day and came back to Tiffin, leaving the Dragonfly with Brad and Kim for the winter.

Henry went out later in the year, fitted a second oil pressure gauge on the nacelle, and found (to our combined fury) nothing wrong with the engine, but a leak in the long tube that connected the engine with the oil pressure gauge in the cockpit. So he serviced both engines carefully and came home.

The following year we went back to Tiffin to collect the Dragonfly, stopped to pick up my brother Desmond near Chicago, and the three of us flew in for a terrific airshow at Oshkosh, where the plane was greatly admired and photographed, even appearing on the cover of the 1996 EAA Oshkosh calendar. Henry and I then flew it back to England, with somewhat fewer adventures than on our way out, but with equally lousy weather, and we even completed the final leg from Reykjavik to Henry's house in Norfolk (including a re-fuelling stop in Glasgow) in one long day – not bad for a more than sixty year old wooden aeroplane.

It was at Goose Bay on the way home that I received the news that a six-month effort to buy the Roundhouse in Chalk Farm might be about to pay off, so there was some pressure to get home quickly.

For the sake of completeness I should mention that having promised myself that I would never do anything as stupid as flying a sixty-two year old aircraft across the Atlantic again, I suddenly got the urge in 2000 to have one more go in my Leopard Moth – sixty-seven years old. I wanted to do something for Geoffrey de Havilland and have one of his aircraft at the millennium Oshkosh air show as he was the man who, with his design genius, has given me more pleasure in life than any other.

Henry as usual did the necessary on the aircraft and the engine, and had a steel tank made up to replace the rear seat with extra fuel. Hugely overweight, as usual, but well within the aircraft's capacity to carry it all and buoyed by the confidence that I had twice the chance of getting there with only one engine to go wrong, I set off from Gloucestershire in July 2000, alone this time. The weather was lousy (as usual). I got stuck in Wick for three days and finally set off for Reykjavik into a 30 knot head wind. But after what I now understand to be the normal hair-raising experiences, including an engine that missed a beat every 30 or 40 minutes across the north Atlantic (my heart missed about seven every time), a failed attempt to cross the ice cap, a close call with an iceberg about 200 miles out of Narsarsuaq, a tempest on the approach to Goose Bay, a delicious, huge, lobster at Chez Omer (he certainly made up for the previous disaster) and a reasonable run across Canada, I eventually arrived at Oshkosh, where Des and Henry, my son Casey and a flying friend of his David Ponte joined me for a wonderful show.

I kept the aircraft at Tiffin during the winter and the following year flew around the southwest USA. I picked up Al who was playing poker at Tunica Mississippi and his wife Anne at Tampa, and together we flew down to Florida to see Bobby and Millicent Monks and then on to the Sun 'n Fun airshow at Lakeland.

On the way north I stopped in Washington DC where I had the rare privilege of flying the famous test and night fighter pilot John Cunningham into Edwards Air Force Base as part of an official visit by the Air Squadron (a club of aeroplane enthusiasts of which I am a member). Finally I arranged to bring it home in a container. It was beginning to display minor faults and there were few people in the USA who understood old de Havilland aeroplanes sufficiently to repair it. At least that was my excuse. I am sure Hubert wouldn't have approved!

I must mention here a lifetime fascination with river barges, which began when I first visited Paris as a young man and was strengthened by later visits with Anne. We used to go there often and enjoyed long walks along the banks of the Seine. I used to sketch the interesting barges that I saw and even reached the point, when I got home from one of these visits, of starting to design one.

About twenty-five years later, when I retired from the toy industry and could finally afford it, I had the opportunity to design and build one for real. I visited Groningen in the north of Holland, which is famous for its glorious canals and its history of barge building. With the help of a Dutchman named Robert Uenk I eventually bought an old 1926, thirty metre luximotor working barge and with Robert's help converted it into something we could live and travel in. Its original purpose was to transport grain and gravel etc. across the Baltic.

It was a three year labour of love, but between us, we created what I believe is still one of the most beautiful traditional barges on the canals. The same design disciplines of fitting a quart into a pint mug, that I had encountered years before in designing our bus, existed in spades when trying to fit everything into the barge. But with wonderful panelling everywhere and a beautiful deck line created in steel by local craftsmen, the first Patricia was beautiful to look at and comfortable to live in. I even found space for a huge bath next to the owner's cabin, and on the foredeck, space for a Renault Twingo. What pure luxury. The old adage about boats, that if you ask the price you can't afford it, was certainly true. I named her Patricia after my mother, who had enjoyed barging in France with friends and it meant that I could think of her even more often.

My idea was that when I became old and gaga, should my children entertain thoughts of putting me in a home, they would first have to find me. There are 8,500 kilometres of canals in France and this would be a difficult task. In fairness, they have shown no such tendencies and I feel very safe.

But when my wife became ill it eventually became impossible to take her to the barge and in the end we had no option but to sell it – luckily to a lovely couple, Barry and Anne Singleton, who fell in love with it and use it constantly – their latest trip being down the Danube.

Later I couldn't resist buying, designing and building a second Patricia (we took the name with us). It is even older (1916) and smaller, but my partner Iga and I can manage her on our own. The original Patricia was too large, too difficult and too complicated. Barry and Anne being younger and fitter, manage brilliantly.

It is the design work that really turns me on. The new Patricia was also built at Groningen, managed by a young man who had worked on the first one. Willem de Vries is one of the most capable men I have ever met. He can do anything, build anything and fix anything (very like Henry) and through years of working together he and his lovely wife Janet have become like family to us. They have also become very close to Barry and Anne. We get huge enjoyment taking friends for trips down the Nivernais and harbour thoughts of longer trips when time allows. At the present rate of progress this may be some time ahead.

Chapter 8
The origins of our idea for the Roundhouse

I should now explain a bit of background to my involvement with the Roundhouse. In 1986 my wife Anne, who was always a wonderful supporter of good causes, had been giving my overdraft away at such a rate that I couldn't keep up with it, particularly as we had five young children approaching school age.

So to try and buy time to catch up, I persuaded her that we should take around a third of our shares in Bluebird Toys and put them into a charitable trust which, if it was successful, would be dedicated to good causes – mostly, we agreed, related to young people. The other two thirds we divided among ourselves and our children. The company was only small at that time (just five years old) so to me it didn't seem a huge sacrifice and Anne was happy with the idea. To our surprise, largely due to the worldwide success of our miniature doll Polly Pocket, Bluebird started to fly from that moment on. By the time I retired from Bluebird, the charity had built up a significant amount of money.

When Anne and I discussed it we both thought the best idea was to devote the money, which amounted to over £6 million, to a large project related to the well-being of young people, rather than spread it around among large numbers of small projects. We felt, for a lot of reasons, that during our lifetime many young people in Britain had received a lousy deal.

I remember as a young man after the war thinking that the country could only get better and that Britain was a wonderful place in which to live and work. It was full of energy, life and exciting ideas and the future seemed unlimited. Thanks to an excellent education and a small amount of capital inherited at a young age following the death of my father, it was clear that my own life had been especially privileged. Although, during the intervening years, the country has got richer, the gap between rich and poor has grown ever wider, and all around us so many young people with so much potential have been poorly educated, remain in poverty and suffer all the problems related to that. Society also suffers as a result.

We wanted to spend our money on something that would demonstrate how to work with large numbers of mostly deprived young people and show them a better way of living their lives. Perhaps over ambitiously, we wanted to build a model that might be copied all over the country – to actually do something rather than talking about it – which could leave young people better off than when we started.

Most of the varied projects which I had worked on during my life had one thing in common. They seemed fairly straightforward in concept but turned out to be much larger, more complicated and time-consuming than I had ever imagined when it came to seeing them through. The phrase 'biting off more than one can chew, and then chewing it' used to occur to me.

The idea for the Roundhouse came to me in the bath. This was where I got most of my ideas (both good and presumably most of the bad ones too). Perhaps it was the hot water that stimulated me. It probably followed something I had read in the local paper. Anyway, I thought I would try to research the ownership of the famous Roundhouse in Chalk Farm to find out whether it could be bought. Anne and I had fond memories of taking our children there for musical performances when they were young, but it had been a pretty wild place in those days and had subsequently fallen on hard times and stood virtually derelict for years, immune to all attempts thus far to resurrect it.

By strange coincidence I was introduced at the very same time to the daughter of one of my Cambridge rowing crew. She came for a drink one evening with her partner, who happened to be a leading London estate agent. I asked, by way of conversation, whether he thought the Roundhouse could be bought. He answered unequivocally that he was pretty certain it could be. I discovered later that his brother, a property developer, was actually occupying the car park adjacent to the Roundhouse. This seemed to me divine intervention, and as a non-believer I guess I shall never come closer to the real thing.

A couple of weeks later I had made an offer to the owners of around £3 million in cash from our Trust, which was accepted, and without any form of due diligence (beyond my wandering around the smelly, pitch-dark undercroft with a torch and inspecting the title) Anne and I, as sole trustees, became its new owners.

It would not be an exaggeration to say that I should probably have been locked up for driving a horse and cart through the charity regulations (of most of which I was blissfully unaware), not only because of the absence of any kind of due diligence but also for assuming a valuation that was in fact incalculable by any sane surveyor – and above all for buying a building with no ownership of the land adjacent to it (the car park), and which consequently had no form of access for heavy goods or anything else other than a few pedestrians off Chalk Farm Road.

I found out that the car park was owned by the Estates Division of the Metropolitan Police, who had originally had the idea of turning it into a super magistrates' court. In fact it took nearly seven years for me to persuade the owners (who had become the magistrates themselves, under the re-organisation of the Greater London Authority), via the government and even the Prime Minister (who must have been rather taken aback when I put an envelope, with a letter asking for his help, into his hands after he misguidedly invited me to a reception at 10 Downing Street) to sell it to our charity for the benefit of young people. And this was at what was described as full commercial value. The magistrates did not consider themselves bound by any rules that applied to 'Non Departmental Governmental Bodies', which laid down clearly that help should be given to causes that involved the public good.

Be all that as it may, we did eventually buy it and in fact we needed all that time (and a good bit more) to raise over £30 million to pay for the construction and the equipping of what has since become one of the finest venues in London as well as a huge creative centre for the benefit of young people. Most of our personal funding was set up as an endowment to support the Roundhouse for the indefinite future. We gave the Roundhouse Trust a 99 year lease on the building and the car park for the particular, defined purpose of supporting work with young people in exchange for what the agreement calls for, 'one red rose'.

I was very pleased that our third son, Caspar agreed to help us, mostly by looking after the hiring of the main space to provide whatever income was possible, but also over the entire development period, helping to work out the detailed conceptual uses for the building.

When I last enquired, the Roundhouse Studios had worked with well over 20,000 young people, many very disadvantaged, from a wide range of social, cultural and religious backgrounds. It is interesting to note that throughout the ten years that we have now been working with these young people, none of the team has lost or had damaged or stolen a single piece of equipment and the young people themselves have been exemplary in every way. It has proved to me what I suspected (but had had no experience of beyond the personal): that young people respond to encouragement, help, support, responsibility and the feeling of belonging in surprisingly generous ways. They grow in confidence and their attitudes change. It is verging on the miraculous how people can change in such circumstances.

We think so much of them that we have set up an arrangement where two young people are appointed as full members of the Roundhouse Trust Board on a rotating basis, which means that they participate in all Board decisions and can give the older members of the Board advice and opinions on policies that affect them.

The other thing that struck me most forcibly when I started to work on the Roundhouse project was the incredible kindness and generosity, particularly with time and advice, but also in many cases with funding support, of people who had had experience of the old Roundhouse in the 60s and 70s. In those days it had been an iconic venue for musical and other extraordinary performances of all kinds that are vividly remembered to this day.

For me it felt exactly as if I were a student applying for a job I particularly wanted. I may not have been the most likely candidate, yet somehow I landed it. With a background in aviation, banking, business, in the toy industry, as a trustee of various charities including the Tavistock Clinic Foundation (Britain's leading mental health clinic), the Fleet Air Arm Museum, chairman of school governors and other assorted activities, I could in no way claim to have had any experience whatsoever of the arts (apart from personal appreciation of art and paintings in particular, due to my wife's influence).

It was often embarrassing, when I explained to people that I knew absolutely nothing about the arts; they always politely professed not to believe me. In fact over the twelve years that I was involved with the Roundhouse I met a huge number of extraordinary people, most of whom were deeply involved in the arts and who accepted me in spite of my utter ignorance. Notable among them were the wonderfully talented members of the Roundhouse Trust board who held my hand and supported Marcus Davey, our chief executive, and me through thick and thin – and there was quite a bit of thin – over many years. Marcus had joined us in 1999 and we worked closely together for almost nine years without ever falling out.

Raising over £30 million was a new activity for me and in the early days I found I hardly dared ask anyone for money. But as time went by and my belief in the project grew ever stronger, and because I felt I had paid my entry fee, it became much easier, and by the end I was a hardened campaigner. But especially at the beginning, when everyone was sceptical about the project, it was a spectacular act of faith for an individual or charity to commit any significant amount. I wish I could mention those that did but there are legions of them and I'd be sure inadvertently to leave someone out. I was to all intents and purposes an unknown refugee from the toy industry, and perhaps this was helpful in a way, as I had no history of having failed with a previous arts project.

Two of my very oldest friends, Roger Gibbs and Stuart Wheeler, will not wish to be mentioned here but I have to say, as this is after all a personal chronicle, that there have never been two better friends to anyone than they have been to me, and as a result, to the Roundhouse. In individually different but massively valuable ways they virtually put the project on its feet and gave us, and my credibility, a huge boost. There is no way that I can adequately express to them my thanks.

For over eight years people would tell me that the Roundhouse had no chance of success, that I would lose all our money and have to give back everything that had been given or pledged and so on. But, particularly when we began to work with young people, it became increasingly clear that what we were doing was a vital ingredient in improving their lives. Marcus's and the whole team's enthusiasm for the project saw it through to a successful conclusion – in fact it became bigger and more important than I had ever dreamed it could be.

People have often said to me how proud I must be of all that we have achieved; in all honesty I have to reply that my main emotion has been one of relief. On the day I retired as chairman of the Roundhouse Trust, Marcus was able to announce that the full sum of £30,140,000 had finally been raised. So, at least I left a viable organisation with no debt and with a reasonable (but nothing like large enough) endowment.

My main sadness is that up to now we have not been able to persuade the Government or others that we have built the model that

I hoped for, and that if it was duplicated at say, six or eight locations in major cities around the country it would be an economical and inspiring way of tackling a lot of the unhappiness, violence, idleness, and poor behaviour of young people throughout Britain. These young people simply have nothing to do, and no creative outlets for their energy, especially if school has not worked for them, so that result is almost inevitable.

The Roundhouse alone is working with around 6,000 young people a year and a network of Roundhouse equivalents could work together, connected electronically and with regular visits, residencies and projects between them.

Just a tiny fraction of the millions spent on abortive government computer projects, wasted on poorly thought out tax credit schemes, endless consultants and quangos etc. would have an enormous impact. Just think of the amount of new untapped creative energy that would be released nationally by say 100,000 young people every year doing music, TV and radio production, theatre, and other creative work rather than slouching about the streets creating mayhem and peddling drugs.

I have even suggested a franchise arrangement with schools, whereby space could be created and equipped in certain schools such that students could work at weekends and after hours on music, media production, performance and so on. Outside instructors and the support of parents would help this along, just as it has in our Roundhouse model – they could even be called Roundhouses.

We have to inspire young people to become creative themselves, rather than passively sitting around, watching their pop idols on TV, listening to their iPods, playing computer games and feeling excluded. They could be designing the games, playing the music and performing on stage! We know this because we have done it over and over again.

I hope the above biography gives some idea of why I feel that I cannot drop off the planet without at least trying to gain support for what seems to be wrong with the way our country is run and with some suggestions for how we might go about improving ourselves.

Postscript

I was surprised a few years ago to have come twenty-ninth in *The Independent* newspaper's list of the country's happiest people. A good part of the reason for this, if indeed it's true, lies in my extraordinary good fortune in meeting my present partner, Iga Downing. She is a well-known and brilliant osteopath, with a family of her own and a very big heart. We have formed a loving yet very independent relationship. Iga is mad about flying and we often go on flying trips together – mostly around Europe but occasionally as far afield as New Zealand and Australia. Iga, my children and ten wonderful grandchildren have been the foundations on which my later life has revolved. So what *The Independent* said is undoubtedly true, (and has been true for most of my life) but I have no idea how they found out!

Part 2

A simple truth

Introduction

Through an interesting and varied life I have learnt a simple truth:

> *Real freedom brings self-reliance and independence of mind which releases unimaginable amounts of energy. Willingness to fail and openness to change focuses that energy towards solid achievement. But equally, lack of freedom, over-control, too much management and too many rules leads to disinterest, apathy and failure.*

With the Government over the past ten years we have had the latter in large doses, combined with a fierce attachment to targeting, a fondness for short-term, off-the-cuff solutions and a willingness to spin and deceive the people with (at best) half truths and the rhetoric of self-justification.

Centralised control has demonstrated complete lack of confidence in the common sense and energy of people to manage anything without the 'nanny state' to direct them.

The growth of the over-complex and pervasive benefit and tax credit systems and the huge over-reliance on means testing has ground out the human spirit from our lives and made too many of us dependent on the state for our very subsistence, while removing much incentive to self-fulfilling work.

This has involved an inescapable necessity to increase taxation – even before the current credit crunch has taken it to unprecedented heights – and the employment by government of large numbers of civil servants to make sure all their complicated rules are adhered to. Poverty is still widespread – particularly among children and young people – and social mobility has been stifled.

The vast amount of money poured into the great departments of state has been absorbed to a large extent by increased wages and pensions but has not had a proportional effect on the quality of the services provided.

What has been lacking is straightforward, honest leadership with a clear vision of how to improve our future and the transparency to encourage and inspire people to believe in it.

So the simple question is: How do we return from our present abyss to the heights of confident achievement? The answer must include: clear leadership with a strong vision of where to take us, empowerment of the people as individuals, simplification of most aspects of our lives, the introduction of transparency at every level, basic good management, plus encouragement and incentive – instead of the endless culture of punishment and the erosion of freedoms.

So I guess the central theme of my book is: Self-reliance.

Tomorrow morning

Just think of what it would be like to wake up one morning in a few years time and find that:

- Parliament had been reformed so that ministers had time to devise policy and do their jobs. Public sector organisations were independently and efficiently run and the Civil Service reorganised to administer our government in a professional non-political manner.

- Members of Parliament had real jobs and real authority, independent of the Whips or anyone else.

- The House of Lords was elected and, through a reformed committee system, was working side by side with the Commons to ensure effective legislation and enlightened government.

- There was no more spin or deceit. Freedom of Information and transparency in nearly everything was the rule.

- Democracy at home had been devolved to local control, where citizens had a strong voice in managing their own schools, hospitals, community centres, prisons and police.

- Young people were being treated as individuals worthy of support, with activities and skills that encouraged them to become strong members of society.

- Youth unemployment was a thing of the past. Communities were running their own affairs and were full of confidence. Serious incentives to work were re-established for all.

- British industry was incentivised to take large numbers of apprentices, to support its growth and aid its recovery.

- We treated our prisoners humanely and looked after their pastoral, health and educational needs in a way that enabled many of them to rejoin their communities as contributing citizens.

- Drug dealers no longer terrorised estates and ruined the lives of many young people. Burglaries fell by 60%. The huge sums spent on petty crime and hunting down dealers were spent on rehabilitating those who had become dependent, to become contributing members of society.

- Means testing had been much reduced and in most areas eliminated completely. The whole of British society was free again to work and contribute to its own prosperity with low marginal tax rates. Poverty reduction was taking place of its own accord – with a vengeance.

- The income tax system had been hugely simplified and tax thresholds were at a level where half of us paid no tax at all. Britain's economy was growing faster than its historical rate.

- The benefit system was massively simplified so that ordinary people could understand and operate it. So that it applied to fewer people, and was administered by a caring government department with a local office that was staffed by local people who you got to know personally (like your doctor), and who sorted out your benefit exactly to meet your entitlement, with a single monthly payment to your account.

- All the endless form filling, discussion, and arguing about the complexities of benefit entitlement, was a thing of the past and more than a million government and other employees were back doing constructive jobs creating wealth for the nation.

- Cheating and fraud against the state was greatly reduced.

- Pensioners, instead of facing poverty, would receive a pension that at least kept them above the poverty level, with virtually no means testing.

- For every new law or regulation that was passed at least one (but preferably more) were removed from the statute books.

- The 'nanny state' was being dismembered with enthusiasm. The amount of surveillance and snooping by numerous authorities was being reduced to more civilised levels, by panels of legal tigers.

Achieving this would surely be worth the effort!

It can't be done overnight. But with determination and the right agenda it could certainly be done within the span of two parliaments.

I suspect no one in authority will remotely comprehend the enormous power and energy that would be unleashed in this country by the combined, huge increase in the tax threshold, the virtual elimination of means testing, the radical simplification of the benefit system and the re-introduction of strong incentives to work through the reformed tax credit system.

Would that I were wrong!

Chapter 1
Why this book?

An effort to promote discussion

When I began thinking about writing this, and through reading quite a few books and articles, what became blindingly obvious almost immediately was how appallingly badly we are being ruled. It was far worse than I had imagined. Some of the failures of our government are systemic, some are down to lousy management, and some have been downright dishonest. Above all, the impression one receives is of total amateurism in most areas of running the country.

I hope my proposals may be of interest in focusing us towards programmes of change that will in the end leave us with a more professional approach to solving our problems and a less frenetic, short-term, incompetent and deceitful style of government.

I should point out that nothing I am saying is original and some of it, dare I say, may even be wrong. I simply want to stimulate discussion about what sort of country we want to live in and hope that in some small way we can influence our rulers towards giving it to us. The inaction towards positive reform over many years is highly dispiriting.

My life has taught me a few simple lessons to do with hard work, persistence, integrity, openness, attention to detail, approaching problems with a certain detached sense of humour and above all an eye to a more inspiring future. (I wish I had more of these virtues but I have at least been attracted to them in others!)

I do not feel especially engaged politically and the roots of many of our problems go back for decades. But I must admit that experience of the past ten years of government seems to have taken most of our difficulties to a higher level of incompetence. However the point is that we are where we are and we must find a way of getting somewhere better.

Unfortunately, while writing this Britain has fallen into appalling recession and, as a result, many of the things that I would like to do immediately are likely to prove a lower priority than dragging our poor over-borrowed country out of the mire.

However, much of what I want to do can be done while actually saving money and doing these things should be encouraging for most of us and should make the job of getting Britain back on its feet somewhat easier. I have pretty much ignored the recession in writing this book. Huge hardship is being inflicted on large numbers of people by our present circumstances and since some of my proposed remedies are fairly demanding in themselves they will have to be handled with great sensitivity and where necessary, introduced slowly. President Obama is demonstrating that fundamental reforms such as (in his case) reform of the US healthcare system can be undertaken in spite of the huge current fiscal problems. It is well worth taking a few risks in establishing the kind of society we want to live in. Continuing the way we are is simply not an option.

The proposals in Part 3 are set out with a short note at the beginning of each chapter sketching the background to the problems, some panels with relevant facts and then short suggestions of actions – or approaches towards actions – we could take that might lead us to better solutions.

Many will consider the assertions and the proposed solutions too sweeping but I haven't the space, time or inclination to consider every argument for and against everything that needs to be done, and I suspect no one would read something of that length anyway. What I am trying to do is set out the issues in a short, simple form and – unlike many of the books I have been reading – provide some ideas for how to go about sorting them out.

I have not dwelt on the good things that have happened – it would be impossible for any government to have spent such huge sums of money without favourable outcomes (although it seems to me far too few) - but have tried to concentrate on the more obvious bits that need fixing.

I should also add that there are many wonderful traits in this country that have survived all the pressures applied to wiping them out. I am sure Parliament, for example, will ultimately be reformed in terms of the lack of ethical values that have recently been exposed and, I hope, also in the way it operates, to make it more effective and more relevant to solving the nation's problems. Our armed forces are second to none in the world, in spite of constantly being over-stretched, ill-equipped and wrongly deployed. The health service has many wonderful people working in it, but deserves better leadership and administration. Much the same can be said of the education system, the prison service, and so on.

In fact in almost every area, this country still has an underlying strength and honesty that is trying to come out. It is just that our leadership has been so lousy and deceitful, and the structure for management is so poor, that it has had very little chance to do so.

Chapter 2
Where we are

We must face the facts. The country is not fit for purpose. We can either just coast along, accepting things as they are, or, get on with doing something about it.

I believe that in Britain we have lost much of the energy, ambition, zest and optimism which was so apparent in my youth and replaced it with higher taxes, endless rules, state interference at all levels, targeting, form-filling and all kinds of complications and inconvenience which have made us demonstrably unhappier, more violent, increasingly materialistic, less irreverent and endlessly weighed down with the mounting cares of simply staying alive and making the best we can of our personal situations.

Britain is a wonderful place to live – particularly for those with the resources to make the most of it – but for many, life is one hell of a struggle. This is because we have been, and are still being, very badly served by successive governments.

Over the past century violent crime has remained stubbornly high, particularly among young people. Gang warfare is rife in our large cities. Mutual respect and social behaviour have deteriorated to levels of which we should all be ashamed. We are at the top of the EU league for alcohol consumption among young people. Care of old people and the mentally ill is shamefully inadequate and poorly supervised, as is the care of young people; young offenders are treated appallingly.

Educational literacy standards have not improved in the past fifty years and neither has the social mobility of children.[1] Four out of ten pupils in state education now leave school without the minimum standards in English and Maths that the QCA deems necessary for 'Life, Learning and Work'. Nursery school provision is still far from adequate and often expensive; we are bottom of the EU league in terms of bringing up our children to be good citizens.[2] We are also bottom of the 'happiness league'.

Our hugely subsidised railway system is out of date, overcrowded and often the most costly to use in Europe – and the method of ticketing is far too complex.

The National Health Service is far down the EU league in many vital areas such as, for example, our cancer survival rates. We top the EU league in the number of hospital infections and have done for years. We have far fewer doctors per head of population compared with other EU countries. We have the largest proportion of drug addicts per head of population in the EU. Proportionally more people in Britain suffer from mental disorders than anywhere in Europe. We have the highest number of prison inmates per head of population in the EU (with the possible exception of Portugal), and our Neolithic, overcrowded prison system has little capacity for rehabilitating them; prisoners' likelihood of re-offending within two years stands at close to 70% (more for young people). Our police force and prosecution service is seriously underperforming in controlling crime and bringing criminals to conviction. At the same time, over the past eight years we have slipped from second to tenth place in the EU table of economic well-being.

The policies of our Government have led people in this country to become the most highly indebted in Europe. Between January 2000 and December 2005, levels of consumer credit rose by no less than 65.8% and mortgage lending soared by 94% to a combined total of £1,157.5 billion. This enormous weight of borrowing means that millions of us are living in a state of anxiety about how to meet the bills every month and has led to a huge growth in the numbers of bankruptcies and 'Individual Voluntary Arrangements' (IVAs). Bankruptcies in England and Wales were up from 21,611 in 1999 to 59,516 in 2006 and IVAs from 7,195 to 38,604 in the same period[3] – long before the credit crunch. Around three million houses are in danger of falling into negative equity. The credit crunch is making most of these statistics worse.

The Government itself (even before the effects of the credit crunch and recession) is also running at record expenditure levels – the highest percentage among developed countries – and building increasingly high levels of national debt. The present government deficit of around £180 billion a year pays no heed to its own new accounting rules, totally ignoring the massive future costs of public sector pensions (total cost estimated at £1,261 billion) the future enormous costs of PFI commitments (£148 billion), future nuclear decommissioning costs

(£73 billion), Network Rail's borrowings (£28 billion) and a massive future liability related to the EU accounting rules (£167 billion). If these were taken into account the effect would be hugely to increase official debt to even more astronomical levels.[4]

The point about all these hidden figures is that the Government has relentlessly understated the real debt position of the country by massive amounts and continued to claim virtue in controlling the economy so that it is prudently managed. When the time comes for it all to be disclosed and added up, the situation will be seen by all to be dire. The Prime Minister has told us that the country's debt is 48.2% of Gross Domestic Product (GDP) whereas one estimate puts the UK's total liabilities at nearly ten times this total (478.6%) which he should be showing on his own books according to his own rules, but doesn't.[5]

His much vaunted 'golden rule' when Chancellor, has been long buried alongside his assertion that boom and bust no longer exist. This was the 'golden rule' that allowed him to increase expenditure and pile up debt during the good times, only to find that when the credit crunch came he had few resources to help the country through the bad ones.

One of the tragedies of the post-war period has been the decline of the UK as a manufacturing nation. In 1973 the US produced an estimated 22% more manufactured goods per head of population than the UK. By 2000 the difference was 91%.[6] Alas, the country that provided engineering know-how to the world for over a century can now barely call itself a manufacturing nation. In 2007 Germany and Japan both produced enormous trade surpluses on their manufactured goods. The UK continues to generate large deficits.

Of course we still have some very fine companies that are world leaders in their fields, but the fact remains that manufacturing output has sunk to around 12.4% of our GDP.

While our manufacturing output has been declining the number of government employees and civil servants has been increasing exponentially. Estimates have put the increase in public service personnel over the past ten years at approaching a million people. It is interesting to note that by mid-2005 those working either directly or indirectly for the state amounted to about a fifth of the working population – close to 7 million.[7] This seems to me a huge number. I have no idea how many of these could be converted back to private employment but the number must be very high. The extra benefit of any reduction to those who currently suffer under their scrutiny is, of course, incalculable.

There has also had to be an increase in the number of advisers, lawyers, accountants and others retained by members of the public to avoid or limit as far as possible the consequences of these rules, and where the rules are unavoidable, show us how to implement them. All this non-productive effort saps the initiative and energy of people who could otherwise be doing something very positive for themselves and for the country.

Recent British governments have entirely misunderstood how to eradicate poverty. They have widened the gap between the haves and have-nots and created many excluded and alienated citizens and groups of citizens (often among young people). On top of this, the current government, as well as increasing our taxes to what I believe are unsustainable levels, has centralised the control of most of the public sector within the Treasury, effectively neutered the Civil Service and shown itself incapable of initiating and seeing through necessary long-term changes in these same public sectors.

In case anyone should gain the impression that I am solely critical of the Labour Government I should mention that it is clear that many of our problems go back for a far longer period. There are many examples, but the one that makes me most unhappy is the callous way the previous Conservative Government sold off many of the country's school playing fields (over 10,000 of them) for development, leaving many of the nation's school children deprived of space in which to play games and exercise. It is perhaps only a sad footnote that, despite promises, the current government has not entirely ceased the practice.

Chapter 3
Amateur government

Most ministers have little practical experience but are given huge responsibility. They are mostly moved on to their next posts before they have either the time to learn about their departments or the possibility of working out a well thought out long-term policy for reform. But it is quickly enough for them to avoid personal responsibility for their past mistakes.

From ample experience, the British people have developed a deep mistrust of politicians, and indeed of the whole system of government and its ability to do anything efficiently. Unsurprisingly, among other consequences, this has had the effect of creating serious voter apathy and general disaffection.

Throughout this book the theme of the 'amateur' nature of the way our government is run is paramount. By 'amateur' I mean the almost complete lack of experience in work, training or special education, of the ministers and civil servants that we rely on so heavily to govern us. I mean too, their use of innumerable (often young and inexperienced) consultants, not to mention the outdated systems they all work under.

We appear in this country to have a genius for complicating almost everything we touch. The statute books and the myriad ministerial orders, rules, statutory instruments and other regulations which grow year on year in number and complexity bear testament to this. Someone surely must have said that true genius lies in the ability to make things simple. Geniuses in this respect we (and the former Chancellor) clearly are not.

A study of the Government's complication of virtually the entire tax and benefit system underscores how far this process has gone. The UK now has the largest body of tax legislation in the world (apparently having recently overtaken India!). *Tolley's Tax Manual* has grown from 2,529 pages in 1997 to 7,838 pages in 2008!

Instead of raising taxes we should have been reducing them, and of course, the government expenditure that requires them, thereby becoming a great deal more prosperous (as well as far more self-reliant).

This same anti-genius for complication is evident in almost every department of state. For example, the Labour government has introduced at least 40 criminal justice bills, apparently creating over 3,500 new offences – with more in the pipeline. Schools are required to achieve and report on innumerable targets – one local authority apparently recorded 350 policy targets and 175 efficiency targets.[1]

The NHS has suffered from relentless repetitive interference, targeting and multiple (often contradictory) reorganisations. Doctors say that many of the targets have nothing to do with medicine and hinder their work as doctors. As well as having relatively fewer doctors than other major EU countries there are now eight administrators for every ten nurses in the NHS.[2] I have spoken to many doctors and nurses and few have anything positive to say about the quality of administration in the areas in which they work. Confusion and lack of leadership seem to prevail everywhere.

Quangos have proliferated at colossal expense despite every party's stated intention, when in opposition, to reduce them. There must be huge possibilities for saving billions of pounds by abolishing and/or merging many of them. Most of them are virtually uncontrolled and many have overlapping functions. Between 1977 and the end of 2004 The Labour Government created 113 new quangos but, apparently, reliable figures since then are not available. It has, however, been reliably estimated that in 2006-07 taxpayers funded 1,162 public bodies at an annual cost of nearly £64 billion.[3] The salaries of quango bosses alone cost over £100 million per year. Taking just one set of quangos, the Regional Development Agencies, they employ 2,500 people and cost the tax payer £2 billion a year.[4]

The point about saving money on quangos is the obvious one which dictates that there can be no saving without abolishing function. There are huge vested interests at work which need removing. Tinkering won't begin to get the job done. What is needed is wholesale carnage among quangos. The current Conservative opposition has made all the old promises about reducing them. If they are elected at the next general election we can only wish Ken Clarke and his team god speed and a strong following wind.

Health and Safety has become a minefield of rules and regulations. Although a few of these have obviously made our lives safer, many have gone way over the top, increasing complications and costs for business and suppressing the rights of individuals to do reasonable things they had previously enjoyed, as well as often denying them opportunity for employment. The activities of young people have been severely restricted. Few now have the opportunity to learn through experience, which is the bedrock of instilling confidence. There must be a limit to the 'nanny state' and we are clearly way beyond it. Further volumes of legislation have been enacted to cover many other areas including for example, employment law and planning. All of this needs heavy pruning so that ordinary citizens can go back to normal activities. It would be good for our children to be climbing trees again.

The problem with all this interference and targeting imposed by central governments, as well as the extraordinary waste of precious time, is that it means that the responsibility for much that goes on is taken away from the professional practitioners themselves – the doctors, teachers etc. – and consequently these professionals have a diminishing sense of pride or incentive to do their jobs to the standards of excellence which they would ordinarily impose on themselves. All this must change if we are ever to improve our current, very poor, standards. Trust and a small element of risk must be allowed to intrude back into our lives at every level, and in most areas of government.

We have to be proud of our nation – not only for how it behaves, but for what it achieves – and for the strength of our self-reliance and self-belief.

Chapter 4
Family life

We must bring back the strength of strong families who support each other and can always be relied upon for help.

Over the past fifteen years, successive governments have pursued welfare policies that discriminate strongly against married and family life, making it economically very beneficial to be a lone parent family. Many lone parents are claiming multiple benefits in order to survive. Amazingly, the system penalises single parents if they live with a partner – thereby denying their children even a slight chance of being brought up with the benefit of two parents.★ Research has sadly, but conclusively shown that children from single parent families are more likely to fail at school, use drugs, become unemployed, and end up in prison.

Along with all these policies comes a huge army of bureaucrats whose job it is to ensure that the massive sets of rules and form-filling associated not only with taxation but also the increasingly complicated benefit and tax credit system and the continually expanded associated system of means testing, are being complied with.

As a result of these supportive policies the number of lone parent families has been steadily growing. A quarter of children now live with one parent, almost double the proportion of twenty years ago. A by-product of this has been to add to the housing requirements which, as we all know, are tremendously overstretched by the shortage of new building and the influx of huge numbers of migrant workers (now acknowledged to be at least 1,500,000 since 1997, but likely to be many more).

The effect of this social upheaval has not only bred feelings of injustice and inequality, causing social division, for example, the

---

★ This incredible policy surely infringes the rights of children and should be brought before the European Court of Human Rights.

winning of two seats in the European Parliament by the BNP. It has also adversely affected a great British tradition: families' willingness to support other family and extended family members in all kinds of ways greatly advantageous to their quality of life and finances (especially in the cities).[1]

It makes me envious to see that other countries in Europe such as Spain, Germany, Italy, Greece and France have managed to maintain the importance and cohesion of family life to a far greater extent than we have. I understand, of course, that these countries also have problems with bureaucracy, sectarian violence, youth disorder and so on, but if statistics are anything to go by, the situation in Britain is far worse on most counts.

These countries also manage to retain a functioning rural society that seems more capable of self-sufficiency than the British countryside, which appears to have suffered more seriously than others from lack of jobs and migration of young people to the cities, over many years.

No wonder so many British people are moving to Europe, Canada, Australia and New Zealand to live. Emigration is rising fast and reached 385,000 a year in 2006, around 200,000 of whom were British citizens. Emigration to Australia, for example, has increased threefold in the past four years.

In Britain, we have created a large segment of young people, with little or no social framework or family to support them, who have turned their backs on society. Our approach to welfare has led to millions of people of working age (including close to 1 million young people) preferring to remain idle, many of them dependent on a means-tested benefit system that has removed much of their incentive to work legitimately, if at all.

The benefit system was originally conceived by Lord Beveridge as a safety net. It has become a cushy way of avoiding gainful employment for far too many of us.

The benchmark for assessing the poverty level is usually taken to be 60% of average income (excluding the wealthiest members of society). I believe this is the wrong way of looking at it. First of all it becomes a moving target as incomes increase, and secondly no one can really say that poverty in 2009 is on a par with the poverty experienced when Beveridge drew up his proposals in 1944. More than half the people defined as 'in poverty' are homeowners and many are pensioners rich in assets but have a low income. I believe we should do more for those in real poverty and less for those who are manifestly abusing the system.

There is no way of measuring the so-called grey/black economy that has thereby been created, but it has to be immense. (For example it has recently been estimated that over 50,000 houses are occupied by people not entitled to them).[2] It has also been estimated that 40% of households – not including pensioners – are relying for income on means-tested benefit.[3] To me this seems a grotesquely huge number.

With such massive numbers discouraged from legitimate work by astronomic marginal tax rates and by strict means-testing criteria, the numbers doing unrecorded work and avoiding tax must be simply enormous – estimates run to the incredible total of 15%–20% of our national income – as high as £200 billion which should instead be supporting the Exchequer.

Chapter 5
Young people and work

Youth unemployment should be banished forever. My new proposals are likely to be far more cost-effective (and get far more done) than the present system of paying people not to work.

I described the Roundhouse project in my biographical note, but I would like to re-emphasise one point:

> *We have proved beyond any doubt that it would be possible to establish a series of say, eight Roundhouse equivalents throughout the larger cities in Britain, working on the model that we have demonstrated works brilliantly in London, giving young people, from all backgrounds, the opportunity to do creative work in a wide range of activities – and, what is more, at a fraction of the cost of locking them up. Those who have gained experience and confidence in working on Roundhouse-type projects are equipped to become highly contributory citizens in their future lives.*

But of course the situation with young people in this country is far larger and more serious than such a scheme could hope to solve on its own. The level of youth and other unemployment has grown under the impetus of the current recession to historically high levels. Those claiming Job Seekers Allowance (JSA) now number nearly 1.6 million, up over 700,000 in the past year (2008). Total unemployment has reached 2.65 million and is still increasing with estimates approaching 3 million by the end of this recession.

Over the years of the present Government, many attempts have been made to try to improve these figures but of course all these have been swept aside by the severity of the current recession. In truth none of the measures looked like solving the problem, although some are helping. I believe something far more creative is called for.

First of all I cannot understand the sense of paying people on JSA £50–£65 a week to look for jobs which either don't exist or exist somewhere far from where the applicant lives. In 2009/10 the total cost of JSA is estimated to be around £6 billion. In addition of course there is the cost of employing large numbers of personnel in local employment offices. When other related benefits are included the total costs are much higher. Working Tax Credits amount to a further £6 billion, plus the cost of attempting to recover overpayments which themselves run into several billion pounds.

It seems wrong that employment offices should try to do both the job of dealing with benefits which are themselves complicated and time-consuming and also the job of finding work for huge numbers of unemployed which also requires a great deal of time and care. It is clear that they are unable to cope properly with both jobs under current pressure. It will be far simpler and they can be better trained if only the job-seeking function is required.

As part of the solution to this problem I have suggested in my proposals a fundamental reform of the tax credit system based on the Earned Income Tax Credit system as developed in the USA. This has the fundamental objective of paying people to work – not paying them *not* to work. It has had a remarkable success in the USA in reducing the number of claimants and also poverty. It is far less costly to administer than our current flawed tax credit system and these savings could be used to support other causes.

Secondly, I have adopted David Martin's straightforward ideas for simplifying the benefit system from over fifty benefits with complicated and sometimes contradictory rules to what amounts to a single benefit paid directly into the recipient's bank account on a monthly basis.

Thirdly, it is clear that when we compare ourselves with say Germany, Japan or the USA our manufacturing base has slipped to becoming a far smaller part of our national output than it used to be and far smaller relative to our competitors. A side effect of this is that our apprentice system has withered away and the puny efforts of the current government to revive it have had little impact.

My final and I believe most important suggestion in this area, beyond income tax changes, is the establishment of **Community National Service**.

I do not mean National Service in the form that I did it for two years in the Navy and RAF during the 50s – encouraging though this would certainly be in bringing back a feeling of self-discipline and purpose to many young lives – but rather a kind of Community National Service taking place all over the country that would be compulsory for those who had failed to find jobs after a certain period, say six months, and after having completed one (or two) serious professional training courses to acquire skills in trades or sectors for which there is public demand. Failing to find a job in these circumstances would make the candidate eligible for local work in a wide range of occupations funded either by state enterprises, voluntary organisations and/or charities and local communities, through appropriate government intervention. Community National Service would be paid at the appropriate minimum wage and the JSA would be considered a set-off towards the overall cost.

I have mentioned in my proposals the importance of re-establishing a widespread apprenticeship system of the sort that around half of young people in Germany undertake. If the government applied the funds that they have been spending on young people through the JSA who do **not** work, to commercial and industrial companies as a contribution towards a well worked out apprenticeship regime, it is more than likely that the number of apprentices learning in British industry would grow hugely. The present government target of 400,000 by 2020, which they are struggling to meet, would look like a gathering in a village hall. We should aim far higher as part of the regeneration of manufacturing industry.

Richard Lambert wrote a very clear piece in the *Sunday Times*[1] setting out the scale of the problem – as it has grown over the past ten years, during the current recession and is projected to grow in the future. As well as remedying the obvious educational shortcomings of many of our schools in teaching the core subjects and skills needed by our children, he suggests creating a large-scale apprentice programme to green the public domain – installing insulation, double glazing and so on. He also mentions the contribution businesses can make in supporting the communities in which they operate. Deloitte's Employability Initiative helps tens of thousands of young people across the country to develop the skills and behaviour needed to get a steady job. I have also learnt[2] of the Microsoft project to help cut the fast growing unemployment queues by 500,000, by providing free IT skills training and at the same time persuading thousands of small businesses they work with to employ jobseekers. I have set out in my proposals many other prospective areas for useful support by Community National Service members.

The principle of this message is clear. There is no excuse for any fit person not working – finding jobs either through their own efforts or with the help of the state. The entire simplified taxation and benefits system set out later in my proposals would be organised to make this possible. At a stroke, a huge amount of Civil Service interference would disappear, replaced ultimately by a strong community network of support for young people (as well as older people) in jobs that would accustom them to working and give them a springboard towards seeking further training or employment. It is clearly understood that not having a job from the age of leaving school, say at 16, to age 18 makes it far less likely that these young people will ever wind up with a worthwhile job. The habit of becoming lazy is unfortunately easy to absorb. Nothing like enough is done for 16 and 17 year olds to avoid this gap.

A word about training: virtually every sector of government that I refer to in this book is managed by groups of employees that have been recruited to do their jobs often with the absolute minimum of training. The training itself is often poorly thought out and badly administered. This is true in hospitals, prisons, young offender institutions, caring establishments, employment offices and I suspect nearly everywhere else. Of course it is an almost impossible objective to achieve when you think of the complexities of modern life and the lack of clear job specifications and objectives laid down by government to oversee it.

But we have to try to do better, spend more time and money and be more concerned about how we train our people. Efficient, thorough, training of people in the jobs they are being taught to do, with clear understanding of the standards and objectives required, is vital to the success of these proposals for ensuring everyone has a worthwhile job to go to. Co-ordination between the countless private, public, and charitable providers of the services to the public and those who are being trained to do the work is absolutely essential. Quick fixes and short cuts to proper training are a recipe for the kind of disasters we are currently facing. The money spent on thorough training is in fact an economy measure towards the cost of running the various services in the future.

It will take time and a lot of effort to organise both the Community National Service arrangements and the co-ordinated training that would go alongside it, but if it were made a top government priority and broken down into local units so that it was carried out at the same time as local democracy was re-established then it could certainly be done.

It would be a fundamental strength for the future of the country's unemployed (boosting their confidence and transforming their attitude) as well as an enormous morale booster when the country became genuinely democratic again.

But it needs someone somewhere to make it all happen. Apathy and incompetence is no longer good enough.

Chapter 6
Localism and democracy

We must get rid of the dead hand of central government control of our lives. We have a right to manage them ourselves – and would do so far more effectively. The by-products would be more confidence and self-reliance.

There would also be a further huge advantage – particularly welcome during these torrid times of massive government over-borrowing. After having devolved government to local authority level, recent international research suggests that there would ultimately be a saving of around £70 billion *per annum* as the system provided more efficiencies and better local control.[1]

During my lifetime there has been a steady and, over the past decade, accelerating, tendency for successive governments to centralise many of the functions of state. The result of this has been an erosion of local democracy in all its forms.

Central government dictates the funding for local authorities and for virtually everything else. The Treasury and other Ministries set numerous detailed targets for every sector including the NHS, schools, transport and the railways, housing, the police, planning (John Prescott stripped counties of any substantive planning role in 2004) and so on. The Treasury negotiates or oversees national pay scales for huge numbers of public sector workers. It is ultimately responsible for setting up quangos and for their cost. It sets public service pensions (acknowledged to be hugely overgenerous when compared with the private sector) and for which the future enormous cost has not even been calculated or, if it has, it has not been included in future borrowing statistics. It sets business property rates (which account for over half local authority revenue) and decides what projects will be financed through PFIs and the scale and terms of the underlying contracts.

In London the Treasury retained the right to overrule Mayoral decisions, for example, by insisting on their version of privatising the London Underground via a Public Private Finance Initiative rather than financing its cost through bonds as many other cities around the world have shown to be effective (at an extra cost to the taxpayers/travellers estimated at something like £1 billion).

Many of these government decisions are taken behind closed doors and policies are changed at will, usually without consultation

When this is compared, for example, to the situation in the USA, France, Germany, Italy and Scandinavian countries where, after the war, real local democracy was re-established with enormous success, Great Britain is in a lousy state and getting worse. The results are clear and manifest themselves through voter apathy, less efficient and more impersonal public services and general unhappiness. Simon Jenkins has conducted something of a crusade to promote the benefits of local democracy over many years but for some unknown reason no political party has taken up the cause despite occasionally praising its merits.[2] The time to do so is now.

The idea is firmly "to take powers from the centre (including the power to raise taxes) and restore them to British counties and cities and subordinate communities in precisely the way that other European States have done with success and to general public satisfaction".[3]

Re-establishing the foundations for a proper solid democracy in which the whole population can become involved must be one of our most important strategic actions. It would involve the abolition of two complete tiers of existing public administration. These would be the regions and most existing rural districts. This is not as radical as it sounds. Regions are new and both the opposition parties called for their abolition at the 2005 election.[4] As Jenkins has said there would be remarkably little difficulty in doing this. Powers effected largely through discretionary clauses in statutes can be restored by executive order in the same way.

Local mayors are a must. Of course they won't all be good, but if they aren't, it will soon become obvious, and then they can be changed by popular vote. The point is that anything is better than the dead hand of central government.

In Doncaster, for example, the election of Peter Davies, one of only eleven directly elected mayors nationwide, was not in the least expected – even by him. But his individualistic and unconventional views proved so popular with the electorate that he polled 24,000 votes. He has remained enormously popular with his measures to cut costs and what he considers as waste in all directions (he has reduced his own salary from £73,000 to £30,000 and sold the mayoral car). Just watching his progress is refreshing. The same democratic dividend should be available to all communities.

In conjunction with all this, Parliament itself needs root and branch reform. The select committees have very limited powers and are in thrall to the whips who appoint their Chairmen. The whips also have great influence in who is selected for preferment as ministers. Legislation is ill-considered, too prolific and often poorly drafted. Power needs to go back to the people and their representatives and the executive needs keeping up to the mark, at all levels, in a much more robust fashion. The Civil Service needs reforming and dragging into the twenty-first century. The political parties need to encourage the entry of new members who have had real experience of outside employment and administration. The selection of MPs needs broadening to a far wider group of entrants – not only women but people of experience regardless of sex. The Freedom of Information Act needs broadening and strengthening. The recent pay and expenses scandals are having the effect of bringing some of these problems onto the parliamentary agenda. It has certainly demonstrated in spectacular fashion the power for change of freedom of information, even in the neutered form we have it in Britain.

Both houses of the UK Parliament require far fewer Members – more than 200 fewer in the Commons if we emulate the United States, and also far fewer in the House of Lords, particularly when it is finally made into a largely elected chamber. The USA has 435 members of Congress and 100 members of the Senate.

With fewer laws, we could have better government, more freedom, and a better life.

Chapter 7
Re-establishing community life

Strong communities should be the backbone supporting all our social services.

It is clear from the press, from my own experience at the Roundhouse and certainly from Iain Duncan Smith's massive research on family life and young people, that we have lost over the past sixty years or so, our sense of togetherness and society.[1] Many of our families are what has been described as 'broken'. There are far more single mothers and children, far fewer married couples and co-habiting couples and much less evidence of communities supporting the people who live in them. This is particularly true in major cities (where, however, elements of it still remain) and in new towns. Families have broken up, often to go to social housing in distant places, and extended families are much less in evidence providing the support they have always given each other.

There have been millions of new immigrants and the benefit and means-testing system has distorted the attitudes of many people and their willingness to work and progress through their own efforts. The schools have grossly underperformed. Around 35% of young people leave school with no significant qualifications and many of them are illiterate. Many more are dispirited and bored.

There is more violence, more drug addiction and worse behaviour among our teenagers. Nursery school provision is definitely improving but remains inadequate and often expensive. Care for young people has in many areas failed systemically and care for the elderly is often appalling.

Prisons and hospitals and many of the services which are provided for the benefit of communities are organised by central control, and many have few links with the people that they are meant to be serving. For example prisoners are rarely kept near their families and are usually shipped around the country where prison space is available. When they are released there is often no one to stand by them and help them. The National Offender Management Service (NOMS) has been shown to be wasteful and not fit for purpose, and the probation service is fundamentally overstretched, often ill-managed and inadequately funded. Primary Care Hospital Trusts which are intended to serve local communities are managed from Regional Health Authorities and often have little real connection with the local communities they are intended to serve.

While there are always exceptions and well-off people are certainly among these exceptions, most of the ordinary people who make up the bulk of our population are becoming worse off and less well-served in spite of the often well-meaning, but ineffectual, efforts of central government to try to assist them. Billions of pounds have been spent in efforts to improve the situation, in many cases they have failed and much of the money has been wasted.

The principle reason for this failure is that our huge benefit and tax credit system and all the means-testing that accompanies it and all the public workers who try to implement the huge resulting volumes of regulation, have had the result of destroying the will of people to help themselves, work together to build their lives, educate themselves and their children, keep themselves and their families healthy and in the end become solid, confident, fully employed, self-sufficient citizens.

Rather than endlessly tinkering with the problems we need a root and branch reform of the way we live.

Establishing complete and thorough localism in government is an essential precondition of this reform. But the second vital condition is to strengthen – wherever possible through the voluntary sector – effective community centres and services to look after the local communities in a friendly and caring atmosphere.

These community services must be organised to look after all our citizens' needs including young people, old people, the mentally ill, drug addicts and those who have been caught up in crime and the prison system. They must ensure that local schools, hospitals and care homes are properly run. Even if some of the services are outsourced from other connected organisations, the community centre must be the principle source of their support. I have tried to set this out more clearly in my proposals.

Part of the community system must include managing and providing work in the community for all those who for some reason have found themselves either sentenced by the courts to community service, or have failed to find a job after all remedies to train them or place them in work have failed. The community should be the hub around which all these activities are based.

Civil servants in some far-off control centre haven't a hope in hell of approaching these problems in any way that could conceivably lead to success. But local, interested and involved people certainly could – and do, all over Europe and the USA.

Chapter 8
The prison system and treatment of prisoners

The appalling way we treat our prisoners, our lack of compassion, our inability to rehabilitate, educate them or to treat their illnesses, has been benignly watched over by countless ministers throughout my entire life.

As I got deeper into my research I found that this is such an enormous minefield of problems that I didn't want to be thought even more stupid than usual by suggesting that I had anything special to say about it. Everything worth saying has already been said by numerous Special Inquiries, Parliamentary Select Committees, women's groups, drug experts and charities as well as many others.[1]

There are many groups such as the Prison Reform Trust, Civitas and the Howard League for Penal Reform who have consistently and strenuously pointed out the shortcomings of the prison system, and some wonderful Chief Inspectors of Prisons, who have been doing the same thing in careful detail every year.

However, I hope I may be allowed a few comments because something very seriously fundamental has got to be done to make our prison system fit for purpose. It impinges not only on young people but also on all strata of society. The problem is that there is much disagreement about solutions and the press usually takes a very inflammatory role when alternatives to prison are discussed. They easily forget that the prisoners they vilify at every turn are all human beings who for whatever reason have got themselves into situations from which they need real help to extricate themselves. One thing is certain – any solution is fundamentally bound up with how we look upon society itself.

It is astonishing to me, that over my entire lifetime the prison regime seems to have changed so little. During most of that period the prisons have been overcrowded and in the last fifteen years this situation has become scandalously worse.

Drugs are also the subject of much discussion and many different points of view. My own thoughts are not based on much experience beyond contact with a number of young people who have used them and some who are still addicted. But our drug culture is the worst in Europe and since the prison population is so involved with drugs I have included a short section on them in my proposals.

So my thoughts are by no means new or revolutionary. Most are well understood ideas which I hope may encourage action to move things forward in a humane and positive direction. I simply cannot understand how regiments of Home Office ministers, over decades, have not found time or sufficient interest to go after the problems with root and branch reform based on a belief in the spiritual value of human beings.

Chapter 9
The 'nanny state' and all that

We have been turned into a semi-nation of indolent softies by endless rules and regulations that control every aspect of our lives. Self-reliance and initiative have been the casualties.

So much has been written about the 'nanny state' that I hardly dare add to the enormous body of literature on the subject. Every year we are apparently required to fill in over a billion forms and the government passes more than twenty laws and around 3,500 regulations amounting to about 75,000 pages, and a further 25,000 pages of instructions.[1]

Unfortunately the government through its thick skinned arrogance has a really pernicious tendency of trying to get its way by fining or penalising us for any infringement that we may make of its endless regulations. It hardly ever rewards us for good behaviour. It is always a fine for speeding, a fine for being in a bus lane, a fine for leaving our bins open a few inches, a fine for putting something in the wrong bin and so on and on.

An area of particularly unacceptable intrusion is via the many huge government databases that monitor every known fact about us and our records including financial, medical and so on. These are regularly left on trains or lost in other ways. The breadth of the collection of DNA samples from non-criminals is highly intrusive – even after the current modifications.

The intrusions include not only the DNA database, but also ContactPoint on which children's records are to be held, a national ID database which is being developed, all health records currently being held by GPs, and endless monitoring of our movements by CCTV cameras most of which have been shown not to work adequately. Our personal liberties are being ground away in every direction.

Regulation doesn't only apply to us as individuals, business regulation too, has mushroomed in exactly the same way. Often as a result of EU regulation but also from a huge amount of home-grown Treasury interference, health and safety rules, targeting and so on.

Martin Wolf discussed this tendency in his totally convincing article, 'Outside Edge':

> *Thanks to the new Independent Safeguarding Authority which is required to carry out checks on the criminal records of all those coming into contact with vulnerable people, about 11.3 million people are now subject to a new "vetting and barring" regime under which it will be a criminal offence, punishable by a £5,000 fine to work with the vulnerable without clearance. This will apply to most people working in the National Health Service, the prison service, education and child care. It even seems likely to apply to people who take children to football matches.*
>
> *But something huge is missing from the legislation: families. Uncles, brothers, step-fathers, grandparents, aunts, daughters and friends can all be a threat. Even criminals have children. What is the government doing to protect vulnerable people from this legion of unchecked, unlicensed and often wildly unsuitable care givers?*
>
> *Homes are dangerous places. According to the National Society for the Prevention of Cruelty to Children, 16% of children experience serious maltreatment at the hands of parents. Tragically around half of the children who are killed are killed by their parents, with the proportion far higher than this for children under 13. Canadian research has also put the risk of being killed by a step-parent at between 50 to 100 times greater than the risk of being killed by a parent.*[2]

Martin Wolf closes with the words "we could admit that child abuse is indeed a terrible tragedy. But to assume that every adult in the country is guilty until proved innocent is an insane solution".[3]

He doesn't mention the huge cost that will inevitably build up over the years as every approval will need renewing at some point and, of course, as they become out of date the difficulties of re-researching the truth of all the applications is mind boggling. The initial cost to the public for *every* application is apparently £46.

I would add that it is highly unlikely that all the "vetting and barring" would in fact be successful in tracking down and excluding all the criminal – or even non-disclosing – elements anymore than the benefit system avoids ineligible beneficiaries cheating at the expense of the state. The delays in granting such clearances by the police (which often takes months) is already deterring many activities with young people that would otherwise have taken place.*

The difficulties of taking other people's children to school and children going on outings, of being forbidden to climb trees, to actually participate in chemistry experiments in school, of hiring a pianist in a pub and so on, are endlessly apparent to us all at every turn.

Children of course have to be looked after. Most are, but a minority are not. Those that are not soon learn things the hard way and are presumably in blissful ignorance of any health and safety requirements – except perhaps to keep their knives sheathed and out of sight.

It is so obvious that it is hardly worth stating: if children never experience anything they will never grow in confidence or become in the least self-reliant. My father took my brother Desmond away from a prep school because he was forbidden to climb trees. As a young man he was always building and attempting to fly home-made gliders down the hill behind our house in Gloucestershire. He became a superb pilot both in the RAF and afterwards, designed and built at least seven original aircraft, several of which are still flying today and flew across Africa, in South America and all over the world. I wonder what he would have got up to if he had been nannied to bits by current government regulations! He would certainly have had a prison record if only for having once stolen a policeman's helmet from off his head one New Year's Eve!

We should take a knife to hundreds of rules that restrict reasonable children's activities and we should encourage children to walk to school, go to playgrounds, play football in the park, go on adventure weekends in the countryside and so on. I suppose there will be a few accidents, but most will be highly educational. The system of police clearance for everything to do with children should be hugely modified to take away all the overzealous efforts at protection.

We should also axe thousands of rules that restrict normal business activities and require forms to be filled in and permission granted for almost everything. Would freedom to do things be so dreadful? These rules also apply to public bodies: soldiers learning to play the

---

* On December 13th 2009 it was reported in the press that the Government was backtracking on some of their proposals, by changing the criteria for applying the act. The effect has been to reduce the number of people requiring to be registered from 11 million to 9 million. Big Deal! Bluntly, this is a typical piece of government fudging which leaves the act in place and with it all the costs and disruption to the lives of those who look after children and have to conform to all the checks and those who are thinking of doing so, but deterred by the act. All the disadvantages of this misguided piece of legislation still apply.

bag pipes are limited to twenty-four minutes of practice a day. A teacher who led a school rock climbing and mountaineering trip was required to sign a form saying that he was safe to go up and down a ladder. There are many regulations restricting the use of ladders for example in the fire brigade and by council contractors.[4] Senior NHS doctors have said that lives are being lost because of the EU restriction that imposes a working limit of 48 hours a week on hospital staff.[5] And so it goes on in huge swathes of regulation.

Reasonable planning laws, laws against making a nuisance of oneself through too loud a noise or malicious behaviour etc, must obviously be respected and enforced. Pub closing times must be adhered to (and perhaps even to some extent re-established). Children on field trips need reasonable supervision. But blanket restrictions on everyone and anything to try to avoid some individual accident that is a normal part of life, is the wrong way to live. Scrubbing these rules would do wonders for our self-reliance.

Millions and millions of people around the globe live happily with *none* of these restrictions. We just succeed in making ourselves unhappy and feeble-minded by having so many rules to observe.

Another enormous infringement of our privacy is the wide prevalence of cameras all over our roads and in every nook and cranny. Apparently only about 20% of them are good enough to identify someone who has done something wrong and only a small percentage of crimes are solved by their use. (But it seems technology is improving – I have been twice caught for entering a bus lane when I shouldn't have done and the picture of me and my car was perfect in both cases!)

On the other hand only around 6% of fatal accidents on the roads involve speeding. When I travel in France there are almost no cameras visible and it is like driving in a new world – or perhaps in an old one. I have a clean licence and normally adhere to speed limits within a mile or two. But it is true that in France and Belgium I have been twice stopped for speeding – in France by a hidden camera near the final exit from a motorway and in Belgium by a motorcycle policeman. I felt it was a fair cop on both occasions. I felt a bit sore about the Belgian incident as a madman in a Porsche went past me at about 150 miles an hour, which led me to wonder if the Belgian speed limit was much adhered to. So feeling that it was safe to exceed the limit somewhat and comforted by the thought that if a speed cop was around he would be occupied with the Porsche, I duly went a bit faster. When I passed the speed cops and one peeled off after me I noticed that there was four of them! I mentioned to the officer that I had been overtaken by a Porsche going at very high speed and he said that they had taken care of him too! He was very polite and kind and made an instant fine notice on me and as I didn't have enough Euros he kindly led me to a cash machine in a nearby village. The weather was fine and the traffic light on both occasions, and no danger was involved. The speed limit on French and Belgian motorways is 130 kph, close to 80 mph.

The British motorway speed limit is 70 mph. These were set over fifty years ago when motorways were first built. Since then the design of cars and motorcycles has hugely improved. Brakes are unbelievably better than in the cars of my youth and steering, handling and so on are also very much improved.

I feel that we should increase the British motorway speed limits to 80 mph as many people go over 70 mph at the moment and I think most of us would feel that at an official 80 mph there would be little incentive to break the speed limit and that in practice the average speeds would not be much different. I understand that this has been tried in America and accidents actually declined.

Of course I am aware the wrath of numerous health and safety and road safety experts will come down like a ton of bricks on my head for even daring to make such a ridiculous suggestion. So in an effort to divert the bricks, I have framed my proposals to try it out on a couple of motorways for a period of, say, six months and see how the safety statistics work out. If they are comparable or better I would extend the higher limit to other motorways. The environmental impact would be negligible.

On the subject of cameras generally I am proposing that we cut out about 80% of them and only retain them on accident black spots, in city centres and where young people misbehave outside pubs etc. and near schools and other places where young people congregate. I would remove any incentive that local councils or others have in maximising the fines, and pass the fines on to the local community. I would make sure that all the cameras we installed took top quality pictures.

I would also replace the cameras on many roads and in cities with the very effective signs that light up if you are exceeding the speed limit as you pass them. I always slow down if I see one of these lit up. I believe most people behave sensibly in the same way. Cameras are just part of the Government's endless wish to punish us, rather than trust us (and to make a few bob on the side).

There is also the matter of large numbers of officials having been given – over the past twelve years – 550 powers to enter our homes: to check if our pot plants have pest, our hedge is too high, confiscate our fridge if it doesn't have the right energy rating and photograph and seize our rubbish and so on.[5] These powers are given to all kinds of people, many from the local council and from other service organisations. Only some are required to be done by the police. In most cases they are unnecessary and overintrusive.

So I have used a section in my proposals to suggest the most radical pruning of as many of these soul destroying regulations as possible. It may take years, but it can certainly be done with the right energy and the right strength of character to ignore the cries of the many do-gooders in our society who would undoubtedly complain.

Chapter 10
The onward march of the EU

The original concept was fine. The EU has unfortunately got carried away by self-indulgent, undemocratically appointed bureaucrats.

In the early days of the Common Market I was, like most of us, completely in favour of establishing a free trading zone where all countries in Europe could grow richer through gaining the benefits, so obvious in the United States, of having a huge domestic market. Order volumes would grow enormously and costs come down. It also seemed clear that when European countries became connected with so many common interests it would be very difficult for them to go to war with each other. (Some prefer to attribute this to the existence of NATO and the unswerving support of the USA.) I still believe in the original Common Market concept, but alas, fifty years later everything is very different.

During most of my life the Common Market and its successor the European Union has been building itself up in Brussels and in Strasbourg in a totally undemocratic way. It now accounts for around 75% of the laws that pass into the UK statute books and its influence continues to grow. This is being done with the active connivance of the current Government (and its predecessors), with the stated support of the European Court of Justice and without the British people being allowed a vote of any kind for over fifty years, or even the referendum which they were constantly promised by both Tony Blair and Gordon Brown and their most recent Manifestos.

The European Parliament has very limited powers to initiate and pass legislation since the majority of decisions are taken by the Commission which is unelected. The enormous €134 billion annual EU budget has been virtually unaudited throughout its existence, particularly the 80% spent by member states. Fraud is rife and is estimated at between 20% and 30% of the total, i.e. up to around

€400 million annually. The present corruption and fraud regarding MEPs' expenses makes the recent UK parliamentary scandals look like a vicarage tea party. The extent of corrupt influence by the huge lobbying groups is opaque and toxic.*

The Common Agricultural Policy which was set up to deal with a problem that existed in the middle of the last century – food shortages in Europe following the Second World War – should be run down over a period of, say, five years and then scrapped. The problem was solved at least thirty years ago when Europe started producing excess food, as evidenced by the huge butter mountains and wine lakes that made the headlines at that time. Over 80% of the CAP budget goes into the pockets of the wealthiest landowners, farmers and agri-businesses. There is no possible justification for even the cost (estimated to be at least €100 million a year) of EU bureaucrats.

Scrapping the CAP would reduce tariff barriers to the benefit not only of its own citizens but also to the world's underdeveloped countries, who would be able to sell their food and other goods into the European Union without import duties. Rather than promote aid into a continent deeply contaminated with corruption, this would be an enormous encouragement to countries to earn their way out of poverty by producing the food that the world so badly needs.

The Common Fisheries Policy (CFP) has existed for over twenty years and although the EU claims it is a huge success it is well understood to be a total disaster. After twenty years of failure and the virtual destruction of our fish stocks it is time for an entirely new approach.

The idea of trying to preserve fish stocks by allocating Total Allowable Catches (TACs) to countries and boats doesn't work and leads to the ecologically damaging discarding of millions of tons of edible fish, massive cheating to avoid quotas and a deliberate decision by many countries not to bother policing the policy to help their own fishing industries. Moreover, the more the EU restricts the TACs the more dead fish are dumped back into the sea and the more cheating becomes the only way fishermen can earn a living.

It is time to abandon the CFP. Fish should no longer be a 'common resource' available to all EU members and instead national waters should be returned to each country with a coastline. These countries

---

* I have relied heavily for my facts in this chapter on the excellent book by David Craig and Matthew Elliott – *The Great European Rip-Off*. See Further Reading p 229 for more details.

should be given back exclusive control of their territorial waters and should have the power to decide who fishes in their waters and how much they can catch. To preserve fish stocks countries should abandon TACs for each boat and replace them by each boat being allowed a certain number of days at sea. With their fishing days limited, boats would be encouraged to bring back as much of their catch as they could (destroying nothing). It is insane to go on destroying the world's fish stocks in the way we are.

Anyone who has seen the documentary *The End of the Line* will understand that we are on the very edge of destroying the blue fin tuna in the Mediterranean, have already totally wiped out the incredibly abundant Newfoundland cod banks and taken fishing across the entire globe to the edge of destruction.

There have been some recent half-hearted efforts to give more power to the European Parliament, and to reform the system of expenses and pensions, but in so feeble a way as to have very limited effect. Fundamental reform combined with complete transparency, are needed.

I had intended to set out some suggestions for improving government in the EU, in my proposals. However the final ratification of the Lisbon Treaty makes this much more difficult since the whole edifice is now set in stone. Future EU creep into all aspects of our lives seems almost inevitable. So I have avoided giving attention to the EU and instead concentrated on my main theme – ideas for sorting out British domestic policy.

Part 3

A non-politician's proposals for change

Chapter 1
Welfare - benefits and means testing

Our entire means-tested benefit system and tax credit arrangements need fundamental reform in at least two respects.

First they need simplification from the complex, completely incomprehensible systems that they have become – as a result of many years of building, changing, modifying and tinkering that have brought them to their present state – to a radically simplified, easily administered and transparent system that would enable government (and others) to understand exactly what the system is achieving and modify it according to the details of people's needs. As a by-product the huge incidence of fraud would be greatly reduced.

Secondly there is the enormous problem of the extent to which the overall welfare system can be brought back to something like Beveridge's original concepts. Welfare payments have increased since 1997 from £90 billion to close to £160 billion in spite of this being supposedly a period of economic boom.[1] This is in itself, a tragic indictment of the way we have run our country.

Nowadays living on benefit has become an acceptable – even desirable – way of life. There is no stigma attached to it as there used to be before the war and during my youth. Well over 2.5 million able-bodied adults take advantage of it. Forty per cent of households (not including pensioners) receive benefits of some kind. To a considerable extent the soul of the country has been gnawed away by the wide availability of so much welfare. It is obvious that a lot of this has to change if we are ever again to drag ourselves out of poverty and become a nation of achievers. So far no government has been prepared to grasp the nettle – and perhaps none ever will. But the whole nation will continue to suffer until something enlightened and inspiring is done. The vital requirement is to make the necessary changes in a way that will not cause undue hardship during the transition period.

In addition to welfare, the poorly thought-out tax credit system as well as the basic tax system itself also needs a fundamental overhaul. I have culled the available advice and found several ideas which could point the way to solving many of these problems. I have set them out in the following pages. They are not my ideas although they conform to principles that I think are important. The people who have developed them are knowledgeable in their fields and I hope that our leaders may feel them worth pursuing.

Benefits

If Albert Einstein had been given the job of complicating our system of benefits so that it became completely unusable he could not have come close to what we have achieved.

Lord Beveridge, when he set up the welfare state, clearly stated that benefits should be at a "subsistence level", by which he meant "a standard of living barely adequate to support life". The benefits should only be basic, as otherwise they would discourage voluntary insurance and savings. Means testing was to have been very limited and subject to conditions about every individual's behaviour. Everyone would make flat-rate contributions to a national insurance scheme. Those who fell ill, became unemployed or reached retirement age would in return receive flat-rate payments. The unemployed would be required to go to a work or training centre. They would not be allowed to stay out of work long term.[2]

He wanted to interfere in people's lives as little as possible and preserve the schemes from other sources such as charities, insurance companies and friendly societies from which millions drew support.

Beveridge wrote, "In establishing a national minimum it should leave room and encouragement for voluntary action by each individual to provide more than that minimum for himself and his family."

However, Beveridge will certainly be turning in his grave at the way successive governments have taken this simple idea and built it into a huge, complicated, highly means-tested welfare and tax credit system on which millions of people rely for their very subsistence and in many cases in order to avoid work. Its introduction also wiped out the huge system of support from non-governmental sources which had been built up over many decades.

For example, since 1997 the Government has introduced the Working Families Tax Credit, Disabled Person's Tax Credit, Childcare Tax Credit, Employment Credit, Children's Tax Credit, Baby Tax

Credit, Child Tax Credit, Working Tax Credit, and the Employment and Support Allowance.

It has abolished the Family Credit and (from among the credits that they themselves introduced) also abolished: Working Families Tax Credit, Disabled Person's Tax Credit, Children's Tax Credit, Baby Tax Credit and are in the process of abolishing Incapacity Benefit.[3] These are only the most recent examples of the constant churning and revision of benefits over many years.

There are now more than fifty benefits, mainly administered by three different agencies – Department of Work and Pensions (DWP), HM Revenue & Customs and local authorities.

The different benefits are complicated. They overlap and confuse. And there seems to be little regard to an overall framework for the benefits system, and how the benefits should interact and fit within that framework.

The DWP issues a total of fourteen manuals, with 8,690 pages, to its decision makers to help them to apply DWP benefits. A separate set of four volumes totalling over 1,200 pages covers Housing and Council Tax Benefits, which are primarily the responsibility of local authorities. The Tax Credits manual used by HM Customs & Revenue is a further 260 pages, even though it omits details of many relevant tax concepts found in other tax manuals. On top of these are huge numbers of circulars, news releases and guidance notes issued to professionals and claimants.

Complexity also exists because of the number of separate benefits. Take the case of a woman with a disabled son. She has to complete 10 different application forms, containing over 1200 questions, to apply for the benefits she needs.

The claim for Housing Benefit and Council Tax Benefit is thirty-one pages long, for Income support forty-two pages long, and although the form for tax credits is only twelve pages long, the guidance notes to help complete the form are thirty-five pages long.

Under David Martin's proposals most of these and many others would be swept away.[4] His booklet covers nearly seventy pages describing the complexities of the whole benefit system in detail and towards the end he sets out a relatively simple way of combining all these benefits under one agency and within the basic tax system. I have set it out in very shortened form in the Proposals below.

Some such system is way past its sell-by date and should be implemented as a matter of priority by whatever Government is in power. In fact it should have been done years ago. Many people have suggested various kinds of reform but somehow the ears of the relevant minister have always been closed. *

Means testing

Make no mistake. Means testing is an invention of the devil. Almost on its own it has turned this country into a toothless tiger who prefers to lie out in the sun and swat flies than get up and hunt for food and shelter for his family.

Means testing has been one of those 'big ideas' that successive chancellors and governments have embraced as an effective way of targeting funds to those most in need. Means testing is inextricably bound up with the benefits system which has evolved since the 30s, but accelerated following World War II, and also, more recently, with tax credits. Tax credits have little to do with the tax system but when they were transferred to HM Revenue & Customs, they had the huge advantage of taking around two million recipients out of the benefit numbers so that these could be spun ever after as having gone down.

Before he became Chancellor, our Prime Minister was dead against means testing – referring to the Tory Government he said, "The Government's real objective is to move from a regime of universal benefits to a regime of universal means testing, jeopardising for millions of pensioners security in ill-health and dignity in old age." Means-testing pensions was "the most serious Government assault so far mounted on the basic principles of Britain's post-war welfare state".[5] I am afraid I broadly agree with his earlier views on means testing, but boy has he destroyed the "the basic principles of Britain's post war welfare state" to say nothing of the pensioners!

As the US Congress Ways and Means Committee said in October 2007, **"When you subsidize people not to work, you get more non workers."**

Means testing is an example of a policy that initially looks attractive because of the ability to target the benefit on those most

---

* Having said this, there are recent signs, because of the considerable outcry at the complexity of the system and the amount of fraud it engenders, that even the present government is starting to consider some simplifications – but as so often, they appear to be mostly on the fringe and amount to tinkering, instead of fundamental reform.

in need while avoiding paying it to those better off, who don't need the help. This is less expensive for the exchequer, but unfortunately it has some terrible side effects for society as a whole when viewed over a longer term.

One way of looking at means testing is as an admission that the basic system of direct taxation is not fit for purpose. It creates infinitely more inequalities and disincentives on top of those already created by the tax system itself.

These are some of the serious problems:

- There is a huge disincentive for means-tested beneficiaries to seek higher paid work as by doing so they lose far more than their benefit income unless their earnings are very substantial. The effective marginal tax rate for a claimant who loses Housing Benefit, Council Tax Benefit and tax credits when their earnings increase is 95.5%. This is typical of the high marginal tax rates involved in almost all elements of the benefit system when a claimant starts to earn money from outside employment. He/she loses almost as much benefit as is earnt in income, taking tax into account.[6]

- After living on benefit for a period of time (and having gone through the complicated ritual of obtaining it) there is a much reduced inclination to go to the trouble of finding work.

- Means-tested benefits discourage saving, and through this discouragement of work and saving, self-reliance and self-respect are also diminished.[7]

- Having started on one benefit there is a strong incentive to go onto others, which is simpler to do once the original complications have been overcome. This in effect makes the recipient totally reliant on the benefit culture for all their income. **"Complete idleness, even on an income, demoralises."**[8]

- Many people who are entitled to benefit don't claim it because they may be unaware that they qualify, or from inability and/or unwillingness to complete the complicated procedures, or from pride, preferring not to go through the indignity of being means-tested. The amounts unclaimed across the five principle benefits amount to the truly astonishing total of between £6.3bn and £10.5 billion.[9] It is hard to imagine a more compelling reason for simplifying the whole system.

- Even if recipients are interested in working it is far simpler to cheat, go onto the black economy, avoid tax etc. and avoid declaring the extra income or increased assets, which in any case may only be of a temporary nature. The black (informal) economy is reckoned to have grown hugely over recent years to a level of at least £120 billion - 12% of GDP![10]

A particularly worrying and important feature of the welfare system (over and above the astronomical complexity of it all) is the way it strongly favours lone parent families over married and co-habiting couples. This has provided a large incentive for single parents to leave their family environment and set up their own households.

In almost every way married couples and families with children, whether with one working parent or two or none, have been steadily and increasingly discriminated against as compared with a lone parent with a similar number of children. This is in spite of the fact that married couples and two parent families have an extra adult to support. Two adults with children − even after the removal of One Parent Benefit for new cases in 1999 − still received the same amount of benefit as one adult with children. A couple's earnings were combined for the purpose of assessing means-testing eligibility but they were denied any right to pool their tax allowances.

The provision of social housing moved in the same direction. The long−term system of qualifying through local ties or by working your way up the queue with patience and good behaviour became impossible when a set of central rules took over priority. These priorities included lone parents either pregnant or with dependent children, and "people who are vulnerable due to old age, physical or mental ill health or some other special reason". Provision for the "unintentionally" homeless meant that notice to quit could be served by a parent on a sixteen-year-old and this became a fully valid reason to be accepted as homeless.

A few facts:

- There are over 700,000 lone parent families. The proportion of births to unmarried parents has increased fivefold since the 70s.

- The parents of a child are five times more likely to split up in the first three years of a child's life if they are co-habiting than if they are married. They are twelve times more likely to split up if they regard themselves as just "closely involved" than if they are married.[11]

- There are now 3.3 million households – one in six – with no-one over the age of 16 in employment.[12]

- There are 1.9 million children living in families without a parent in work.[13]

- A least 2.5 million able-bodied adults have not worked at all since 1997. This is in spite of ten years of boom, when the economy created something like 1.5 million jobs that immigrants happily filled.[14]

- There are higher levels of child poverty and worklessness among families headed by a single parent than among families whose parents are married.

- The higher levels of poverty occur despite huge welfare transfers (benefits and tax credits) to lone parent families.

- The UK spends £10,000 more than the EU average of £80,000 on each child from birth to the age of 18. But in a table that constructs an overall measure of child well-being for twenty-one countries, the UK came bottom, alongside the USA.[15]

- Lone parent families depend on benefits and tax credits for an average of 66% of their income.

- One in six adults aged 18–24 in England are so called 'neets' (not in education, employment or training) according to recent Department for Children, Schools and Families statistics. This amounts to more than 835,000, up around 100,000 since this time last year. Around 37% of those aged 16–17 are also considered to be out of work.

- Lone parents on income support are allowed to earn twice the amount that couples are entitled to earn before benefit is affected and two and a half times more when on housing benefit.*

Not surprisingly, the proportion of lone mothers heading up their own households doubled between 1974 and 1989. In the 1990s three quarters of lone parents were housed in the public sector, compared with around a fifth of two parent families.

There is also a strong incentive for a lone parent not to disclose co-habiting with a partner so as not to risk losing benefit, particularly

---

* As Patricia Morgan says – the logic is elusive!

when the lone parent is on out-of-work benefits or a low wage. This brings about the utterly bizarre situation where the Government is in effect paying lone parents *not* to live with a partner and thus removing whatever slim chance the child might have of growing up with the support of a two parent household! There are approximately 1.8 million couples who are affected by such a penalty. Depending on whether both mother and father were unemployed and taking into account the level of declared income they earned between them, the benefit of 'faking' a non co-habiting lifestyle varied in 2006/07 between an average of £1,336 and as much as £9,000 per annum.

An indication of how hostile to families the child and benefit system has become is illustrated by the fact that only when joint income reaches around £50,000 per annum is a couple better off in declaring their relationship.

It may surprise some people to know that over 20 million people in the United Kingdom are means-tested annually. Around 17.5 million are means-tested in conjunction with the pensions and benefit system and around 2.5 million for tax credits. Forty per cent of UK households receive *non-pension-related* welfare benefits – an enormous figure.[16]

The Tory Government in the 80s shifted a large number of the unemployed off the unemployment register onto disability allowances. This had the effect (no doubt politically desirable in terms of statistics) of reducing the headline figures for unemployment – the same game as Labour more recently played with tax credits and the benefits system. It is an area where fraud is considered to be rife. The number of claimants has more than doubled over the years, and in February 2006 2,727,290 people were receiving disabled, means-tested benefits. The Labour Government has been trying to reform the system – so far with only limited success, and the new system has not yet had time to work through.

Means testing at present levels carries a huge responsibility for changing us from a hard working, energetic, ambitious, productive, can-do society into one that expects hand outs from the state for far too large a part of its subsistence. The recipients of these handouts also include immigrants and I noticed that a Polish newspaper published a guide showing how to take advantage of the UK benefit and tax credit system as well as useful advice about changing telephone numbers etc. to avoid being contacted. Apparently benefits are even routinely paid to Polish immigrants and their children who have returned home!

So my conclusion is that where there is a will there is a way. The advantages of establishing over time a society that is self-reliant with a simplified benefit system and lower levels of taxation – even if it takes several years – has got to be worth it. The advantages of having less government interference are incalculable and long term.

Since the whole tax system also needs a fundamental overhaul the complications in deciding exactly what to do, and in what order, do require careful thought. I have also set out some ideas for modifying the approach to direct taxation and the tax credit system to do away with as much means testing as possible, which I hope will receive serious consideration.

Proposals for *change*

The whole tax and benefit system is indeed capable of being reformed into a simple straightforward system provided by one agency and simplified so that a single coding arrangement can make all tax transactions transparent and relatively simple to understand.[17]

The simplified system would also have the great advantage of dealing a body blow to the level of cheating and fraud that currently exists from people whose tax affairs are not 'married up' with their benefits claims, and it will also have the further advantage of making it obvious when the government is trying to take stealth taxes from taxpayers by failing to index allowances etc.

It would hugely reduce the cost of all the civil servants and other advisers trying to administer the complexities of the present system and support claimants to ensure that everyone receives the correct benefit to which they are entitled – an almost impossible job at the moment in view of the different criteria that exist for almost every claim, and where more than one benefit is involved.

The fact that most benefits could ultimately be handled in direct contact with claimant beneficiaries by local offices of the Department of Works and Pensions and its existing network of Jobcentre Plus offices together with its Pension, Disability and Carers Service would mean that the basic premise of strengthening local communities and personalising democracy would at the same time receive a major boost. Staff and expertise would also be moved into the DWP from local authorities and HMRC.

This would be a major logistical exercise but it could be done if carefully planned. The present system whereby tax credits can be dispensed with virtually no personal contact would come to an end. Also the army of snoopers that ensure that all the archaic rules about co-habitation etc. are adhered to and means testing limits are not infringed, would be greatly depleted.

Where it was decided appropriate for the single agency to effect the payment of a benefit through the claimant's PAYE code, the amount of the benefit would simply be added to the claimant's personal tax allowances by HMRC in order to obtain the desired result. The employee would therefore receive the net amount in his or her pay packet after tax due had been deducted and any benefits due had been added back, so reducing the 'churn' of separate tax and benefit payments being treated as separate transactions in opposite directions. In cases where benefits are paid to non-employees these would be paid to the claimant directly by the DWP (without reference to HMRC) by means of a code related to the benefit amount.

This approach could also be extended to other matters such as student loans and maternity pay, which are currently handled by employers as part of payroll management. A single PAYE code could be calculated to reflect all these amounts. It would be far more efficient for government agencies, with their specialised personnel and computer systems to assume a larger administrative role. Employers and especially small employers would then obtain significant relief from some of the burdens currently imposed on them.

David Martin's proposals for integrating the tax and benefits system could be implemented in four straightforward stages.

1. Identify where the separate pieces of the benefit system might be simplified;

2. Eliminate overlaps between benefits;

3. Combine the pieces together to form an integrated system and to establish a single entry point for claimants into the benefit system;

4. Review and propose reforms to the current system for National Insurance Contributions and the payment of contributory benefits.

There is a choice about whether to incorporate the NIC system into the tax system or make it into an honest system where NIC contributions would only be used for the purposes of paying out pensions, maternity pay and sickness benefit, instead of being simply used as a stealth tax by the government for whatever purpose they dream up as important. I believe it is vital to return the NIC system to one where every contributor knows for certain that all of his/ her money is going into a fund dedicated and ring-fenced for the provision of state pensions and closely related purposes.

The government's policy of allowing it to be used in practice for other general taxation purposes is in my view dishonest and a fraud on contributors.★

★ Any serious consideration of this whole subject should include careful study of David Martin's *Benefit Simplification*. Summarising parts of this excellent work does no justice at all to the details of the simplification that is proposed. It is inconceivable that we can go on living any longer with an insane system of the sort that has been developed over many decades by civil servants working piecemeal by 'Topsy's law'.

Chapter 2
Tax credits

As a system for paying people *not* to work it is successful.

As already mentioned, means testing, the benefit and tax credit systems and the overall tax system will have to be tackled at the same time.

Part of any such review must obviously take into account a reform of our appalling tax credit system which is still subject to massive unrecoverable overpayments every year in spite of the HMRC ignoring increases in individual income of an amazing £25,000 a year. It is obvious that many claimants no longer need the benefit, even though they are legitimately entitled to receive it.

Although the motives for introducing and expanding tax credits were honourable, the whole tax credit scheme has been an expensive fiasco as highlighted recently by the House of Commons Committee of Public Accounts (22nd report 2006/7) whose conclusions include the following:

- £5.8 billion was overpaid to claimants during the first three years of the current tax credits scheme. (It seems that most of this will never be reclaimed.)

- Tax credits suffer from the highest rates of error and fraud in central government. (It is interesting that 200,000 more single parents claimed tax credits than were believed to exist!)

- The Department does not have up to date information on levels of claimant error and fraud in tax credits.

- The design of the internet system for tax credits was deficient from the outset and left it vulnerable to attack by organised criminals. (It was closed in December 2005, after estimated losses through fraud of around £5 billion.)

- The Department also failed to design the basic tax credits scheme to give proper protection against error and fraud.

There are a number of precedents abroad for far more effective tax credit systems that provide useful models. Gordon Brown set up his own UK tax credit system and ignored good practice as carried out, for example, in the USA.

The US system, which was developed by a Democrat senator and signed into law by a Republican President, was expanded by Ronald Reagan and again substantially expanded during the Clinton presidency. It has been largely responsible for lifting 4.3 million people and 2.2 million children out of poverty.*

- The key feature of the US system (known as Earned Income Tax Credit) is that it encourages and rewards the low paid to *work* their way out of poverty, with a tax credit of 40c for each $1 of pre-tax earnings.

- In the UK by contrast, despite all the rhetoric on rights and responsibilities and the importance of work, only a part of the UK system (Working Tax Credit) requires the claimant to work (including part-time work) to receive tax credits. The other, far larger, part of the UK system (Child Tax Credit) has no compulsion to work at all – 1.4 million people in the UK are not working but are receiving tax credits.

- UK tax credits have extremely high marginal rates of tax (around 70%). These create a huge disincentive to the low paid in seeking full-time work. A single mother on earnings 25% above the minimum wage can see her after-tax-and-benefit income fall to just £1.89 per hour, depending on the number of hours worked per week – little more than a third of the Minimum Wage.

- UK tax credits *give* money to poor families but discourage them from *earning* it.

- They are socially divisive, helping to create a stratified, two class Britain – one class of advancement and achievement; and the other a class of dependency, passivity and social breakdown.

- Tax credits in the UK have other disadvantages:

---

* I am indebted to Rupert Darwall for kindly reviewing the figures used in this chapter to bring them up to date. It is hard to understand how the Government has failed to implement something along these lines already!

1. they discourage full time work;

2. they are complex;

3. they are more generous to lone parents than to couples and thereby penalise mothers and fathers who live together;

4. administrative problems relating to over payment are designed into the system.

- Tax credits are expensive. The Working Tax Credit was estimated to cost £5.92 billion and the Child Tax Credit £15.68 billion in 2007/8. UK expenditure on tax credits is around 0.9% of GDP, compared to 0.3% in the USA.[1]

Proposals for *change*

The UK tax credit system needs to be completely redesigned. The objective should be similar to President Clinton's: **"If you have a child at home and if you work 40 hours a week, you will not be in poverty."** This objective can be delivered by means of a British Earned Income Tax Credit (BEITC). Under this system, low paid families with children would:

- Receive, say, an additional 40p for every £1 of earnings for the first £10,000 of pre-tax income. The BEITC could be phased out at a rate of 25% up to £24,000, depending on family size.

- This would give a powerful boost to incentives for those working more than 16 hours a week and earning less than £10,000 a year.

- In this range, the current marginal tax rates of up to 70% would be replaced by substantial net payments from the tax man as the 40% tax credit is greater than the combined rate of the 20% basic rate of income tax and the 11% rate of employee National Insurance.

- Above £10,000 a year, incentives are also improved for most of the income range, as the 25% withdrawal rate of the BEITC is less than the 39% first withdrawal rate of the existing tax credits (see proposed changes to income tax threshold in chapter 4, pages 144–146).

- As in the US, nearly 99% of BEITC recipients will be paid after claims have been finalised, removing a key weakness of the UK system. The exchequer instantly benefits from the almost total elimination of the design flaw that leads to tax credit over-payments (which has been disguised by the £25,000 income disregard).

- The proposed BEITC would cost only around £6 billion, compared to, currently, around £20 billion. After taking into account additional spending on welfare benefits (for example, workless families would be supported by welfare, not by tax credits) the reforms would yield around £8 billion in savings.

- These savings could contribute to the cost of raising tax thresholds, which would have an impact on further simplifying and improving our income tax system and giving incentive to those on low incomes to seek work, thereby reducing the dependency culture.

- In addition to providing a powerful boost to help the low paid out of poverty, the BEITC would increase the supply of labour, improve output per head and improve national economic performance.

Chapter 3
Pensions

Henri IV said he wouldn't rest until every French family had a chicken on the table every Sunday. This is how we should feel about decent life supporting pensions for all Britons.

We used to have a pensions system that was the envy of the world. Most companies had well managed defined-benefit pension schemes that paid a fixed percentage of final salary as a pension – usually two thirds. Both the company and the employee paid into these schemes. By 1997 Britain had more money invested in these private schemes than the rest of Europe combined.

Alas, most of these schemes have now been abolished. Of the 98,000 that existed in 1997, less than a third have survived. By the end of 2007 there were a million less active members of occupational pension schemes than just three years earlier.

The government slipped into its first budget in 1997 the ending of dividend credits on advance corporation tax. It was a typical Brown stealth tax (there were many more to follow), the impact of which, hardly anyone understood at the time. By this means almost £5 billion was taken out of private pensions in the first year alone. In the past twelve years over £175 billion has been taken from pensioners for the benefit of the Treasury.

On top of this, new rules were announced (without debate in Parliament) that loaded onto the trustees of company pension schemes a huge amount of extra regulation and cost, including new solvency and disclosure rules. The effect of these was to accelerate into closure many pension schemes that the tax changes had helped to force into collapse.

Less than half of those who work in the private sector are now paying into a pension and the number is still declining. The slow death of this once-thriving savings sector is a reason why more and more people now face hard times in retirement. As Eamonn Butler has said, the whole affair has been a tale of political greed, deception and incompetence.[1]

While the number of people on private pension schemes has plummeted, the opposite has happened in the public sector. There has been a rise of about a million civil servants employed by this government and the large majority have defined-benefit pension schemes providing about two thirds of final salary. What is more, most of these pension benefits, unlike many of those in the private sector, are index linked to inflation which roughly doubles the cost of providing them. A survey by the Institute of Directors shows that in the private sector only 12% of its members are in final salary schemes, compared with 90% in the public sector.[2]

There are now about 5.4 million (up 200,000 during 2008) public employees from policemen, judges, BBC employees, firefighters and Whitehall mandarins who are members of 313 public pension schemes. The cost to taxpayers of these schemes was £21.4 billion in 2007 (£2.7 billion more than Brown estimated in his budget two years earlier – an astonishing degree of miscalculation).

By contrast the number of active members of private sector defined benefit schemes in 2008 slipped by 100,000 to 2.6 million from the year before.[3]

Private sector workers now pay more to fund public pensions than their own. The average private sector worker now retires with a pension pot – if they have one at all – of £25,100, enough to fund a pension of about £1,700 a year! The average public sector worker retires with ten times that – an index linked pension of £17,091 per year.

Civil servants pay just 3.5% of their salaries into the Civil Service pension scheme, but the government pays a whopping 22% on top.

The estimated future costs of public sector pensions have risen from around £360 billion in 1997 to well over £880 billion today. With the increase in numbers of those who live to be over 80, some have put the cost as high as £1,200 billion simply to pay the state pensions of those who are currently retired.[4]

Compared with other European states the British state pension is equivalent to just 17% of average earnings, against an average EU figure of 57% of average earnings. What a massive problem, and none of this potential cost is factored into our government borrowing figures.

The result of this is that the government finds it necessary to top up the poorest pensioners – nearly 3 million of them – with a means-tested Pension Credit averaging around £41.67 a week.

A further 1.8 million pensioners who are entitled to it don't claim it, because they find the whole process too complicated, do not know it exists or feel too proud to do so.

It is this means-tested benefit that makes saving irrational for around a quarter of the population. If you save through your life time, it does you absolutely no good at all. You simply lose this means-tested benefit when you retire – another huge reason why I feel means testing is such a thoroughly pernicious practice.[5]

My tax proposal for raising the tax threshold to £15,000 (see chapter 4, pages 144–146) would have a dramatic effect in almost wiping out the number of pensioners being means-tested. It would incidentally have the same effect throughout the benefits system.

In the early days of the Blair government, Tony Blair appointed Frank Field to think 'out of the box' on welfare and pension matters. But when he started to do this Blair took fright and, allegedly at the instigation of Gordon Brown, dismissed Field before he could bring forward any concrete proposals.

However, in 1999 Frank Field founded the Pensions Reform Group and it has been pursuing pension reform ever since. The group produced a series of papers promoting the Universal Protected Pension which seems an admirable approach to providing a defined pension of 25-30% of average earnings (in itself a low percentage) throughout retirement. It is aimed at ensuring that future pensioners can retire with a pension above the poverty level. As things stand at the moment huge numbers of future British pensioners will be living in poverty, and even the proposed level seems thin to me.

Frank Field recently wrote to the *Financial Times*, setting out the basis for his suggested pension reform:

> *The Government, with taxpayers' money, supports pensions in three ways but, even when the latest reforms are through, 40% of pensioners will remain poor. Already, £30 billion goes in subsidising pension savings; £15 billion is spent on means-test support for poorer pensioners. Public sector pensions will cost taxpayers a staggering £90 billion [a year] by midcentury.*
>
> *A truly radical government would introduce a pension reform along the lines advocated by the Pensions Reform Group. A funded scheme would be built around the current pay-as-you-go state pension, aiming to give every responsible citizen a minimum income to take them off means-tested assistance.*

The reform would take time to become fully effective but over this period the means-test budget would fall, before being eliminated. A reforming government would also be able to close all public sector schemes including that for MPs, to new members.

This reform alone would transform our public accounts but would do so while achieving what no other government has achieved, namely abolishing pensioner poverty.[6]

I don't fully agree with some of the aspects of the Pension Reform Group's Universal Protected Pension – for example I believe public sector pensions will have to be modified, in spite of the long-term arrangements that have been agreed with public sector employee unions, in terms of both increased contributions by the pensioner, reduced contributions by the government and later retirement dates. I think it is grossly unfair that private sector workers are having to lose or modify their pension rights (mostly already far inferior to the equivalent public sector pension) in order for their employers to survive financially during the recession, while the public sector sails merrily on with generous index linked pensions and early retirement intact.

However I do fully agree that if the State Second Pension is introduced as planned it is totally wrong that it should be propelling ever more pensioners into the means-tested net. Means-tested benefit has grown by nearly 40% in real terms between 1997–98 and 2003–04 and no doubt it has continued to grow since then (I can find no up to date figures).

The Dutch pensions arrangements have been praised as a model for others to follow. The Association of Consulting Actuaries, the CBI and others have lobbied the Government to allow Dutch style pensions under forthcoming UK rules. The Dutch scheme includes a stable and consistent state provision and fiscal support (in total contrast to the UK which constantly changes the tax treatment and adds complexity at every turn). It also allows a proportion of the benefit to be made conditional on investment returns which allows investment in equities as well as other assets without the downside risks to sponsors inherent in the UK system.

The Universal Protected Pension has the laudable objective of lifting every worker above the means-testing benefit criteria by the time he/she retires. This becomes true far sooner with the reforms proposed in this book for the income tax system through raising thresholds, and when further combined with the reformed working tax credit system and the simplification of all the benefit arrangements, would help the entire community as well.

Proposals for *change*

- Set up a working party of people who understand pensions under a tough knowledgeable chairman for the purpose of agreeing a pension system that is fair for all the people of this country, including both public and private sector employees with similar retirement ages and broadly similar contribution arrangements. Some initial sacrifices – with the impact spread over several years – would have to be made by the public sector to ensure fairness.

- Take into account the flexibility and consistency of the Dutch pension system and use it as a model for simplifying our own arrangements.

- It would also be useful to try to re-establish some form of defined benefit scheme incorporating a minimum guaranteed pension, combined with an additional defined *contribution* scheme. Cartain safeguards would of course be required, covering such things as the categories of investment and measures to ensure that recipients maintained both elements of the scheme. Such arrangements are, apparently, working well in Australia[7].

It used to be that lower public sector pay was used as a justification for paying more generous pensions. This appears no longer to be the case and in fact many public sector salaries are now ahead of the private sector equivalents.* The independent working party should of course take this into account

This should be done in an agreed time span – say a year – and then put before Parliament and enacted into law. ★★

---

* Recent figures show that in 2008 a typical state employee was paid 7% more than his/her private sector equivalent compared to 3% in 2005. Public sector wages are rising at 2.8% compared with 1.1% in the private sector. In 2008 the average public sector worker worked 35 hours per week, 2.5 hours less than their equivalent in the private sector. The average state employee enjoys three or four more days of holiday a year. (Robert Watts, "Public pay races ahead in recession." *Sunday Times*, 3rd January, 2010).

★★ I am aware that Lord Turner has already been through such an exercise but I don't think the time span was urgent enough and I don't feel that it has solved the problem of giving our future pensioners something that they can reasonably survive on. I suspect this was more the government's doing than Lord Turner's!

Chapter 4
Our taxation system

People with the lowest 20% of income pay an all-inclusive tax rate estimated at 38% and those with the highest 20% of income pay 35% in tax. No wonder poverty persists![1]

Since I have no specialised knowledge about taxation beyond what a normal taxpayer might, I am concentrating on the areas that concern me most. I have mentioned means testing, benefits simplification, tax credits and pensions. However the reform of the income tax system itself is also long overdue and could be highly beneficial to the country's prosperity. In fact it is crucial.

Background note

There is a body of research which seems to me compelling that has established that when government expenditure exceeds about 35% of Gross National Product, the economy's performance is strongly adversely affected. For example, if the UK had maintained its 1960 level of expenditure (32.2%) until 2005 the size of its output by then would have nearly doubled. Ignoring the current recession the level of government expenditure has grown pretty steadily to above 40% over that period. So the hugely increased level of expenditure, with its higher taxation to pay for it which we now have, has massively complicated our taxation and benefit systems (in fact our entire lives!) and reduced the potential for the prosperity of the British economy substantially. This is a thought that I can't escape when thinking about our current problems.[2]

What politicians forget is that for every penny of tax they raise, and for all the endless occasions they tell us what wonderful things they are doing with it, there is someone, often a rather poor someone, who is paying it.

The result is not an increase in our national wealth, but often a negative impact when they waste it – as alas, they often do. Even if the result is positive, the growth overall is very small, because they also forget that the person paying the tax does not have that money available to spend, and so the economy suffers.★

A better way to make poorer people better off is to free them from paying any tax at all. This is also very good for the future prosperity of the country.

Income tax – where we are now

It is clear to any objective observer that the UK tax system has become so huge and so complicated that it now represents the economics of the madhouse.

Integrated with means-tested benefits and tax credits, it imposes an extraordinarily heavy series of burdens on a large part of the population. It forces people to conform to all kinds of petty rules, to fill out enormously complicated and lengthy forms, to employ lawyers, tax advisers and accountants at huge expense and/or to seek advice from citizens' advice organisations and charities. It is a major reason that the government employs about 20% of the working population on what, for many of them, is essentially unproductive work.

Taxation's original purpose was to pay for services that individuals could not reasonably or efficiently provide for themselves such as defence, education, police, hospitals, prisons and so on. But it has developed into a kind of all-embracing life-threatening system, the effect of which is to deny people the most basic human rights – the right to work and the freedom to determine their own spending priorities. Whether intentional or not it is immoral to lead the country down such a path to unemployment and poverty.

As more and more people become dependent on the state, the phrase 'dependency culture' has become a widespread description of how so many people have become reliant on the welfare system. Many of us are losing the will and confidence to become responsible for our own lives and to do things for ourselves rather than being

---

★ Recent figures from the Office of National Statistics show that output grew by 1.7% during the period 2000–2009 compared with 3.1% during the 1960s. Manufacturing output actually *declined* by 1.2% annually during the later period.

spoon-fed. In Britain today there are proportionately more children than anywhere else in the world that are born into a household without a wage earner and that is primarily dependent on the state for its purchasing power. Yet thirty-five years ago fewer than one household in ten was workless.[3]

People are liable to income tax at 20% as soon as they earn more than the annual allowance of £6,475.★ They also have to pay National Insurance contributions (NICs) of 11%. On top of this their employer has to pay NICs at the rate of 12.8 %. It is widely held by economists that if employer NICs were abolished then wages would rise by the same amount, so the total burden on the lowest paid is in the region of 43%.★★ It is absurd that such high rates should apply on such low incomes.

It is estimated that in 2008/09 there were 1.6 million people earning less than £10,000 p.a. paying tax, and a further 6.7million people earning between £10,000 and £15,000 p.a. also paying tax.[4]

It is also absurd that most of this money then needs to be refunded in benefit payments. Non-retired households in the lowest fifth income bracket have earnings of less than £14,500 p.a. Average earnings of these households are only £7,500. But these households bear the burden, on average, of £1,491 each in tax and employer and employee NICs. (Incidentally they also pay an average of almost £3,300 on other indirect taxes, such as VAT, tobacco and alcohol duties etc.) The Government then repays these households an average of almost £6,000 in cash benefits! What a pointless exercise in paying billions of pounds back and forth.[5]

At the same time there is an array of special allowances and exemptions for giving tax relief, many of which are only in practice available to the better off. For example many private equity managers and others in the City of London are able to arrange that, by holding shares of a special class in their companies, they only pay tax at the capital gains rate of 18% when they sell their shares, even though these gains are, in substance, earnings. UK resident individuals who are domiciled overseas may escape this tax charge altogether.

In 2008/09 the gross income of companies and individuals amounted to £741 billion. But an amazing £237bn, almost a third of the total, is given back in the form of reliefs and allowances.

★ The Taxpayers Alliance and David Martin have kindly helped me to update the figures used in this section to the present day.

★★ An element of grossing up has been ignored to simplify the calculation.

Included in this is a complex system of business–based capital allowances, which is always changing. A recent example was the abolition of industrial building allowances which disadvantaged some companies who were already contractually committed to construction programmes on the assumption that they would get allowances. It would be much better simply to allow tax relief for all business depreciation costs.

In the past, UK governments have often taken credit for lowering the basic rate of income tax. But in spite of this the personal tax burden has increased substantially (irrespective of other declared tax increases) due to the erosion of the real value of the allowances, leaving a rising share of personal income liable to tax. This has been particularly evident under the current Labour Government. Invisible tax increases cannot be seen and consequently are hardly felt. No Chancellor can resist this temptation.

The solution to all this is to remove most of these allowances and reduce tax rates.

Proposals for *change*

Raising the tax threshold

I believe that the threshold before *anyone* starts to pay tax should be raised from the present £6,475 to £15,000. This would have the immediate effect of releasing an additional 8.3 million people from the burden of paying tax.

As a result, *exactly half* of the adult population would pay no tax at all! This would create a truly incentivised, forward-looking and highly successful society.*

A major programme to raise the initial tax threshold would not only bring this drastic reduction in the numbers of tax payers, it would also eliminate millions of small payments by various government agencies to individuals and bring a major simplification to the system. The amount of 'churn' – that is the government paying many billions of pounds to existing tax payers who then return it to the government, would be almost eliminated.

---

* Adult population in mid-2008 = 47.4 million less 32 million tax payers = 15.4 million non-tax payers plus 8.3 million dropping out of tax from the higher threshold = 23.7 million = 50% of 47.4 million – amazing!!

If David Martin's proposals for simplifying the benefits system, were, as I am suggesting, combined with raising the threshold at which tax is payable, it would mean that governments could no longer hide from the political consequences of their tax actions. By exchanging the mass of complex allowances for lower tax rates the huge gulf between the gross and net tax system could be greatly reduced.

Raising the threshold for income tax to £15,000 would reduce the number of taxpayers by close to a third and wipe out tax for the large majority of taxpayers over the age of 65.

The cost to the Exchequer of doing this would be a gross sum of about £45 billion but this would be reduced to a net figure of around £6 billion once the many savings on counterbalancing allowances and benefits were taken into account.

It is difficult for a lay person to work out the numbers precisely but with David Martin's enormous help here are our assumptions:

1. Every tax payer who has become a non-taxpayer and earns more than £15,000 a year will become £2,000 better off as a result of the rise in the threshold. We have assumed that they should keep £1,000 of this and the government will take back £1,000 by some other mechanism such as raising somewhat the basic rate of tax or reducing the 40% threshold or similar. The principal objective, of course, is to help the members of our society on lower incomes, although others would also benefit. The effect of this clawback is to reduce the deficit by around £19.5 billion.

2. We have estimated that the savings to the tax credit system by reforming it so that it is concentrated on those in work, is about £8 billion.

3. Table 16A of "The effects of taxes and benefits on household incomes" tells us that 3.72 million non-retired households in the bottom quintile have incomes of less than £14,505 and pay tax on average of £761 or £2.8 billion in total. Assuming that the large majority of these households are on benefits, we would reduce their benefits bill by £1,000 each, still leaving them better off and making a clawback of around £2.5 billion.

4. Non-retired households earning more than £15,000 will be £1,000 better off. These households receive about £6 billion in income support and pension credit and about the same in

housing benefit. It seems reasonable to assume that these benefits could be reduced by at least, £5 billion.

5. The potential clawback from retired households would be far smaller since there are far fewer of them and they pay less tax. We feel we could claw back around £1 billion from this group – again still leaving them better off.

6. From the above saving of £36 billion about £9 billion would be released to the economy meaning an increase in the amount of VAT collected of around £1 billion.

7. There should also be administrative savings from the simplification of around £2 billion.

8. The net effect of all this is a total saving of £39 billion making a net cost of £6 billion.

The £6 billion would evaporate over two or three years and turn into a substantial surplus, as these people poured their energy and ideas into the economy for the first time. It would have a major impact on poverty since everyone earning less than £15,000 a year would be better off by a substantial amount of up to £2,000 and those earning more would be £1,000 better off. The huge but incalculable cost of the grey/black economy would be reduced enormously – probably by several tens of billions of pounds – a hidden bonus.

Most current benefits would continue to be paid to those entitled to receive them. For those working part-time or in low paid jobs (see working tax credits reform) the range of income over which social security benefits would be phased out would no longer overlap with the threshold for payment of income tax. By separating the ranges of benefit withdrawal and income tax payments, the problem of very high marginal tax deduction rates would be greatly diminished. People would typically receive benefits or pensions, or pay income tax; but seldom both at the same time.

There would also be huge savings for all the voluntary and charitable organisations who will no longer be needed to advise many thousands of people on the benefits and means-testing systems, and who could bend their energies, for example, to sorting out youth unemployment.

A modern day Beveridge

Come back Lord Beveridge – we need you more than ever

Means testing, benefits and tax credits are such a huge subject and the changes that need to be made are so fundamental that I believe there is no alternative but to identify another highly experienced entrepreneurial team in the field of taxation, benefits, tax credits and means testing to form a commission to examine all the elements of the problem and come up with finite recommendations.* One or two experienced politicians** should be members but on a non-partisan basis and with a brief to get it sorted quickly. Above all it will need a tough and sympathetic chairman (or woman).

The brief should include going back to the main principles laid down by Beveridge of providing a safety net for those in real need, scaling down the cost of the overall system substantially, greatly reducing the impact of means testing, providing real incentives for young people to work and a system of community national service available to those who have failed to find work or training and otherwise would receive no support. The seriously disabled should be properly looked after with more community support.

There will be areas such as childcare, young people and caring for the aged which will inevitably require considerable additional expenditure and the funds should be available from within the overall savings.

A year could be allocated to the task (possibly with an interim report) and then firm steps should be taken to implement the main recommendations. The tax changes could be brought in over, say two years. When one thinks about the astronomical sums that have been used to bail out the banks and support the entire financial system a mere £6 billion seems chicken feed when the powerful and beneficial effect on 8 million people, as well as the economy as a whole, is considered.

It may seem far-fetched to wish to change such fundamental systems so completely. But since it is obvious that the present system has been crying out for such changes for many years, the government should finally have the courage and drive to undertake them – not to fudge them or to take half measures. Nothing less than our long-term

---

* David Martin should certainly be a key member of it!
** Iain Duncan Smith.

influence as a nation and the well-being of our society – perhaps even the existence of our society as we know it – is at stake.

This is all about changing and inspiring Britain to become a strong nation of achievers again.

Not having been aware of the Centre for Social Justice's work on benefit simplification when I began formulating my ideas, I have concentrated my own reform suggestions on David Martin's proposals which in some ways appear simpler to operate in terms of making the benefit payments.* Underlying changes in terms of criteria, funding levels etc. should be the subject of the working party suggested above – including the proposals for reforming the tax credit system so that it concentrates on helping people who are *in* work rather than paying them *not to* work, as has proved so successful in the USA.

The simplified benefit system will not, of itself, change radically the criteria for receiving benefits but, rather, make it easy for the government and others to see exactly what they are doing and modify it accordingly. I believe, in fact that there are further substantial savings to be made, particularly from avoidance of fraud, and savings from personnel, who will no longer be needed to explain and police the system, with all its complications and abuses. A very important side effect which will benefit millions is that the huge sums that are not claimed from the tax/ benefit system will finally be able to reach their intended targets.

However there are also many areas where more money will be needed and I hope the working party will address some of these at the same time. The provision of properly organised and universal child care facilities will be one of the major requirements. The entire system of benefits and services has to be rebalanced.

It won't happen overnight but we have to start somewhere. At least when we have a simple system to operate we can work the rest out over time. This is a time for boldness and an end to tinkering with a clapped-out system.

---

* The Centre for Social Justice (Iain Duncan Smith's think tank for addressing problems relating to broken families and welfare reform) has recently published a major study on simplifying the benefit system. It is clear and well thought out. It is amazing to me how quickly and abruptly the present government turned down these carefully researched proposals without apparent reflection. How can they be so obtuse? (I suspect they can't be and are simply laying low, like Br'er Fox so as not to have to attribute any changes to the Tory party.) Their own tinkering over a decade has contributed hugely to the mess we are in. I hope whatever government is in power will respond to David Martin's excellent parallel work on benefit simplification, but also of course to the many proposals along similar lines from the Centre for Social Justice.

Chapter 5
Total Place – finding the value of local services

A method of finding out how much cost we should move from central to local control.

The reorganisation of our entire system of democracy and the establishment of vibrant community responsibility for most of the local services, gives us the opportunity of assessing the value of the services we are providing at the moment, and the necessary cost or benefit of changing them to local control.

There have been some interesting approaches to this already and the conclusion seems likely to be that the same services can be provided far more effectively and at lower cost at the local level than under our present centralised system.

The latest big idea is called Total Place.[1] The concept involves adding up all the public money that goes into an area – covering local government, police, courts, probation service, health, education, benefits, housing subsidies, the Learning and Skills Council and the like – then considering whether it could be better used.

The exercise is deceptively difficult, according to Stephen Taylor, a former chief executive of the Leadership Centre for Local Government, and now a consultant who helped undertake one of the first of these exercises in Cumbria in 2008. Yet the results, he says, are "gobsmacking".

The amount spent in Cumbria was a whopping £7.1 billion, or £14,000 per head of population. In Birmingham the results were an also impressive £7.3 billion, or around £7,500 per head.

In a report on the project in the *Financial Times*, Stephen Taylor goes on to say:

> *Just doing this exercise prompts some hard questions. How much is being spent on prevention of problems, how much on cure? How much is going on delivering stuff as opposed to overheads from simply running*

all these organisations. How much is actually making a difference? How much of this money is influenced locally so that it could be spent better? How much is directed to national bodies?[2]

In Cumbria the answer was that less than a quarter was influenced locally.

Apparently the idea has received heavyweight support from Sir Michael Bichard, a former Whitehall permanent secretary and now head of the Institute for Government, a charity campaigning for more effective government.

He strongly promoted it as his contribution to the Treasury's latest efficiency review, arguing that even a 1% improvement in the use of public money in an area where £7.5 billion is spent amounted to £75 million.

John Denham, the Communities Secretary, has now launched thirteen pilot programmes.[3]

Proposals for *change*

Continue with John Denham's research, and assuming the results are helpful, expand it as fast as possible, but in conjunction with the programme devolving democratic government to local communities as suggested earlier. Of course this is an enormous exercise, if carried out nationally. It is clear that it can only be done properly once a decision has been taken on political grounds to return democracy to local levels. Doing it beforehand would produce results without the local organisations and administrative set ups to make them work.

But done properly it will enable local organisations to be put in charge of how these services are run and the proportion of them run locally will likely reverse to, say, 75% being run locally, and the balance provided by central government. The setting up of the alternative methods of running these services would be in the hands of the communities. They will benefit from running them efficiently and economically – exactly what is needed in Britain to restore confidence in government and raise the morale of the country.

Chapter 6
Prisons and the treatment of prisoners

The way we treat our prisoners is utterly shameful. We wouldn't treat our dogs the way we treat our prisoners.

The prisons were designed to hold around 65,000 prisoners. The present prison population is around 85,000 which has led to severe overcrowding. The prison system has been at the bottom of every government totem pole when it comes to expenditure – I assume because prisoners have no votes and no leverage to complain.

The last Tory government instituted a building programme, but the current government, over the last ten years, has done very little to increase it. This in spite of virtually doubling the overall level of taxation and on top of that, lavishing billions of pounds year after year on PFIs related to hospital and school building programmes. They are talking about catching up now with a PFI prison building programme amounting to £4.2 billion, but it is a question of too little too late, and from what is being suggested the new prisons will be much too large and in the wrong places. Fingers crossed, I have heard recently that this programme may, thank heavens, have been quietly laid to rest.

And yet it is a shameful fact that overcrowding has reached such a state that prisoners (often dangerous and violent ones) are being let out of prison before the end of their sentences in order to make space for new prisoners coming into the system. Many prisoners are 'banged up' for 18–20 hours a day, or even more, often two or three to a cell, often in cells designed for single occupation. Conditions are cramped and unpleasant and severe overcrowding makes operating the prisons properly virtually impossible.

The same appalling conditions also apply to the growing number of prisoners on remand who haven't yet been convicted of anything. There can be nothing more dispiriting or destructive to someone's character than to be confined for twenty hours a day in a small cell. I would become seriously mentally ill after a few weeks of this inhuman treatment. No wonder the ill become more ill, the violent more violent and the desperate more suicidal.

Around 13,000 remand prisoners are in jail, many for over ninety days, often with little idea of their future or when they will be tried. Many wind up being found not guilty of anything but nevertheless have had their lives ruined. Putting up with overcrowded prison conditions and fellow convicted inmates, violent or otherwise, is a tremendous strain.

The tragedy is that prisons, in the same way as Young Offenders Institutes (YOIs), should be an opportunity to help disadvantaged people while they are segregated and get-at-able.

The pressure on the loyal and hard-working prison officers who have to look after them is enormous. Most of them haven't been trained to look after young offenders, the mentally ill or those addicted to drugs, but are required to do so. It is a miracle that in the present overcrowded conditions they are able to cope at all.

It is officially admitted that 13% of prisoners have schizophrenia and a further 70% have diagnosable mental disorders. These are mixed up with violent prisoners, sex offenders, and non-violent prisoners some of whom are young. Many of these are on short sentences and should have been dealt with by community sentences. Those coming into prisons for shortish periods (including those on remand) find their lives completely destroyed, losing their jobs, their homes, their partners and friends. But they are often there long enough to pick up appallingly bad habits from hardened and habitual criminals. Prisoners are constantly moved round the prison system in an attempt to utilise capacity to the maximum thus taking them far away from their families and support groups.[1]

And the irony of the whole system is that between 60% and 70% of prisoners who are released offend again within a period of two years and many much more quickly. For burglary and theft the figures are 78% and 73% respectively. For young offenders the percentage increases to nearly 80%.[2] It is interesting to note that in, for example, Sweden and Denmark the figure is between 20% and 30%. Even in Britain in 1992 when the prison population was around 40,000 and before the big expansion of prison populations began, the figure was 48%.[3]

One of the most serious failures of the prison system concerns the lack of preparation and care for prisoners at the time of their release.

Many come out with nowhere to live, to broken homes, without family support, without money, without jobs to go to or people to help them. Many of them are drug-dependent or alcoholics. The "monolithic and absurdly expensive and wasteful National Offender Management Service (NOMS) has been proved to be a complete failure".[4] No wonder they fall quickly into bad company and bad habits so that they soon offend again. Often prison appears like a refuge.

One is bound to ask what on earth is the point of it all? We are told by some that it is to keep criminals off the streets and away from society. We are also told that it is to reform and rehabilitate prisoners so that they can play a constructive role in society. Our inability to do either properly is shameful.

Prison sentences are being given more often and for longer periods in spite of the fact that the number of community sentences has also been increasing over the years. The enormous pressure on the prison system persists and gets continually worse. Somehow the public has little confidence in the usefulness of community sentencing and feel that the rules for early release mean that sentences are ineffective.

The cost of maintaining the prison service is huge. In 2006 it amounted to £3.2 billion, equivalent to about £40,000 a year for each prisoner. On top of this is the cost of the probation service, which itself is stretched beyond reasonable limits in many places and in need of serious reform.

The whole operation involves tragic suffering for large numbers of people, many of whom are young, ill-educated, mentally ill or have special educational needs, the victims of broken families, many from underprivileged backgrounds, violent childhoods and poverty.

By 'ill-educated' I mean that less than half our young people leaving state schools in 2008 did so with five good (A-C) GCSE grades including the vital subjects of English and Maths.[5] For the prison system this means that 60% of prisoners have a reading ability below that of a six year old child – and most leave having learnt nothing.

It is tragic that in spite of endless government initiatives and a huge increase in educational spending the situation seems to be getting no better. It is like a cancer at the centre of our entire society.

If anyone in this country had the guts to undertake a complete long-term reform of the entire prison system it would bring enormous benefits to Britain as a whole. We would be perceived by other countries as a far more civilised place in which to live, and I suspect it would have the knock-on effect of making ordinary people less aggressive in their dealings with one another. It would provide an enormous boost to the country's morale. The fact that they have tamed the problem in Scandinavia means that with the right resources, training and understanding we should be able to set ourselves on the right path in Britain.

Keys to the solution

I feel there are certain keys to resolving this almost impossibly complicated problem.

Local communities

The problems should be tackled against a background of political reform that re-established local communities as the arbiters for much of the running of the country as opposed to the faceless, incompetent, centralised control that is practiced throughout the UK at the moment.

The Centre for Social Justice proposes that NOMS should be abolished and the job of commissioning and managing custody places and offender rehabilitation services should be taken over by a new network of Community Prison and Rehabilitation Trusts (CPRTs) which would be the prison and offender management equivalent of local NHS Trusts. This seems an excellent approach but I hope they become much more involved with the local communities than the typical NHS Trust.

Local amenities and services

It should be part of an overall process of dealing with local policing, building local prisons and hospitals, managing local schools and setting up serious community centres and facilities dealing with all the necessary local services including care of young people, the aged, the disabled, drug addicts and so on. These should be managed by voluntary organisations with government support. When local democracy was fully established the local elected councils would be given power to raise funds through various forms of local taxation which would supplement government funding of the local community services.

The recent Fiona Pilkington tragedy, in which a disturbed mother took her own and her disabled daughter's life because neither the police nor the local authority or anyone else paid any attention to her calls for help over several years, is an all too frequent example of what should never, ever happen.

Surely this could not have occurred if there was a locally elected mayor and Chief of Police and elected members of the local community, meeting regularly to discuss all the community problems? We simply must get democracy back to life at local levels. The bad behaviour by local youths and families that caused Mrs. Pilkington's death is not a one-off situation. It occurs all over the country.

Community National Service

A form of Community National Service supporting many aspects of public life should be set up so that no unemployed person who is fit enough to participate can have an excuse for sitting at home. These activities could include hospital work, community work with the aged and with young people (helping to organise get-togethers, club activities, music sessions, exercising etc.), supporting meals on wheels, projects to beautify our towns and cities, tree planting, clearing up waste and rubbish dumps, service with some parts of the armed services, help with the railways and canals, maintaining railway stations, clearing footpaths, working in schools, catering and many other community projects. As Richard Lambert has suggested, a large scale apprenticeship programme to green the public domain – installing insulation, double glazing and so on should be included.

Those coming from a background of unemployment should of course be paid the minimum wage and those from a custodial background should be paid their transport/living costs and the balance of their pay should be saved up for them to receive when they had satisfactorily (in terms of good behaviour, time keeping etc.) completed their community service sentence. They could continue to work at community service on a fully paid basis if they had no job to go to at the time of the completion of their sentence. The key to the success of this programme would depend on the quality of supervision and training that could be provided by the authorities, the voluntary organisations and the probation service. The fact that these young people would be working beside young people who had committed no offences should be helpful to them understanding the value of the process. I cannot believe that young people would not be hugely influenced and interested working with all these deserving causes.

These activities should be connected with a tremendous drive to set up normal work opportunities with voluntary organisations based mostly in local communities where many kinds of activities could be centred. These exist already in some areas such as Newham and other London boroughs.

After all, if we were capable of organising the lives of every young person in the country for National Service in the 1950s we should be able to organise a new Community National Service today and in addition a better system of training non-academic young people into vocational jobs.

It would be great to have a system of Community National Service that included *all* young people so that there would be a mix of all classes and backgrounds. But it seems that the electorate as a whole would not approve of compulsion in spite of its obvious merits in bringing young people from different backgrounds together. Perhaps if my suggestions are adopted, it might eventually become sufficiently interesting for a broad section of the population to support it.

The Government is trying to set up a National Apprenticeship Service by 2020 for under 18s which is intended to benefit 400,000 young people. On their past record this will not happen. The lack of proper apprenticeships in this country is a long-term disgrace. In Germany for instance around 50% of *all* young people are involved in apprenticeships in a wide range of occupations and industries. It is one basis for that country's enormous success as a manufacturing powerhouse.

It is vital that we get on and sort out the work possibilities for our young people as quickly as possible. And we should start by taking most of the form filling and targets out of education and letting schools and other organisations get on and provide the learning and education that they are well capable of doing.

The tax/benefit system should give solid financial support for a huge range of apprenticeships throughout industry perhaps along similar lines to my suggestions for the reform of tax credits. The vital thing is not for the Government to do everything, but to provide a framework and funds targeted at the companies who will employ apprentices so that there is a real incentive for them to do it all.

Young people

Some miscellaneous facts regarding crime by children and young people:

- In November 2006 there were 11,862 under 21 year olds in custody, and close to 3,000 were children under 18.[6]

- Children in custody have very little access to fresh air and exercise, many have none at all.[7]

- Physical control (handcuffs) and strip-searching as well as segregation (solitary confinement) is common in both prison units and young offenders' institutions. A recent HMIP report[8] raised concerns about the application of adult strip-searching rules on children, forcible strip-searching and high levels of use of force.[9]

- Children are serving longer sentences: the average length of custodial sentences at magistrates' court for 10–17 year olds nearly doubled between 1995 and 2005 to 6.4 months. At crown court they rose from 17.6 to 22.1 months during the same period.[10]

- A recent study reveals that over 18,000 assaults have taken place in the eighteen YOIs which were studied between 2003 and 2006.[11] Young offender institutes have a majority of 18-21 year olds. It is clear that YOIs are hotbeds of violence. The majority of the 18,000 plus assaults, over 15,000 of them, were one prisoner on another and over 2,500 were prisoners on prison officers. These numbers look even more horrifying when one understands that YOIs house only around 2,700 offenders in total. They differ in size, the smallest holding sixteen offenders and the largest 400. The balance of young offenders are housed in Secure Training Centres run by private contractors and secure children's homes run mostly by local authorities. Some are sent to prison. It is also interesting that, as in prisons, many of the offenders in YOIs can neither read nor write.

- The Howard League's submission to the United Nations Committee on the Rights of the Child and the treatment of children in prison found that the government is failing its obligations in at least ten articles of the UN Convention on the Rights of the Child.

- England and Wales in particular continue to lock up more children than any other country in Western Europe. According to statistics published by the Council of Europe in 2005, England and Wales were found to have jailed an average of 2,274 children in any one week compared to 1,456 in Germany, 628 in France, seventy-three in the Netherlands and nine in Norway.[12]

- Of the 120,000 young offenders annually in England and Wales, about 75% are given pre-court or first-tier interventions such as curfews or fines. Around 17% are subject to a community sentence and around 4% are sentenced to custody.

- On recent figures 78.2% of young people sentenced to custody reoffend within one year and for community sentences the figure is 70.3%. Around 90% have taken drugs in the past year and around 40% have mental health disorders. Only 30% live with both parents and over 40% have had experience of care.

- Education is a vital element in the cause of offending. Excluded young people according to Mori are committing twice as many crimes as their peers in mainstream education. The number of young people excluded from school has almost doubled since 1995.

- And yet the results from those few offenders who have been re-introduced to education immediately they have been released back into the community have been excellent, with very few reoffending.

- The YOI at Ashfield near Bristol, managed privately by Serco, has recently been praised by Anne Owers, Chief Inspector of Prisons, as a model of how to deal with young offenders. She said 'the amount and quality of activity available is a model of what ought to be expected and available for all 15 to 18 year olds'. It has been described as 'an educational establishment with fences'[13]. This is exactly as all YOIs and other young people's secure training centres should ultimately be described. The Director of the prison, Wendy Sinclair, appears particularly enlightened as other YOIs (including those privately managed) fall very far short of these standards. As usual it is a matter of leadership, training and inspired supervision.

Proposals for *change*

Much of what I am proposing is already being done all over the country by many wonderful voluntary and other organisations. But alas, it is on a scale that will take many years to have a widespread effect on the whole system. I believe that much more support must be given to these organisations by an administratively well organised and well funded unit in the Ministry of Justice – or similar – so that change can take place on a truly national scale with the spectacular results that are sorely needed – but which are clearly well within our grasp if experience in Scandinavia and best practice European countries is anything to go by.

The whole effort ought really to start in primary schools. Young children learn bad (and good) habits so fast that we should not wait until they are sixteen or more before trying to encourage them into a positive way of life. Not only teachers but outside professionals including nurses, the police, prison and probation officers should show these youngsters how to behave in terms of alcohol, drugs, knives and so on. If they learnt the dangers and the problems of such habits early on, there would be less chance of them being led astray by bad role models either within or outside their families.

At least they would recognise bad behaviour and would, hopefully, come and talk to someone in the school if they were worried at home. The system for pastoral care in schools should be further developed in such a way that it was easy for pupils to come and talk to a designated teacher.

We must find a way to lock up far fewer young people (as other countries manage) and provide better supervision and control by the probation service and voluntary organisations. We should also set up other activities and services for non-violent young people. Expensive and unproductive short sentences are being discouraged, but should be virtually discontinued for non-violent offences. We should remove all young people from the adult prison system and provide additional young offender institutes to accommodate them.

The YOIs, which are so violent and unproductive, should be completely reformed. After all, we are talking about fairly small numbers of young people – not huge numbers. We need to get the young people out of a culture of being locked up and bored and into something far more positive. Staff who man these prisons need to undertake a major training programme to teach them how to provide basic educational and rehabilitation opportunities for the young people and above all how to manage them. We must ensure that best practice, as demonstrated by Ashfield, is improved even further – with more resources – and that all are included in the process.

More professional teachers and youth workers should be brought in to work on projects within the YOI framework. The programme should also be aimed at reducing enormously the appalling record of violence in these institutions, providing real pastoral care and supervision for the inmates and of course solid rehabilitation.

All young prisoners should have regular classes in reading and writing taken by professional teachers. It is scandalous that the present education system does not teach them this at school, but it is even more scandalous that it should be neglected while they are in prison. We should look upon YOI and similar time as a priceless opportunity to rectify the educational shortcomings of these young offenders.

There should be real imagination given to other activities for young people, such as training in sailing ships and other well supervised outward bound activities that might encourage a different outlook and a more constructive life for these severely disadvantaged young members of our society.

Outcries by the popular press about 'holidays for young offenders' should be ignored, but equally the outward bound regimes should be aimed at making young people fitter and generally more positive so that they have much improved self-confidence and 'holiday' elements should not be part of the programme. On the other hand it must give them satisfaction and pleasure – why not? – hard work usually does!

The government should cause to be set up – with the help of a wide range of charitable and other organisations and experienced personnel – an initial number – say six to begin with – of outward bound camps in remote areas of Scotland and Wales where these young people could live a hard outdoor life and learn survival skills, thereby becoming more self-reliant, tougher and finding ways of learning to look after each other.

Each camp could be affiliated to designated YOIs and other youth detention centres, and the camps would be open from say March to October each year, during the period of better weather. If each camp could handle say 120 young people at a time over a thirty-six week season, and if each young person spent, say, twelve weeks at a camp, then a total of 2,160 young people could be accommodated in six camps. The most promising young people would be encouraged to stay on as active (paid) volunteer peer managers of the training programmes. Following their time at an outward bound camp they would be encouraged to return to compulsory community service, but if this was not suitable, to the YOI, which by now should have been reformed to enable a full rehabilitation/educational programme to be in place. The number of camps could be increased as they were seen to be successful.

Consideration should also be given to building/acquiring four or five sail training ships, not only for training young naval personnel but also so that a number of young prisoners could have the opportunity of joining the crews for extended periods during which they would become extremely fit and learn a completely new way of life with different values and a work ethic.

Sail Training International has affiliated members all over the world. The UK has members operating fifty-five sail training vessels but as far as I know, none of their crew members are drawn from the prison system. But we have a large infrastructure of operators with whom we could form a partnership. By contributing say five tall ships to the fleet we could support many places for young offenders to find a better route in their lives. Two or three weeks on a sailing training ship can do wonders for one's character and self-belief.

Young offenders including those who are doing time in YOIs should be given the opportunity voluntarily to go to these camps and to these ships and should be encouraged to do so with the promise of reductions in their sentences for good behaviour and other benefits when they are later released into the community. Obviously from the young person's point of view this programme would be treated with great suspicion initially (and heaven knows what they would think of physical exercise and outdoor life!), but over time, and assuming they were encouraged into the harder life with care and understanding, they would ultimately find it a more constructive way of spending their time than being stuck in a YOI. The people running the outward bound camps could even become role models if their backgrounds were as marine commandos, climbers and other 'tough' professions. They would hopefully find youth work less stressful than, say, active service in Afghanistan!

Magistrates should be given the power to recommend such sentences to young people convicted of relatively minor offences as part of a YOI sentence or as part of community service. I feel Magistrates have a too limited number of sentence options at their disposal. ASBOs, for example, have been largely discredited and should be mostly discontinued. What is needed are projects that are more pro-active and inspiring.

It will take time before YOIs are sufficiently reorganised to provide high quality rehabilitation and a caring environment, but a programme of reform and proper leadership and funding would mean that they could be improved enormously over a period of, say, three or four years.

There should also be opportunities for young people to participate in theatre, music and other cultural activities that would stimulate their interest. Experience at the Roundhouse – which works with a local YOI – has shown that such programmes are extremely beneficial to these young people and give them training and confidence to lead highly constructive lives. We have learnt that this is not a far-fetched idea but a practical way of helping them. It is simply a way of finding interesting and stimulating activities in which young people would otherwise have no opportunity to become involved. The facilities and trained personnel to help them must be created and be made available.

Local authorities and charities already arrange all kinds of activities for young people from all walks of life during the holiday periods. I feel these activities should be greatly expanded and incorporate more general outdoor activities so that children could enjoy a wider range of experiences and in the process become fitter. No doubt there are chapters of health and safety regulations that would conflict with this but they should, quite simply, be scrapped. There will be some accidents but how otherwise will young people learn to become more self-confident. Without any statistics it seems to me the French are far better than us at this kind of thing. We should team up with them.

A new approach to dealing with young offenders

What I am seeking is a totally different approach to the handling of young criminals and potential criminals. After all no baby, when born, is a criminal. It is environment, upbringing and bad example and discipline that turns too many of them towards bad habits. Proper supervision should be involved, but the emphasis should be on their future and how to make the most of it. Our present approach is often threatening, negligent and inhuman.

I will doubtless be told that all of the above and the rest of these suggestions will be expensive and beyond our means to fund.

Research has calculated that the total cost of recorded crime by ex-prisoners is around £12 billion. Since crime by young people is about 4% of this we are talking about a cost of £480 million. In 2006 the

Youth Justice Board spent £281 million on secure accommodation. According to the Audit Commission early intervention to prevent young people offending could save public services more than £80 million a year. This would pay for the outward bound camps and the sail training ships many times over.

It sounds a bit trite, but I bet one war in Iraq would pay for all of it and a great deal more. We seem able to pay for the wars abroad but what about at home?

Since that money has already been spent and we have to look forward, please consider carefully the tax proposals (above) for lowering our percentage of national expenditure, raising tax thresholds and reducing government interference at every level – all of which stunt growth and cost huge sums of money. It may take a decade but with the right spirit and national commitment it could be done. We need to look over the horizon and embrace a clearly thought out future.

We should also reform the way we arrange the original contacts which we make after young people are apprehended for offending. In Finland for example, young people under the age of fifteen are dealt with by child welfare authorities with the criminal justice system being applied to those aged 15-17. The criteria for all child welfare interventions is "the best interests of the child" and juvenile crime is viewed as arising from social conditions that should be addressed by further investment in health and social services.

In Germany only a small proportion of juveniles who appear in court are ultimately sent to custody. Instead they are sent on 'social training' courses which involve regular meetings with social workers and intensive weekend arrangements with sporting activities such as sailing and mountain climbing to foster development of social skills and appropriate behaviour.[14]

Somehow I feel we need a combination of these approaches in some brilliantly well organised way.

Managing crime

A study by one of Britain's most distinguished criminologists, Professor David Farrington of Cambridge University, in conjunction with Patrick Langan of the US Department of Justice, compared the USA with England and Wales between 1981 and 1996. The study was subsequently updated to include the estimates for England and Wales to 1999.[15]

The study found that the chances of being imprisoned increased in the USA between 1981 and 1995 and during the same period fell significantly in England and Wales. During these years crime fell in the USA and increased in England and Wales.[16]

The details of the study seem compelling:

- In comparing the figures between 1985 and 1996, the US robbery rate as measured in the victim survey was nearly double that in England and Wales in 1981, but by 1995 the English and Welsh robbery rate was 1.4 times America's.

- In 1981 the English and Welsh assault rate was slightly higher than America's but by 1995 the English and Welsh assault rate was more than double America's.

- The US burglary rate was more than double that in England and Wales in 1981 but by 1995 the English and Welsh burglary rate was nearly double America's.

- The English and Welsh motor vehicle theft rate in 1981 was 1.5 times America's but in 1995 the English and Welsh rate for vehicle theft was more than double America's.

- Between 1950 and 2000 the likelihood of a crime being cleared up by the police in England and Wales decreased by 46.2% to a clear up rate of 24%.

- From 1950 to 1999/2000 the percentage of recorded indictable offences in England and Wales leading to a custodial sentence dropped over 72% from 5.4% to 1.5%.

All the above statistics lead to the clear conclusion that part of the problem is the ineffectiveness of our police and prosecution service in bringing criminals to justice, convicting them and locking them up.

Recently there has also been a large increase in the issue of cautions and fixed penalty notices as a way of avoiding the courts and dealing with 'minor' crimes and misdemeanours. It amounts to a 'slap on the wrist' by magistrates. Unfortunately this is having a bad effect on criminals' belief that they will go to prison for their crimes and the system is being increasingly used for crimes that are serious or violent and where the Crown Court is the proper solution. Around 39,000 penalty notices were issued in 2008 for those who have committed, rape, mistreatment of children, burglary or actual bodily harm a charge, for example, that could carry a jail term of up to five years. Those receiving two cautions increased between 2000 and 2008 to 34,785 and those receiving three or more cautions also increased substantially.

As Sir Paul Stephenson the Metropolitan Police Commissioner said "attempts to reduce the pressure on the courts had distorted the traditional role of policing. Police Officers found themselves responsible for handing out punishments and were being distracted from their proper role of detecting crime and catching criminals … the outcome has been an almost uncontrollable increase in cautions and the introduction of the fixed penalty ticket which in the public's mind equates to a parking ticket which should not be used [for] theft and thuggery". He also said "I point out that the public is aware of how, even when persistent violent offenders are given custodial sentences, they are kept in jail for a much shorter period than the term stipulated by the courts, as prison governors attempt to ease the pressure on space in their cells."[17]

Official figures show that only 22% of first time burglars are sent to prison, Only 20% of third-time burglary offenders get what is supposed to be the minimum three years. Fewer than two in five members of the public have confidence in the criminal justice system.

It is a sad, but not surprising fact, that only 50% of those that are given fixed penalty tickets actually pay them on demand. The rest have to be pursued through the courts with limited success. It seems ironic that the tickets are issued to save court time and then court time is squandered in pursuing them!

This policy is also sending a totally wrong message to these (many of them) young people. They should go through court and receive either a strong community sentence (for the less serious cases) or a (rehabilitating) prison sentence. Violence must be shown to be completely unacceptable.

So at the same time, reform of the police (as well as the Crown Prosecution Service and Probation Service) is also vitally necessary. Professor Farrington's study is compelling evidence that criminals who fear they will be apprehended and sent to prison are far less likely to commit crimes than if they have little fear of being caught and even less of being sent to prison. This clearly appears to be the situation in Britain, which has a low level of prisoners per 100,000 recorded crimes. It has been much improved in the USA which shows that it can be done.

Reform the police

Much has been written about police reform. A glance at some of the relevant websites makes this abundantly clear. The vital thing seems to be that the morale and effectiveness of the police could be hugely improved if the current approach of centrally imposed crime targets was scrapped and tick in the box crimes and misdemeanours forgotten. The amount of time-consuming paper work must be severely reduced. Modern technology can obviously play its part, but the reduction in the endless reports etc. is vital.

The key is surely local community control and not some central system of interference from afar in the interests of endless reporting of crime statistics – most of which are unreliable.

In 2008/9 3.6 million antisocial behaviour complaints were reported – about half the number that actually occurred. They are not dealt with by the police as criminal offences and according to the police one quarter of those who complain are not even visited.

Many years ago society used to look after its own local behaviour. Neighbours were close enough and strong enough to ensure that young people behaved themselves. Much of this seems now to have gone and the problems with badly behaved young people are so huge that the police are simply incapable of carrying out the job. Communities must be re-established so that the old system can come back. Parents must be helped, even as early as school and pre-marital counselling, and encouraged to look after their children. Rowdy neighbours and gangs of young people should be dealt with by community action backed up by prompt police intervention whenever it occurs.

Proposals for *change*

The Government has been trying to further amalgamate the Police Authorities that remain – 43 of them. Thank heavens they were not successful! The police themselves should put a stop to it. The opposite is where the future should be.

The police should be released from the shackles imposed on them by the Home Office and the targets inspired by central government control. It is encouraging that Boris Johnson has been strong enough to get rid of Sir Ian Blair, the controversial and highly political head of the Metropolitan Police. (It appears that almost no one in the police service can remember a Chief Constable ever being removed.) He should now ensure that Home Office influence on local policing in London is ended and fully passed to local control as well. This is exactly what should also be happening all over the country.

Control of local police authorities should be based at local level with the Chief Constable being elected at regular intervals by those resident within the Local Authority boundaries. The Tories with their proposal for elected Sheriffs may be along the right lines. This is closely connected with the overall necessity to devolve democracy down to the local level wherever possible.

Each Police Authority would then have to review and adapt its own organization bearing in mind that officers on the beat, close relationships with local communities and control at the lowest level possible are the ideals to be striven for. A bit of local democracy at grass roots level would do wonders for the way communities take control of their policing and clear up their neighbourhoods. New York precincts are a good guide of how our inner cities should be policed. So is the Japanese system, Tokyo for instance has small two-man police stations all over the city. Japanese police officers know all the families and businesses in their precincts. Crime in Japan is well below the levels in the UK and young people's behaviour is infinitely better.

A clear overall co-ordinated policy should be worked out for dealing with youth crime and how cautions and penalty notices should be used and when prosecutions should take place. At the same time (assuming, by then, that the prison capacity allows it) a policy of zero tolerance in matters of drug and alcohol-related crime, knife and gun crime and other serious crime should be established and adhered to.

But alongside this attitude of zero tolerance should come many more constructive activities for young people who are not yet hardened criminals and in cases where different, but well supervised, activities might be good for them and alter their sense of values. The Roundhouse provides a good model for how this can be done, but outward bound experiences would also be very beneficial.

In Glasgow new methods of dealing with the gang culture, based on a successful 'Ceasefire' project developed in Boston, USA, has been proving successful.[18] In Boston they sought to engage directly with gang members and to dismantle their powerful street code. A large group of gang members were summoned to face-to-face forums, referred to as call-ins, at the local courthouse. The object was explicit moral engagement. They were told that what they were doing was causing huge damage to their families and communities and that the violence must stop. The police said that that any further violence would result in the whole group being punished. In emotional appeals, members of the community, victims' relatives and ex-offenders spoke of the consequences of gang violence, and youth workers said that if they wanted out of gang life they would be given help with jobs, housing, training and addiction problems.

This radical approach worked. Over the five month period between the first two call-ins there was a 71% drop in youth homicides. When the strategy was used in Chicago the homicide rate went down 37% within eighteen months in some neighbourhoods. Nine months after the first call-in in Cincinnati, gang-related homicides were down by 50%.

In London and Glasgow's deprived inner cities the drivers of gang crime – poor parenting, fractured families, youth unemployment, school exclusion – are the same as in the US.

The police in Glasgow have followed the Boston project to the letter. After four months, 119 gang members had taken up the offer. Recently the programme was expanded from the east of Glasgow to the north. It will undoubtedly now be more widely used elsewhere and government should see that it is.

Obviously there will continue to be national organisations to deal with terrorist threats, paedophile activity etc. and there would have to continue to be close links between police authorities and local police stations (across boundary lines).

I imagine that at some point the present government will come up with a huge national IT system that will be a disaster in terms of cost but with luck, and after a long passage of time, will be an improvement on what exists now. It is impressive how in the USA technology is used to check instantly on the backgrounds of suspected criminals and their records.

For instance Sir Michael Bichard in the Soham Enquiry slammed the police IT system. He said "an IT system capable of allowing police intelligence to be shared nationally is a priority".

Since it is clear that the likelihood of being caught, prosecuted and jailed in England and Wales has gone down substantially over many years, it seems certain that it is not only the police, but also the prosecution service that is responsible.

Some reports I have read indicate that the Crown Prosecution Service (CPS) has itself been responsible for slowing down and reducing the number of prosecutions and therefore convictions. So somehow the CPS and the police, with appropriate guidance from the Government and the law officers, must simplify and make more effective the ability of the State to bring offenders to justice. Some strong and effective lateral thinking is needed. Unless criminals have a real sense that committing a serious crime will wind them up in jail, the crime rate will not reduce as it has in the USA.

There are efforts being made to increase support for victims of crime which should be encouraged and become part of the strength of community arrangements nationwide. These efforts could go hand in hand with more efforts to bring convicted criminals together with their victims. Where this has been tried seriously it has apparently been a considerable success. Of course it will be time-consuming but for crimes of violence and intrusive crimes such as burglary it could become part of normal practice and over time would have a real impact on the attitudes of those offenders and would certainly contribute to reducing the reoffending rate. It might for example be a fixed element in the release programmes for offenders.

The mentally ill

It is estimated that nine out of ten of the prisoners in England and Wales suffer from one or more mental disorders. This suggests that the Prison Service has become a catch-all social and mental health-care service, as well as a breeding ground for poor mental health.

A recent study by Professor David James found that when you send mentally ill persons to prison instead of hospital they become 50% more likely to reoffend.[18]

The current assessment of prison healthcare by those who deal with it every day is bleak. More than half of healthcare professionals surveyed said that prison mental healthcare was average or poor – (surprisingly low for a self assessment). A panel of experts which included the current and previous Chief Inspectors of Prisons also acknowledged that prison healthcare is still not working properly despite some improvements.

Spending on mental healthcare in prisons, at around £24 million (2008-09), is not only inefficient but also insufficient. Primary Care Trusts (PCTs) are responsible for the healthcare budgets in their areas. Budgets are based on past practice, rather than any definition of current need. These budgets amount to only 11% of the total prison healthcare budget compared with 15% in the community at large. This is in spite of the high concentration of mental illness in prisons. One consequence of underfunding is chronic understaffing.

If compared with Department of Health guidelines for community health teams, the staff allocated for the same work in prisons should be around three times the size.

The report "Out of sight, out of mind" suggests that whatever the costs necessary to achieve these proper staffing levels, they would be far more than offset by a reduction in offending.[20]

The authors also believe that it is very necessary to fund a robust system for diverting offenders away from prison. Not only would this ease the crisis of overcrowding, but also ensure that offenders with mental illnesses were provided care and treatment in an appropriate setting, whether in the community or in a secure health facility.

The biggest drivers of reoffending – lack of employment, suitable accommodation and access to healthcare – need to be carefully considered in an offender's resettlement plan. Ensuring that everyone with a mental health problem who is released from prison has a proper, appropriate care plan as well as the specialist premises where treatment can be given and continued, is crucial in decreasing offending rates.

Although the clinical staff are vital in delivering effective mental healthcare, prison officers have the most contact with prisoners day to day. It is essential that they have the skills to identify and deal with mental illness and in their turn ensure that proper action is taken.

Surveys have shown that one of the biggest improvements that could be made would be to increase health awareness training for prison officers, and also, let it be said strongly, of Prison Governors who play the most important role of all in determining the atmosphere of a prison.

An inspiring Prison Governor can make a huge difference to the activities of the inmates and the morale in the prison. One of the steps that could be taken which would have a huge effect on the prisoners' state of mind is to expand and encourage work by prisoners with local companies and for their own account, and allow them to keep more of the proceeds. Some of their earnings could be used with the active support of the prisoners themselves for the improvement of facilities in the prison and the balance as a fund to be given to them on their release. It seems there are not many such Governors although some have been outstanding, receiving commendations from time to time by Chief Inspectors of Prisons.

In Liverpool prison for example, there was a brilliant scheme where prisoners were taught construction skills and then used them to do up an abandoned council house which they used as accommodation when they were released. It's what Johann Hari, who saw it, called a crime-busting double whammy: work skills and a house nobody else wanted. As he says, why isn't this being done in every prison?

There are some very good rehabilitation projects in all too few prisons. The Open Book Project has been used by an ex-prisoner Joe Baden to encourage creative writing among inmates, taking them from illiteracy to gaining degrees. Only 2% of the people he works with reoffend. Yet he has said that "most rehabilitation today is just crap".[21]

Responsibility for prison healthcare was transferred fully from the Prison Service to the Department of Health in 2006 but offender health is managed by a separate directorate of the DoH.

In 1996 Lord Ramsbotham, then Chief Inspector of Prisons wrote a report that was heavily critical of prison healthcare services – their lack of suitable training for medical and nursing staff; isolation from new clinical developments; inadequate care for the mentally disordered in prison; failure of continuity and care between prison and community; and a lack of consideration of the care needs of specific groups of prisoners such as women and young people. Although matters have improved since then, progress is slow. "Out of sight, out of mind" argues that Lord Ramsbotham's findings are as relevant today as they were thirteen years ago.[22]

This is typical of the massive output of well researched and well argued studies of various aspects of our prison system by many concerned voluntary organisations, that have been seeking improvements for years.

It is just so tragic that minister after minister in government after government has not felt it necessary or found a way to set about improving the prison system in a seriously fundamental way.

Proposals for *change*

- We should review all mentally ill prisoners and grade them in terms of the seriousness of their illness and their propensity for violence etc. We should then remove the seriously mentally ill and the violent from the general prison system and secure accommodation should be converted or built to work entirely with such prisoners. Full teams of staff and doctors, trained specifically for the purpose, should look after them. Segregation of the potentially violent from the non-violent and the seriously ill from those less ill, is fundamental. Those less ill prisoners that cannot be moved due to space and other constraints should receive proper care from the same kind of fully manned teams of trained carers within the prison system. Over time the whole system should be reformed.

- Exactly the same approach should be taken with those on drugs (see chapter 7, p. 178).

- Prisoners should be found jobs that would occupy them constructively and enable them to earn money for both their own subsequent use when they are released, and for the benefit of the amenities in the prison. (This already happens to a limited extent but should be much more widely practised.) What amenities they pay for should be decided by the prisoners themselves. This would greatly improve their morale as well as their surroundings.

- The responsibility for all healthcare in prisons as well as mental health of offenders should be transferred to a single unit away from Primary Health Trusts and adequately funded and manned. Someone who can make things happen should be put in charge. As the numbers of mentally ill prisoners reduce and therefore the space to work is created, the job of rehabilitating 'normal' prisoners should be undertaken in a way that means that they have a chance of becoming good members of society after they come out. This of course means that they need full pastoral care, educational help, a job (both before and after release) and a place to live on release. They also need their health and, where necessary, drug dependency needs supported by easily accessible local health facilities.

- Present prison officers are clearly insufficiently trained, unqualified and have few resources to look after mentally ill prisoners. Prison Governors should all be trained in the requirements of mentally ill prisoners and should make it their duty to see that conditions improve fast and that the most serious cases have been moved to separate specialised accommodation.

- Finally, following a successful new arrangement developed in Pennsylvania, we should set up an entirely separate 'mental health court' system for the mentally ill and drug offenders. When, say, Sally Judson – a diagnosed schizophrenic who developed a heroin habit – was picked up for disorderly conduct, she was taken to a mental health court. Instead of jailing her, they drew up an action plan with her. They found her a doctor, a therapist and a waitressing job. If she relapses onto heroin there is a rehab place waiting for her. The system is working. Mentally ill people in Pennsylvania have a 55% reoffending rate in the normal courts, but in the mental health courts it is just 10%.[23]

I wish we had established such an enlightened approach in this country to our similar problems. We should do it at once!

Women prisoners

There are around 4,300 women in our prisons, only a minority of whom are in jail for violent offences. An increasing total of 8,862 were jailed last year. We should find entirely different ways of managing and helping women who are convicted of non-violent offences.

Proposals for *change*

- Obviously the suggestions for working with the mentally ill and drug addicts could be useful for women prisoners as long as they were based on women only facilities.

- Short-term sentences for women should be abandoned altogether. Further efforts should be made to avoid sending women to prison for short (expensive) sentences and care for these women should be undertaken by voluntary organisations.* Here again community service should become an important facility, as well as other activities that would encourage their rehabilitation outside the prison environment including where necessary appropriate treatment for drug dependency and other illnesses such a mental health.

---

* The Asha Centre in Worcester, and Calderdale Women's Centre in Halifax are just two fine examples.

- New centres should be set up on a regional basis through properly funded voluntary organisations, based for example on the Asha and Calderdale's women's centres, so that it is not necessary for women to be shipped miles from home and family to receive proper care.

Prisons and the prison building programme

The state we have got ourselves into through inadequate investment over decades in appropriate prison capacity has meant that almost nothing is possible in the very short term in achieving the deep reform of the prison system that is required.

So the vital work of planning the prison system that we would like to have in 10–12 years time must begin as soon as possible. The objectives should of course be prioritised, perhaps on the basis that the first new facilities to be built should be for severely mentally ill patients which would free up something like 10,000 places in the present prison system. Simultaneously the work should begin at once on YOIs and other youth facilities. If these two issues could be addressed over a period of say five years the whole problem will soon begin to appear more manageable.

Proposals for *change*

- A new prison building programme should be started based on a long-term plan for situating smaller prisons in local communities. If this was combined with finding ways of reducing the prison population – such as women prisoners, the mentally ill and drug addicts – with more appropriate accommodation, then headway could start to be made. The Ministry of Justice is apparently committed to spending £4.2 million to create 10,000 additional spaces by 2014. This programme should be held back and used to fulfil the above programme for providing accommodation to these needy groups. Also many more community-based sentences should be used to reduce the overall prison population.

- The present government appears fixated on building a small number of huge prisons some of which might also contain separate units for the mentally ill. I believe this approach is totally misconceived. Prisons, like hospitals, police stations and schools, should, in general, be local institutions where prisoners can be close to their families and friends. Community centres could help with their rehabilitation.

- While this detailed work is getting started a separate group should be visiting Denmark, Sweden, Finland, Germany and other countries that manage their prisoner affairs far better than we do to bring back the very latest management information and specification for facilities, so that every new prison or detention centre that we build is fit for purpose with state-of-the-art facilities and properly trained management. Ministers are always trying to cut corners (they are rarely successful!), but the one thing they shouldn't try to alter is the proper level of accommodation. Cells that were originally designed for one person should revert to single person occupancy – not two or three.

- The other background factors and policies that prevent people committing so many crimes in the first place in these countries should also be studied carefully. This would impact the way we work with children, families, schools, the police, the courts and so on.

- A far-reaching and rigorous overhaul of management and management training and systems should be undertaken generally to make sure that the bulk of our prisons are brought up to a state where overcrowding is eliminated and a full programme of reform and rehabilitation is undertaken. No excuse should be accepted for not doing this on a timely basis.

- New thinking is required on how the top management of these facilities is set up. I believe the blueprint mentioned in chapter nine should be considered so that whatever organisations are established to see these changes through will be completely independent of day to day government interference. Management should have appropriate incentives to succeed based on the successful achievement of the required criteria. There are almost no cases of prison governors being dismissed for incompetence and yet Her Majesty's Chief Prison Inspectors have, for years, been criticising (although sometimes praising) the managements of large numbers of prisons.

Organising proper release arrangements

It is well known that prisoners when they are released suffer from extreme difficulties in getting jobs, accommodation and finding healthcare and pastoral care facilities. The overstretched probation service, and the non fit-for-purpose NOMS are incapable of carrying out this work adequately. It needs more funding, more training and less autocratic systems. It should also be based at community level where they are in closer touch with the people they serve.

Proposals for *change*

- Make sure prisoners are kept in touch with their families. The evidence shows that this is the single biggest factor in keeping a prisoner from reoffending. If you manage to keep your partner you are 20% more likely to stay out of jail. But our prisons make this impossible for around half the inmates. 37,000 prisoners are held more than three hours journey from their homes and 5,000 more than six hours. Prisoners are constantly being moved where capacity has become available. Families simply cannot afford to keep in touch so nearly half of male prisoners lose touch with their families and loved ones. Around a third of prisoners are released to 'no fixed abode'. No wonder they reoffend.[24]

- A special unit should be established to ensure that every single prisoner who is released is supported by all these services. The system should be analogous to finding a bed for a seriously ill patient in the NHS. Probably the most difficult to arrange is the job element but of course, once it is fully established nationally, the Community National Service system should look after that.

- Consider as a fixed element in the release programme a conference to bring the offender into a meeting with the victim of his/her crime. If all the other support arrangements were in place such a face to face conversation should contribute over time to the reduction in reoffending rates.

- Having a system of local prisons would make all these problems more manageable. Small prisons, are also easier and quicker to build and manage except of course for seriously violent and high security prisoners. Such factors should be considered during the process of planning the future prison system.

- Above all, make sure prison is for violent and sexual offenders only. All the rest need specialised treatment and thorough rehabilitation.

Locked up potential

While going through my final drafts I have seen the paper "Locked up Potential" on prison reform produced by Iain Duncan Smith's Centre for Social Justice with a committee chaired by Jonathan Aitken. I could not have believed that in my lifetime I would read such a detailed, well researched and enlightened set of proposals for dealing with every aspect of our prison system. It is what should have been suggested decades ago and by now fully implemented.

It made me wonder whether I should continue with my own proposals at all, after reading such a comprehensive work.

I have decided to go ahead with setting out my own ideas because some of them go beyond the proposals in the Centre for Social Justice's paper and I come at the subject from a very individual perspective.*

The point is, of course, that the subject of fundamental prison reform must be put high on any future Government's agenda and a powerful managerial team must be enlisted to make sure it all happens. It is a huge job.

The chances of it happening, based on history, still seem slim although there is now even less excuse for the next Home Office Minister (unlike so many predecessors) avoiding his/her clear responsibility!

---

* I have however incorporated a few of their statistics.

Chapter 7
Drugs and reform

A few facts:

- Figures are hard to come by but drug use has become very prevalent in Britain. The latest survey I have found, 2003/04 suggests that 35.6% of people aged 16-59 in England and Wales have used drugs at some time in their lives (around 11 million people), 12% have used drugs during the past year and 7.5% in the past month.[1]

- Nothing the government or the police have been doing has succeeded in getting a grip on this business.

- The cost of drugs is lower in real terms than it has ever been. A gram of cocaine a few years ago used to cost £80–£100 whereas more recently it has been as low as £40–£50.[2]

- Three quarters of the people in this country say drugs are a problem in their area.[3]

- 60% of serious crime – including burglaries and car theft – involves use of drugs or alcohol. Much of it is committed in order to obtain funds to feed the habit.

- Prisons appear to be wide open to drug use in spite of apparent tight security. I assume much of this is a reflection of corrupt practices.

- Cocaine (776,000 users) and crack/cocaine (53,000) are the most prevalent class A drugs on the street with Ecstasy (502,000) fairly close behind. These figures are most likely underestimates. Some estimates published in 2005 put the number of crack users in London alone at 46,000. The number of heroin users has been estimated to be as high as 200,000 with 88,000 receiving treatment.

- Cannabis (2,655,000) (now class B again) has grown in potency in recent years and is now considered to be a dangerous drug if taken in significant amounts over a long period. It causes hallucinations and panic attacks and may affect the brain in terms of ability to concentrate. It is a major cause of clinical depression and consequently psychosis and schizophrenia. It is considered by some to be a stepping stone to class A drugs.

- Treatment centres have widely used methadone as a heroin substitute but this treatment is criticised by many as being ineffective in taking addicts off the habit. There is a feeling that treatment centres are more concerned with using methadone as a substitute than finding ways of taking heroin addicts off dependency altogether. Methadone users are often tempted to other drugs such as crack and the combination can be very bad for their health.

- The Home Office estimates that three quarters of crack and heroin addicts steal to fund their habit. Chris Allen of Sheffield Hallam University says that heroin addicts are often more able to control their need for the drug than is widely assumed: many have periods of being "Giro junkies" who wait until they receive their benefits payment before buying their fix.[4]

- Cocaine seizures more than doubled in 2003/4 to 20,727 kilograms. Around 12% of heroin and 9% of cocaine was impounded by law enforcement agencies during the period 1996–2005, but in a report the government "agrees that enforcement in isolation is not effective".[5]

- The same report estimated that between 60% and 80% of drugs would need to be seized to put major traffickers out of business. Nothing on this scale has yet come close to being achieved.

- It has been estimated that the criminal justice costs of class A drugs alone (i.e. not cannabis) is around £4 billion a year. The drugs market in the UK has been estimated at £5.3 billion.[6]

- The Home Office has said that every £1 spent on drug treatment saves £3 in less crime.[7]

- The UK is one of the few countries that allow heroin to be prescribed for addicts but it can only be done by a doctor with Home Office approval, amounting to about 0.5% of those in treatment. New pilot projects are expected to increase this number.

There is a huge amount of anecdotal evidence connected with drug use and the opinions of addicts and reformed addicts. There are many who say that being prescribed heroin by a doctor transforms their lives from a situation where getting their next fix dominates everything they do, into a position where they can live a normal life, plan normally and do regular work. Their health improves and they can become normal functioning members of society. They can plan their actions like normal people and this gives them a real feeling of stability.

Diamorphine (heroin) prescribed by the state is pure and avoids all the risks of overdosing, unsafe injection and infection including HIV, hepatitis, abscesses and ulcers.

It also means that users have the time and surroundings in which they can form a view about coming off drugs and undergoing detox treatment. Many of those receiving doctor's prescriptions for heroin have, over a period of time, done this successfully.

However, at the moment all new heroin trials are heavily supervised and very rigid in structure. Addicts have to turn up twice a day, seven days a week to a clinic to inject their heroin, but the rigid nature of the regime means that it allows none of the clients to attend work or college and lead an otherwise normal life. The results, however, are better than methadone treatment for crime committed, use of street drugs and mental and physical well-being.

One thing is clear. If treatment centres are oppressive or heavy-handed, prescribe too little heroin to satisfy the addicts' needs or try to bully addicts into actions that they find unacceptable, they will find additional drugs outside with all the health dangers and increase in crime, implied. Addicts refused treatment have in some cases committed suicide.

So the characteristics of the treatment centre and the form of the treatment is vitally important. The regime for treatment must be more adaptable to the working and outside life of the users. Doctors and nurses cannot be judgemental but must try and work closely with the addict to encourage their wish to come off drugs altogether.

I well understand that saying anything about drugs is entering a virtual minefield. But since it is so important an element in crime and prison, I am venturing to support opinions put forward by those who are dissatisfied with the quality and extent of our present efforts to solve the problems, and who support deep-seated reform of the current drug policies.*

---

* For example Johann Hari, who writes for *The Independent* and posts many internet articles on drug use as well as prisons and the treatment of prisoners.

"The drug war hands one of our biggest industries to armed criminal gangs, who unleash terrible violence across the country. When alcohol was prohibited in the US in the 1920s it didn't vanish."[8] Under prohibition alcohol use became more hardcore. The writer Richard Cowan called it "the iron law of prohibition" – whenever a substance is criminalised it becomes stronger. It has happened to cannabis and it is why the dealers invented crack in the 1980s.

Where there is a huge profit to be made in a black market – it's 3000% on drugs today – people will fight and kill to control it. Arrest a dealer, and you simply trigger a new war for his patch. The Nobel Prize-winning economist Milton Friedman calculated that there are 10,000 murders in the US alone caused by these wars. He also said "Prohibition is the drug dealers' best friend. Legalise and you bankrupt most organised crime overnight".

It has been thought by many (myself included) that by legalising drugs the amount of drug use in the country would soar. This doesn't appear to be the case.

"On July 1st 2001 Portugal decriminalised the possession of **all** drugs including heroin and cocaine. You can have as much as you like for your own needs. If you are caught the police might refer you to a rehab programme but you will never get a criminal record. Supplying, dealing and selling these drugs remain illegal."[9]

In fact "the overall use of drugs fell a little. A major study by Glen Greenwald of the Cato Institute found that among teenagers the fall was fastest: 13 year olds are 4% less likely to use drugs and 16 year olds 16% less likely. As the 'iron law of prohibition' predicts, the use of hard drugs has fallen fastest: heroin use among the young not yet addicted has come down by nearly 50%".[10]

The Portuguese have switched the huge sums they used to spend on chasing and jailing addicts to providing them with prescriptions and rehab. The number of people in drug treatment is up by 147%. Almost nobody in Portugal wants to go back. Indeed many want to take the next step: legalise supply too and break the back of the gangs.

Portugal is no fluke. It turns out that wherever drug laws are relaxed, drug use stays the same, or where spending is switched to treatment – falls. Between 1972 and 1978 eleven US states decriminalised marijuana possession. The National Research Council found that the numbers of dope smokers stayed the same.

In Switzerland, a decade ago the government provided legal centres where people could safely inject heroin – for free. The burglary rate fell by 60%, and street homelessness ended. A study by *The Lancet* – one of the most respected medical journals in the world – found that the rate of people becoming new heroin addicts fell by 82%. Why? "Heroin addicts didn't need to recruit new addicts to sell to in order to feed their habit. The pyramid scheme of heroin addiction was broken."[11]

The present war against drugs clearly does not achieve its goal of reducing addiction – in spite of vast cost in terms of expenditure, huge police time and effort. Addicts still commit many thousands of serious crimes. It also does little to assist the health of many thousands of addicts which could be greatly improved by diverting some of this huge cost to their treatment and rehabilitation.

I have suggested a slightly modified approach which I hope will achieve the required ends and might be followed by more extensive policies when they are proved successful.

Proposals for *change**

- The same approach towards moving mentally ill prisoners from prison should be taken for those on drugs. For example, 12% of prisoners are heroin addicts, imprisoned for either possessing the drug or committing property crimes to feed their desperate need. Rather than spend the £40,000 a year to keep them in prison we could prescribe a legal supply for £4,000 a year. They could then live full healthy lives. Arthur Conan Doyle and the father of modern surgery William Halstead did. When the Swiss did this, burglary fell by 70%.[12]

- The present network of drug treatment centres should be reviewed and new centres planned wherever it is necessary to ensure that all places where class A drug use is known to be significant, are properly served. Centres could be run by the NHS, by private voluntary organisations or subcontracted to existing private drug rehabilitation centres.

---

* I have been deeply influenced throughout this report by the very perceptive writings of Johann Hari, introduced to me by Aly Boyt. I may not have gone far enough to satisfy him, but compared to him I have very little experience – just a burning desire to improve the way we treat drug dependency at the moment.

- The review should take into account the provision of adequate staff, staff training, doctors and facilities to manage the likely number of users.

- Heroin should be administered free of charge to all heroin addicts. It is not, I imagine, normally sensible to give out prescriptions to addicts, as control of the use may be lost. However as users became comfortable with their arrangements it may be contemplated.

- Every patient should be examined, assessed and counselled in a friendly manner before being given their first free injection as part of an ongoing programme. It should always be the timely objective to get addicts off the habit if possible. Attendance at private rehab centres for this purpose should be encouraged – usually for fairly short periods and perhaps on a partnership basis. Methadone would not normally be part of this process. The important element in all this is that the addict should have someone that he or she trusts available at all times for counselling through a friendly centre.

- I have no idea whether such an approach could be useful for addiction to cocaine and/or crack cocaine. But obviously private rehab treatment centres work with these addicts and although it might be a very expensive option, the government must have a policy for dealing effectively with such cases. There has recently been some encouraging news from a company in Texas that appears to have developed a vaccine that has a beneficial effect on half the cocaine users who have tried it.

- There should be the harshest possible treatment of drug dealers and sellers. Those caught selling and trafficking drugs of all categories should certainly go to jail.

- The amount of publicity and counselling given to explaining to children the dangers of drug use both in schools, from primary school onwards, and other media that they read, should be stepped up.

- In any case, prospective mothers and young mothers should be helped with mothering skills even more assiduously than happens at the moment – through community activity – so that they would be better informed about how to bring up their children and of course advice on the dangers of using drugs should be part of that help.

- If we changed our court system so that young drug addict offenders – as well as young mentally ill – were seen by special 'health courts' whose job was to make sure these offenders received the help, rehabilitation and/or medical support they needed, wherever possible within a family setting, I believe we would be on the way to a more effective and civilised solution to our general problems connected with young people.

Since the use of heroin in this country is involved with so much crime, the fact that the state provided it free, in a supervised environment, should have an even more dramatic effect on the amount of such crime committed than in Portugal and Switzerland, and result in a substantial saving of cost related to all the overheads involved with the paraphernalia of taking criminals to court, locking them up etc. as well as the benefit to the public from less burglaries, car thefts and so on.

It seems to me that our treatment of drug addicts and the related problems is symptomatic of much else that we try to do in this country. It is not done with enough planning, investment, thoroughness and training and winds up being only half achieved. It is over bureaucratic. It is this approach that we must learn to improve everywhere. Long-term planning and proper funding is essential so that what we do, we do well. This is at the root of solving many of our problems.

Chapter 8
The nanny state: time to grow up

Alas, our state is aptly named.

I have set out in Part 2 my concerns about the many ways in which the state intrudes into the lives of all of us in this country. This intrusion has been gathering pace for decades but has accelerated enormously under the Labour Government. The problem with the intrusions is that they are not only expensive but also spiritually corrosive.

A House of Lords Committee has reported unequivocally that monitoring every day the activities of innocent individuals has become "pervasive" and "routine". The peers noted that this intrusiveness had altered the relationship between the state and its citizens and represented "one of the most significant changes in the life of the nation since the end of the second world war". The peers also observed that most Britons were unaware of the extent of these surveillance policies and did not fully appreciate their potential consequences. One of the reasons for this is the lamentable record of the Commons in curtailing these developments. The Coroners and Justice Bill currently before Parliament contains powers to let Whitehall departments and other state agencies use and share personal data for whatever purpose a minister sees fit. This removes protections that exist in statute precisely to stop this happening.[1]

These 'activities' include numbers of people and government departments who have databases which hold our criminal and financial records, our DNA and almost every known fact about us. The amount of information that is on file about us far exceeds what is reasonable. It does little to solve crimes and lots to incur unhappiness. It often involves considerable expense for us, individually, in the time, for example, that it takes to fill out the endless forms, and via our taxes, through the enormous government expenditure in building up and administering the databases. Thank heavens after several long expensive years the ID card system seems finally to be being laid to rest.

The number of intruders that are legally allowed to enter our properties and the endless harassment on the roads and by local authorities and others is a serious imposition. It makes living in Britain a stressful experience for many among us.

So my proposals are directed at hacking back some of this cloying legislation.

Proposals for *change*

- The first thing, obviously, is to identify the areas of law that we want to cleanse. These would include Health and Safety in every respect, laws relating to schools and young people and their protection, laws to do with local authority regulation for everything from dustbin collection to cameras, speed cameras (and traffic calming measures!), laws related to the collection of electronic information about us and many, many others. I have no idea how to start going about this as there will be endless conflict between anyone wishing to cut out legislation and the ministries and departments concerned, who set up the complex systems in the first place.

- Perhaps there should be a powerful Central Committee of experienced legislators who are ideologically committed to cutting down the number and scope of these laws and a series of temporary sub committees, responsible to the Central Committee, looking at each of the major areas for attention and making recommendations. These might each operate for say four years (being reviewed for progress on a quarterly basis) and then pack up having done all that they could. The Government and Parliament would have to give them the necessary powers to make a real difference.

- Quangos and other non-departmental public bodies (NDPBs) should be included in this major culling of unproductive interference by unrepresentative organisations. As a first step all such organisations should be asked to set out the reasons for their existence and the success or otherwise they have achieved in fulfilling their objectives. They should also quantify fully the cost of the results they achieved from their work. They should set out details of any other organisations overlapping/duplicating the work they do and the situation that would occur if they ceased to provide the services they render. The Central Committee should consider all these and any other pertinent factors and then, first assess whether the organisation can be wound down completely or secondly, be reduced in size. Any overlapping organisations should be considered at the same time. As mentioned earlier, saving can only be achieved if there are real structural changes.

- We should get rid of the Independent Safeguarding Authority and improve the care and protection of young people through reforming the existing channels, better parenting education and through better understanding of the problems in schools.

- We should also follow the Dutch example – as also proposed by the Tory opposition – of making sure that for every new law or regulation passed, a similar existing law or regulation was cancelled. I feel we are so deep into this malaise that we should have a moratorium on passing any law that entailed new penalties or restrictions for say one year, while these committees got to work deleting laws. We could then operate the Dutch system, but with the requirement that two or three regulations should be scrapped for every new one proposed. Ultimately if we ever got it cleansed we could go back to a law for a law.

- It would be important for the Central Committee to solicit ideas for which laws to cancel from the general public and different sections of industry. This would provide an enormous head of steam to get the whole system up and running.

- I mentioned in Part 2 that we should increase the speed limit on major motorways from the present 70 mph to 80 mph. I do not believe that in practice the speeds would increase much if at all. But I do believe that motorists, feeling that the speed was sensible, would be inclined to keep to the higher limit with less differential between the speeds of the fast and slower drivers. The new limit should be tried out on a couple of motorways for say six months or a year to assess the impact of the change. If favourable it should be extended to the rest of the motorway system. While doing this it would be sensible to improve the signage on the major roads to make clear what the speed limit actually is. At the moment many dual carriageways are restricted to 60 mph but the signs do not make clear whether on many of them the limit is in fact 60 mph or 70 mph.

Chapter 9
Our outdated system of parliamentary government

The blind leading the blind.

Perhaps the major cause of our difficulties over at least the past twenty years has been the lack of training and experience and the incompetence of the people who pass the ever-increasing number of laws and regulations that we are required to obey – that is the politicians and their advisers, the civil servants, and their advisers, the consultants.

Linked to this is the problem of short-termism. Most worthwhile projects take many years to come to fruition, but the way our government and its ministers work there is a strong pressure to achieve instant results. Both short and long-term projects are often ill-thought out and hurried into legislation with harmful consequences. This short-termism has to be resisted if we are to achieve success in much of what we do.

Part of the problem is the very short time span that most ministers spend in any one job, and the short-sighted approach forced upon them by the media and, via the media, by the public, who have come to expect instant solutions to almost everything.

The number of outside professions and interests represented in Parliament has declined by over half in the past fifty years[1] and, as MPs get younger this trend is likely to continue. Even the number of practising lawyers among them has declined substantially.[2] It is sad that Parliament now offers so narrow a range of experience. Every possible step should be taken to reverse the trend.

This state of affairs has been encouraged by the abolition of evening sittings, which used to allow MPs time during the day to do other jobs. Since the pay, expenses, allowances and pensions which MPs have voted themselves have risen so dramatically, the job has become a profession in itself (encouraged by the scandalous system of accounting for expenses), thereby attracting younger and less experienced 'career' politicians.

The recent scandals exposed by the *Daily Telegraph* of the extent to which MPs of all parties have abused the confidence we put in them by, in effect, stealing (if not illegally, certainly very unethically) huge amounts of money from the tax payers, has made clear how far Parliament has fallen in terms of the quality of its members.[3] The House of Commons used to be filled with men of renown in their professional activities. Sir Christopher Wren was an MP, as were Sir Isaac Newton and John Stewart Mill. More recently we have had politicians such as Disraeli, Gladstone, Winston Churchill, Nye Bevan, Ernest Bevin, Clement Attlee, Margaret Thatcher and Tony Benn. There is no doubting the quality of their contributions to our political development and our standing in the world.[4]

For half a century or more Britain has lost power at the executive end of government, becoming far less influential in the world. To combat that, it reluctantly joined what it thought was the Common Market, but which became the European Union. Thus Britain found itself subject to massive direction from Brussels. At the same time Westminster sucked power from below, reducing local government to a cipher. Deprived of serious influence on events, backbench MPs mutated into glorified councillors themselves, sorting out their constituents' visa problems and leaky drainpipes. Over-whipped, and in some cases overworked they became less and less recognisable as genuine parliamentarians.[5]

Politicians in the US Congress wield immense influence over legislation and the budget due to the way the Congress has been set up to give their committee system real information, authority and power. In France many deputies have real power from the tradition which encourages local mayors and other people of influence to stand as members – including civil servants. In the UK overcentralisation of power in the cabinet and in the Prime Minister has destroyed much of Parliament's influence.

The Cabinet Secretary Richard Wilson (now Lord Wilson) commented on politicians' lack of experience in 2001 at a meeting with Tony Blair and Gordon Brown: "Your problem is that neither of you or anyone in Number 10 has ever managed anything."[6] The same is true, alas, of most of the Government.

MPs have shown foolish tenacity in trying to avoid even the limited scope of current Freedom of Information legislation. Led by no less a person than the then Speaker, Michael Martin, they have attempted to keep their expenses and how they use their allowances secret, and several of them have been found out employing their children and other family members to do little or no work for substantial salaries at taxpayers' expense. Many have manipulated their housing allowances to buy second homes on free mortgages that have grown enormously in value and some have even invented non-existent mortgages themselves.

A further example of Britain's amateurish approach to government is the very short period of time that most ministers have to get a grip of their departments before setting up long-term plans to improve performance and change policies.

It is almost unbelievable, for example, that the recent Home Secretary John Reid had no less than nine ministerial posts in the nine years up to 2006 – covering Defence, Environment, Transport, the Regions, Scotland, Northern Ireland Party Chairmanship, Leader of the Commons, Health, Defence (again) and recently Home Secretary. I cannot find in his CV any relevant experience to qualify him for taking any one of these jobs.

How on earth could Reid be expected to master the detail of all the problems and opportunities in each of these enormous posts in the span of a year? What chance did any of his seven ministries have of establishing continuity of policy or management? In private industry he could never have achieved responsibility at anything like this level for even one job and certainly not for nine of them. If it wasn't so serious it would be laughable.

There are limitless other examples. Nearly every minister has had little relevant experience in terms of work outside parliament and few have had their jobs in a single ministry for more than two years.

The US system, by contrast, is quite different. It has been hugely instructive to watch the new President, Barack Obama, choosing his cabinet from among the best-qualified candidates in the country for the relevant jobs. He has kept Robert Gates as Secretary of Defence, a Republican who proved himself under George W. Bush and appointed Steven Chu a Nobel Prize-winning scientist as Energy Secretary. His Treasury Secretary is Tim Geithner, previously Chairman of the New York Federal Reserve Bank. Geithner's predecessor was Hank Paulson a hugely experienced ex-chairman of Goldman Sachs.

Other than Prescott, Gordon Brown is the one minister who kept the same position throughout the Blair government's tenure of office.* He did this through what seems to many (and to me) a thoroughly

---

* There have been a few other exceptions including Jack Straw, four years as Home Secretary and five years as Foreign Secretary and Clare Short six years on International Development.

unprincipled agreement with Tony Blair, who gave him a virtual monopoly over domestic policy in exchange for not competing with Blair for the leadership of the Labour Party following John Smith's untimely death. It is well established that communication between them was often poor and spasmodic. On occasion Blair apparently heard of the budget measures only a day or two before the budget announcement in Parliament. What a way to run a country!

If only our chancellors had had something like Geithner's or Paulson's training and experience before they started, I feel sure they would have been able to make many of the changes simpler, the tax system less onerous and complicated and the economic management of the country more efficient.

We have to find a way in Britain of bringing similar experience and efficient administration into running the great departments of state, while reorganising Ministers' responsibilities so that they can concentrate on policy and good quality legislation. This has to be done while at the same time preserving their long established responsibility to Parliament.

I would like to emphasise that the following ideas are not intended as a blueprint for exactly how each Department of State should be managed. At the moment each department is managed on a different model. For example, the NHS is organised in such a way that some NHS Foundation Trusts have achieved considerable autonomy while others are working towards achieving it. It is intended that in the end all hospitals should ultimately become free-standing foundation trusts. At the same time there is an independent regulatory monitor to ensure that it all works, and this brings it into conflict from time to time with the Department of Health. On top of this there is the Care Quality Commission, an independent NHS inspectorate. No doubt there are many other elements as well. It has recently been reported by the monitor that the Health Minister Andy Burnham is "seeking to re-impose central control" over NHS Foundation Trusts.[7] This makes my point perfectly. From press comment it appears as though a future Conservative government if elected would encourage a more arms-length method of running the NHS but this would only be fully effective if it were combined with devolving government to a local level.

I am not trying to get into the huge minefield of suggesting exactly how all these organisations should be changed across government but rather I am going back to first principles as a kind of blueprint that should create a much leaner more efficient system based on a simple proposal. It should also have the effect of removing some of the independent regulators and inspectors since management of the whole system will itself become independent.

While proofreading this book (January 2010), two new reports have been published, almost simultaneously, that cover the perceived deficiencies of the present system of government, parliamentary organisation and responsibility, and re-organisation of the civil service. These are *Shaping up: A Whitehall for the Future*, by the Institute for Government, based on evidence from sixty-one highly qualified top civil servants and carried out over the past year, and *Good Government: Reforming Parliament and the Executive*, also by a (smaller) group of highly qualified civil servants and ex-civil servants, which traces its origins back to 2006.[8]

These two independent (but mutually aware) studies set out strong criticisms of the way, during recent decades, government, the cabinet, the executive, ministers and their special advisers and civil servants have operated and the shortcomings of Parliament in terms of the amount, quality and effectiveness of the legislation it has produced. If after the forthcoming election Parliament was to implement all the detailed recommendations from these two excellent studies, then indeed the government of the country would be hugely improved and reformed.

The erudition and experience of the authors and the clarity of the civil service approach to reform is very impressive.

To a non-politician there remains a concern, however, that after one party has won the election and decided that root and branch reform is not needed, the machinery of government and parliament might still look rather as it does now, although no doubt working somewhat more effectively. Perhaps this is all that is needed. I find civil service drafting incredibly clever but sometimes a bit too academic and ministers more interested in headline-catching initiatives than boring old reform or time-consuming change.

I take comfort that the detailed analysis carried out by both organisations of the deficiencies in the way the country is governed at the moment has much in common with the criticisms I have set out in this book.

Logically I should pack up and go back to flying, but I have continued with my own approach to government reform, as in some ways it is more fundamental and, I hope, convincing in lay terms about what should be done. I have tackled the changes in ministerial responsibility, the role of the civil service and the managing of the great state enterprises in a straightforward way, keeping in mind the basic principles of simplicity. But I have also covered a number of other areas such as freedom of information and lessons from the US select committee system, which, if dealt with together, might have a broader impact.

Proposals for *change*

Leadership

A massive overhaul is required in the way most major government departments are led and managed and direct ministerial responsibility for the minute detail of everything done by their departments must be changed.

Policy

Ministerial time should be converted to creating and thinking through policy (using outside help where necessary), but also to working closely with Civil Service advisers, overseeing the creation and passage of legislation through Parliament until it becomes law, and communicating policies and options they have been considering, and their vision for the (long-term) future of their sector, to Parliament, fellow ministers and the general public.

But politics must be completely expunged from the Civil Service and so-called 'special advisers' should become a thing of the past. A totally independent non-political Civil Service, as it always used to be in the old days, must be re-established and Civil Service pride restored.

Reorganisation of Ministers' Departments

Ministerial Civil Service Departments (I have called these MCSDs – simply an indicative name) are those elements working directly with each minister and by definition **strictly not** those running the principal Public Sector Departments of State (which I have called PSDSs – also an indicative name). These are the major departments that actually manage the huge public services. These, of course, should be organised in an efficient manner, with a strong Chief Executive, clear chains of command, and normal incentives and sanctions to make the system work in broadly the same way as large private corporations.

Most likely, ministerial advisers would be organised into those who work on policy, those responsible for seeing through legislation★ and those who troubleshoot for the minister. There will no doubt be others (e.g. researchers, press officers etc.) but the overall result should be far less people who are more focused and more efficient. At a guess the service would be infinitely more effective and have more pride in what they do as a result of a reduction in numbers of, say, 30% to 40%.[9] Years ago I had to take the difficult decision after a period of acquisitions and growth to reduce the numbers at Bluebird's head office from 120 to just over 80. This was a worrying time for all of us. But after biting the bullet, the work rate among those remaining increased substantially alongside the morale and it became an altogether more efficient organisation going on to greater success.

Reorganisation should also mean the employment of far fewer extremely highly paid (and often inexperienced) outside consultants, at a gigantic saving, and enable much of the work to be carried out in-house.

In this way the Civil Service as well as becoming smaller would be much more knowledgeable and efficient. It would have to recruit into its ranks specialists such as lawyers, cost accountants and others to enable it to take over elements of the work currently being mindlessly farmed out to often untrained consultants. This practice has in fact been growing recently to the point where around 25% of new civil servants are recruited at higher levels from the private sector. In addition, on-the-job training for civil servants should be a core element of their employment.

Ministers will have more than enough to do and with any luck the amount of legislation will at least halve, as it will no longer be formulated on the hoof in response to daily pressures, e.g. breaking news stories, but according to carefully considered, well-researched and agreed plans.

Reorganisation of principle public sector Departments of State

In tandem with the reorganisation of MCSDs, the PSDSs should be reorganised from top to bottom with a 'Permanent Secretary'

★ Co-ordinated with the House of Lords including any scrutiny arrangements that come out of reform of the committee process – see below.

(by whatever name) who has had broad experience of managing successful enterprises, often in the private sector, as Chief Executive in charge of each one, supported by strong Boards of Directors

These Permanent Secretaries would in turn be responsible for organising their departments into appropriate units with proper chains of command and reporting systems, including a proper system of incentives for managers and others at all levels based on their individual and departmental performances.

Care should be taken that every decision should be delegated to the lowest level at which it can be taken, with the interests and involvement of the public and consumers always uppermost. There should be the fewest possible layers of management between the central directorates and the consumer.

These basic changes would also involve, of course, completely new thinking about how the Civil Service is structured: out would have to go security of tenure (except perhaps for very senior members); long-term employment contracts; the tradition of sourcing from university; the old-fashioned grading system, privileged pensions and so on.

Instead the best available people would be hired from outside the Civil Service as board members and for individual jobs. Normal employment policies and pay scales as operated in the private sector would apply (this is already practised for some civil servants). It should be policy only to contract with outside consultants where a particular expertise is required or particular research undertaken and then only on a short-term basis. (Think tanks and similar could and should, of course, be consulted if necessary in the early stages of considering options for dealing with policy matters.) The final policy decisions must be taken by the Permanent Secretary and his/her senior advisers in consultation with the Minister and his/her senior advisers. The management decisions remain the responsibility of the Permanent Secretaries and their boards.

If it was felt advantageous to privatise any of the PSDSs then that would be a policy decision for the Government and the organisation of the PSDS would make this a relatively easy matter to achieve. The Post Office comes to mind as an obvious example. The procurement agency for the Department of Defence might be another (in the light of the recent amazing exposure of the present system's rank incompetence).

Minister/Permanent Secretary relationship

The relationship between the minister and the department for which he or she is ultimately responsible needs very careful working out. There are one or two clear principles that should be adhered to if the system is to work: the PSDS's Board of Directors should be made up of directors from within the department plus some strong, experienced, outside directors with long experience of industry, finance and commerce.

The department must be seen to be clearly independent in the running of its day to day affairs and the minister should not be allowed to interfere in the detail of what is being done. This is vital so that he/she doesn't try, after the event, to claim responsibility for all the small things that go on – whether successful or not – and therefore be perceived to be responsible for them. The permanent secretary and his/her team must be seen to be in complete control of the management of the department. No permanent secretary worth their salt would stay for a moment if ministers constantly interfered. But many would also, no doubt, be compliant, and thereby make a nonsense of independent management control.

The minister must nevertheless be responsible in terms of policy for the department that he/she represents. There must be a close relationship with the permanent secretary and regular discussion of strategic matters of policy and finance.

But the minister must take great care not to become so involved that the permanent secretary cannot do his job or feels hectored or bullied into doing things that he and his team object to. He cannot go behind the permanent secretary's back and speak to other members of the board or to the staff unless by prior agreement with the permanent secretary. It will be difficult for politicians to behave like this but there are plenty of examples in industry of successful, large corporations working on the basis of a Group Chief Executive and a separate Non-Executive Chairman (in fact the Cadbury report objects strongly to the jobs of Chairman and Chief Executive being combined). This is the same principle.

But it should be possible for information to pass between the department and the ministry in such a way that the minister can answer parliamentary or press questions about the workings of the department, taking care to devolve those matters that don't pertain to policy (e.g. matters of management) to the departmental press officer and his/her colleagues. If in doubt the board's view should prevail.

Outside consultants

The last Conservative government was lambasted by the then Labour Opposition for spending up to £500 million a year on management and IT consultants. This was said to be a disgraceful waste of taxpayers' money, which should have been spent on front line services such as schools or hospitals rather than handed over to a few already wealthy consultants.[10]

It has since been estimated that the nation has been committed to spending the astonishing total of around £70 billion on consultants during Labour's three terms in office – more than £20 billion for management consultants and at least another £50 billion for IT consultants[11]. The consultancy industry itself has estimated that about 40% of its entire output is now in the public sector.

A large proportion of this expenditure has, alas, been responsible for some of the country's largest computer foul-ups and for centralising many financial functions where the effect has been a huge and unanticipated increase in costs. The PFIs also 'benefited' from much 'consultants' work. They seem to me a very cumbersome, inefficient and expensive way of managing projects with what looks like an astronomical cost legacy to be borne by future governments.

In future, whenever outside consultants are employed, care should be taken to ensure that contracts of appointment are drawn up in such a way that the consultants are responsible for the work they do. If – as so often happens – they make a complete mess of a contract, they must be made responsible for putting that mess right at their own expense. If there are reasons for both sides being responsible then normal arbitration clauses should be used to allocate blame and apportion cost.

Copyright in the work consultants do should, in most cases, become the property of government so that the government is not obliged to employ the same consultants, if they prove to be incompetent, to put matters right. Examples of government having taken such an approach to recovering cost overruns seem very sparse.

Alice in Wonderland would have felt quite at home in this world. The Treasury was responsible for approving much of this expenditure, which seems an exercise in uncontrolled power that should bear closer scrutiny, with proper checks and balances imposed.[12]

Financial targets

The setting of financial targets and limits between the Treasury and the department, and the monitoring of budgets should be the subject of regular (monthly?) meetings based on an efficient reporting system. The minister, preferably with some financial experience and/ or qualifications, could be present at the more important of these meetings but a junior minister might be responsible for monitoring this aspect of communication and control.

The example of the Bank of England managing interest rates and inflation has proved (in this limited respect) to have worked well. If only Gordon Brown had had the foresight and the courage to continue with this form of devolving management with other sectors of government, the country might be very different (and more successful in terms of public services) today. But hasn't it been wonderful for ministers to be seen not to be involved in the difficult decisions of raising or lowering interest rates in the run up to elections and constantly adjusting the money supply, for example, in response to political factors? We need much more of this ministerial non-involvement. (I wrote this before the Prime Minister and the Chancellor used obvious political pressure to influence the Bank of England's decision on interest rates towards the end of 2008 and subsequently. But it least at became obvious when they did so!)

It is a shame also that the tri-partite arrangement for managing the banking and financial system which the Government set up after taking power (including the Bank of England, the FSA, and the Treasury) was not better thought out and tested so that there was one clear entity in charge of continually monitoring and managing the behaviour, performance and liquidity levels of individual banks and organisations so as to avoid disasters such as the Northern Rock debacle. All of this is now coming under much closer scrutiny as a result of the worldwide banking crisis.

The role of the Treasury

The present system whereby the Treasury and other government departments interfere in everything, set targets, employ enormously expensive outside consultants and so on will have to stop. The Treasury clearly has a central role in the overall control of government expenditure, but it has been utterly unsuccessful in managing everything from the centre. The result has been a large increase in expenditure and far too much interference with each department, for example, the foot and mouth settlements, Civil Service pensions, doctors' pay contracts, IT disasters, PFIs, the London Underground, tax credits and endless targeting to name but a few. I don't think anyone believes that the recent huge spending increase on the various major departments has brought anything like the benefits it should have done. It has certainly brought over-manning and a horrendous waste of precious resources.

The Treasury should be 'downsized' so that it becomes a far smaller unit: "a bureau of the budget" in the American fashion.[13] In this way, instead of creating huge costs by ill-advised meddling in every aspect of every public sector business, it could concentrate on seeing that whatever contracts were agreed by the individual departments of state were properly set up and monitored and that spending limits were carefully adhered to, instead of themselves negotiating all the huge consultancy agreements. It should fulfil its proper role as devil's advocate, and make sure that the agreements are sound commercially and carried out on a timely basis. Where departments overrun costs the Treasury should examine what remedies are available to recover as much of the excess as possible and make sure matters are put right by the relevant department in the most efficient way.

The Treasury has shown itself impossible to control while it has so many functions, and only by letting the individual departments take back the running of their own businesses can efficiency be restored. The highly trained personnel that have been wrestling with these problems at the Treasury could be redeployed to the Permanent Secretary operating departments where they could become far more entrepreneurial instead of inquisitorial.

This should be an early priority of the next government.

The role of Cabinet

Whichever Prime Minister bites these tough bullets should re-establish Cabinet as a strong executive unit and ensure the Cabinet Office manages its affairs, encourages proper communication between ministers and keeps proper records of its decisions and of decisions taken by other committees.

Undoubtedly he/she will also wish to have a personal support staff and a private office to carry out research and advise on policy, but if these people are not civil servants they should not become involved in any executive sense as *part of* the Civil Service. As mentioned above, the days of special advisers telling civil servants what to do must be ended. The Civil Service should be reformed so that highly experienced and qualified independent (non political) civil servants provide most of the important support and advice that ministers need.

Managing civil servants

Civil servants destined for important roles as ministerial advisers to the principle departments of state should all be required, after, say, a couple of years of learning how government works, to undertake a solid stint of work experience in the industries or sectors that they are involved in managing, for anything up to two years. (This would be without loss of seniority, pension rights etc. and would cover all aspects of the work in these areas.) Any urge to shorten these assignments should be strongly resisted.

Those destined for higher authority should no longer be continually moved to other duties and/or departments but should stay in the sectors where they have most experience until they reach a level of seniority where a broader remit would be beneficial. There is no substitute for direct, hands-on experience, and far too little of it happens at the moment.

For example, if they worked in the health sector they should start travelling with ambulances, working in the emergency wards, the general wards, the admissions office, organising the allocation of beds, with the cleaners, in the pharmacy, in administration and accounts (with time spent understanding the computer systems), in the operating theatres (as observers, of course!), with doctors and consultants, in all areas of doctors' surgeries and finally they should spend two or three months at Primary Care Trusts and at a Strategic Health Authority and the NHS Executive.

Health Department civil servants would then have a real understanding of the problems of admission, the red tape so endemic in hospital administration, the problems of shortages, doctors' and nurses' workloads, doctors' working hours, when and where outsourcing makes sense, overmanning and bureaucracy at management levels, the complications of administration, the computer failings, equipment shortages and so on. They would also have real knowledge of hospital failings in fighting MRSA, the advantages of bringing cleaning under the direct control of the hospital, the problems of care homes for the elderly, mental health provision, the care of young people and the many other areas where the NHS can be improved. They could also be sent abroad to health services where standards of excellence are higher than our own so as to bring back valuable lessons we might adopt. They should also in passing take a special look at the NHS complaints procedures which at the moment work very slowly, very unfairly and produce a great deal of patient dissatisfaction at enormous cost.

This process would make these important civil servants aware of the many strengths of the NHS as well as the areas that need support. They might also form views on some of the fundamental problems, such as whether to have large centralised hospitals or strong local hospitals, new centralised healthcare centres or provision of more services closer to the patient within existing doctors' surgeries. They would have seen at first hand the effectiveness and cost of operating PFI schemes and their benefits and disadvantages. Then they could go to work with their ministers trying to sort out the problems with far greater understanding and a better chance of success.

It would of course also give civil servants a clear hands-on view about the advantages or otherwise of hospitals and other health service entities being sold off to voluntary and other owners.

The same principles should be applied in all sectors. For example, working in the Home Office/Ministry of Justice would entail working with the police, on the beat and in the back office, with patrol cars, on late night police sorties, in the courts (magistrates and high courts as well as young people's courts). The same system would apply in the prison service at every level from prison warders to prison governors, in all areas of the immigration service and so on. The list makes it sound like a daunting task – which of course it would be – but also makes it sound urgent and necessary, which it is. It seems to me amazing that we have struggled on for so many decades without doing these jobs far more thoroughly and on the basis of direct, in-depth, hands-on experience and infinitely better trained management. Close scrutiny of how PFIs perform would be part of this curriculum.

Just think what a difference this level of experience would make to the quality of advice provided to a minister. It is a certainty that the advice would be far more germane than the advice given now on the basis of little or no direct experience and reliant on similarly deficient outside consultants and academic theory.

Training

The French École Nationale d'Administration (ENA) undoubtedly provides very high calibre graduates for entry into the elite ministries, such as the French equivalents of the Treasury and Foreign Office, but I believe the British system would not favour this kind of elitism, and the idea that such a school should have a legal quasi-monopoly on access to some of the most prestigious positions would set up a 'them and us' culture that would be counterproductive in our system.

I have no direct understanding of the work of the Civil Service College but in its short life since 2005 it has clearly worked to improve the knowledge and skills of civil servants.

If it is not already done, I would set up an induction course for all higher grade civil servants before they take up their jobs, to underline the importance of a non-political Civil Service ethos and show them how the various departments work – particularly the difference between the roles of the MCSDs and the PSDSs. At some point before leaving the college they should make the choice of which kind of department they wish to work for and the last period of training would specialise in the structure and working methods of that department.

In addition, I can see no reason for not allowing civil servants to stand for Parliament, as happens in France (if not elected they could resume their Civil Service posts without loss of seniority), particularly if the civil servants in question had done their stint in learning about their areas of responsibility first-hand. It would have the effect of humanising the public attitude towards the Civil Service as well as encouraging more knowledge and efficiency in serving politicians.

Practicality

Reading the journals and blogs of ex-civil servants, one is left with a feeling of despair that anything fundamental or useful to reduce numbers and improve management, efficiency and expertise will ever be carried out. But if we are to have a really effective system of government this problem must be tackled, and fast. My problem still is: by whom? Very few politicians have sufficient experience to initiate this process and see it through.

But I feel strongly that these proposals – with suitable flexibility and adaptation – are practical and can be introduced. It would take a few years before the new arrangements began to have real impact, but this is a time span that we should be prepared to accept for all kinds of initiatives. When up and working, this system would have a permanent and fundamental influence on government's future competence.

Since it is the Opposition which has the golden opportunity to research and think through policy it is high time that an Opposition Leader took this matter carefully and thoroughly in hand. It was the opposition in New Zealand that prepared the way for the ultimate reform of the New Zealand government, and the civil servants were encouraged to help them.

David Cameron has initiated very useful research into many different areas of future government policy as well as some interesting changes which a future Conservative government might bring in. But on present showing it is not clear whether their proposed changes go deeply enough to the root of our problems.

I have no idea if this kind of Civil Service reform would prove a vote winner at an election but I suspect it is the kind of root and branch policy change that would be enormously appealing to the electorate. Courage and a lot of hard explaining will be necessary to reap the full benefit and then of course a huge amount of planning and detail to make it happen.

Constitutional Manifesto

Perhaps ideas for such deep-seated reform should be the subject of a separate 'Constitutional Manifesto' from one of the political parties, which would draw attention to the fundamental importance of reform and give it special emphasis for the public.

By this I mean a separate Manifesto to be issued (ideally) well before any election is called, setting out the principles that a new (or existing) government would follow.

A 'Constitutional Commission' of wise men and women with the relevant experience, under the chairmanship of a tough independent-minded chairman, might be what is needed to start the ball rolling. Alternatively it might be set up by a government in power who had a strong wish to improve radically our system of government.*

---

* I understand that a new Constitutional Bill has been drafted and is being considered by Parliament. I have no idea what this draft bill includes or whether my comments here are relevant.

Chapter 10
Party funding

Neither the rich nor the trade unions should be so powerful in their funding influence that they can demand and receive favoured policy changes.

One subject – party funding – sits on its own, but I feel requires a mention. It has been a bone of contention among the parties for years and, in spite of various attempts to solve it, entrenched interests have always meant that no solution has been found.

The support given to the Labour Party throughout my lifetime by the Trade Unions has been enormous and is easily explained by the close roots the two movements have in common. But the recent scale of this support and the influence consequently exercised over Labour Party policy by the Trade Unions has become too pervasive and powerful and should be controlled in the interests of democracy.

The Times recently reported "Ten Whitehall departments have revealed that they employ 46 full-time and 87 part-time officials to work exclusively for the unions at taxpayers' expense. Their salaries cost between £150,000 and £4.5 million per department. They are also given access to office space, computers and photocopiers worth an estimated £1.2 million each year."[1] If this is true the relationship has clearly overstepped the bounds of probity.

All the main political parties have become heavily reliant on donations from rich individuals. The Conservatives having been through a lean period when they were clearly unelectable are awash with funds from well off donors and the Labour Party has recently been losing rich donors and have consequently fallen back on the Trade Unions. The Liberal Democrats are also increasingly reliant on rich donors. The whole system clearly needs thorough reform.

Proposals for *change*

- The reforms suggested by Lord Hayden Phillips in 2007 seemed a reasonable basis for negotiation between the parties. Such negotiations should be urgently re-established until a fair compromise is reached. I believe the public would welcome some such agreement.

- The proposed cap on individual donations should be reduced to more like £10,000 per annum than the £50,000 he suggested, and the total government contribution to say £10 million rather than his suggestion of £20 million.

- President Obama has demonstrated through his brilliant use of the internet that it is possible to raise large sums in small donations of around $200 per person, and we should work in the same way over here – thus involving a much larger group of donors and thereby strengthening democracy.

- Care must be taken that the Trade Union support for the Labour Party is phased down over a reasonable period – say three years to avoid bankrupting the party and giving the other parties an unfair political advantage.

- Giving tax relief on small donations, say, up to £100 or £200 a year plus a firm cap on overall levels of support might prove a way forward.

Chapter 11
Parliamentary Select Committees and the US Model

They are not perfect but they give individual Representatives and Senators real clout.

A further aspect of government that urgently needs reform relates to Parliamentary Select Committees and other committees such as the Public Accounts Committee. These committees often do a useful job exposing malpractice, cost overruns and inefficiency in the areas they cover, but if they were given the necessary powers, timely information and authority, they could do a great deal more and make the MPs themselves far more effective.

The present Parliamentary Committee system was set up in 1980 and has developed in such a way that today there are over thirty committees covering a wide range of subjects. The purpose of Select Committees is to inform Parliamentarians on government initiatives, and to hold government more accountable. They were designed to restore to backbenchers a sense of purpose and encourage their participation in parliamentary matters.

Unfortunately, successive governments have seen advantage in keeping the Select Committees in an ineffective, toothless state and under the firm control of the whips. In spite of this, committees do useful work (one example of the most effective was the Transport Committee under the formidable leadership of the late Gwyneth Dunwoody). But in the main these committees are mere shadows of what they might be if they were given the requisite powers and authority; they often, for instance, receive information far too late and are therefore very slow to act.

A far more effective method of using Select and other Committees is operated in the US Congress where, for example, they have the power to subpoena witnesses and documents under oath. Unlike ours, the US system of Congressional Committees is vital and central to the working of its government. Congressional Committees are the centres for policy making and supervision of federal agencies, as well as instruments of public education (largely through public hearings). Without committees, 100 Senators and 440 House Representatives would need to go through 10,000 bills and 100,000 nominations.

Congress has several types of committees, including Standing Committees, Select (or Special) Committees and Conference Committees. There are also Joint Committees and important committees like the Rules Committee which acts as the House's 'traffic cop'.

Standing Committees are central to the working of Congress. They process the bulk of Congress's daily and annual agenda of business. Measures are rarely considered on the floor without first going through committee. Much of the work is performed by subcommittees whose rules and procedures vary widely.

Select or Special Committees in the US model are usually temporary panels that dissolve after they have served their purpose, or at the end of a congressional term.

Joint Committees are formed when members of the Senate and House form a committee for investigation, study, oversight and/or routine activities. Two important joint committees, for example, are the Joint Tax Committee and the Joint Economics Committee.

The Conference Committee(s) are often called the 'third house of congress' and are responsible for reconciling any differences between similar measures passed by both chambers. They are composed of members from each house. This committee is actually responsible for writing the final legislation (bill) that is to be signed by the President.

Woodrow Wilson said "Congress at work is Congress in committees."

It seems clear that the US system of congressional committees holds real power in Congress and is responsible for an enormous amount of work which enables a country many times the size of Britain to be run effectively.

To summarise:

- Committees shape the House and Senate Agendas: the bills they write largely determine what each chamber will debate and in what form.

- Committees often develop an *esprit de corps* that flows across party lines. Members usually fiercely defend their committees against criticism, jurisdictional trespassing (overlapping committees) or any attempt to by-pass them.

- Committees typically operate independently of one another; they let other committees get on with their work.

- The committee system contributes fundamentally to policy making, as well as to specialisation in policy areas.

I have gone into more detail than perhaps I should regarding the US system. I wanted to draw attention to the importance of a strong independent committee system to provide proper scrutiny of the Executive.

However, the US system is far from perfect. Elements such as the outside funding by pressure groups (for example the insurance industry) for members and the chairman of the Senate Committee considering the new healthcare reform legislation and the general gridlock and delay that the system often creates would not, I hope, be tolerated in the UK Parliament – nor of course should the endless addition of expenditure projects to obtain the votes of individual Senators and Representatives be countenanced.

The majority party in the UK Parliament has far more control over the legislation it wishes to pass compared to the US Congress. There, the Senate is shackled by the filibuster rule which has the malign effect of turning a huge Democratic majority of 59–41 into an effective minority. Recently we have witnessed how dysfunctional and powerless the US Government can become in these circumstances. Happily this is not the case in the UK.

It is hard to avoid the conclusion that a similar system Select Committee properly adapted to the Houses of Parliament, including a reformed House of Lords, would solve a lot of the problems of 'amateur government'. A great deal of thought and probably the deliberations of a Royal Commission (or similar) would be required to make the proposals workable. I understand★ that the cross-party "Reform of the House of Commons Select Committee", under the chairmanship of Tony Wright MP is considering a number of reforms including the very important reform of giving Parliament the right, without interference from the whips, to appoint members of Select Committees and especially the chairman by secret ballot. Another innovation that is currently being considered is pre-leg scrutiny: that is the publication of bills in draft, in time to allow Select Committees to take evidence from interested parties, giving the Government a chance to make changes before the bill is set in stone. I agree that this approach has real potential

---

★ Chris Mullin has kindly given me advice after reviewing my proposals on government reform.

– particularly if fewer but more interesting bills made up the legislative programme. I hope Mr. Wright's proposals (the First Report has just appeared, November 2009) will be well received and start the serious process of reforming Parliament in all respects.

The Committee also recommends a range of other changes in the way the business of the House is managed including the setting up of a Backbench Committee responsible for all business which is not directly of Ministerial origin. It also suggests that the House should be responsible for deciding its own sitting arrangements for itself. Finally it concludes that opening up the process of legislation and giving the public a real opportunity to influence the content of draft laws should be a priority in the new Parliament.

If reforms such as these and the approach I am proposing are adopted, it would have the effect of giving MPs real jobs and serious responsibility, with a vital link to both the House of Lords (when finally reformed) and, crucially, the Opposition. It would bring more careful review of legislation in Parliament and encourage compromise in working out the details of legislation. It would allow for far more interesting and wide-ranging debate about policies and perhaps remove some of the accusations of 'short termism' that affect us now.

If the UK Parliamentary Select Committees were given these stronger powers, various important benefits should follow:

- A system of 'checks and balances' would be created which would contribute hugely to transparency in government as well as to better legislation. Consequently, government would be held much more strongly to account.

- Backbench Members of Parliament would wield substantially more power and the job of being an MP would automatically assume more importance and be more exposed to the public eye. Committee chairmen would become very important Members.

- MPs would be encouraged to study their briefs more thoroughly and become far more involved in creating policy.

- Legislation, some of which currently receives no scrutiny by Parliament at all, would be more thoroughly reviewed before reaching the statute book.

- Spin would be reduced.

- Higher quality candidates seeking to be MPs would come forward, possibly from more varied backgrounds.

This system would even justify paying MPs in line with a more detailed, worthwhile and important job, but the difference is – they would certainly have to earn it!

The chances of any government voluntarily conceding so much power to its backbenchers may seem fanciful. But it happened in the USA and it looks as though it could conceivably happen in Britain. So perhaps the intention to introduce such a system might also be included by political parties in their manifestos or in my suggested Constitutional Manifesto

Let the public decide. It is quality of government we need, not the ability to keep policy decisions hidden behind closed doors and away from public scrutiny.

Proposals for *change*

- We should follow the example of the US Congress and strengthen our Select Committee system so that UK Parliamentary Committees, no longer under whips' control, could become far more influential in formulating policy, reviewing detailed legislation, reconciling differences with the House of Lords and generally holding government to account.

- Select Committees could, when they wished, hold their meetings in public, have access to up to the minute information, and the power to subpoena witnesses and compel testimony under oath.★

- Pre-Leg scrutiny should be adopted to give Select Committees the opportunity of taking evidence from interested parties and changing proposed legislation before a bill is set in stone.

- Tony Wright's Select Committee work should be welcomed and supported in Parliament so that deep and sensible reform is initiated promptly, and *continues* until a reformed House of Lords can play its part and Parliament as a whole can become highly professional and effective.

★ The introduction of some kind of Fifth Amendment protection might be needed so that witnesses could avoid self-incrimination.

I suppose it would be churlish to question whether a Select Committee of the kind set up by the present government will have enough clout to achieve all this, but if it doesn't - and history is not always so positive - then a Constitutional Committee of the great and the good might be required.

Chapter 12
The Freedom of Information Act

We only did half the job last time around. It is time to give the FOI real teeth and timely delivery.

A further example of recent British governments' fear of diminishing their own authority is the way they have approached the subject of freedom of information – a facility that ought to be a pearl in the crown of British democracy.

Freedom of information was originally proposed in the Labour Party manifesto of 1974 but when they lost the election the proposal was also lost. It reappeared in the 1997 manifesto and was quickly followed by a White Paper dated December 1997: 'Your Right to Know'.

Meanwhile, the Conservative Party had, in 1994, brought in the 'Code of Practice on Access to Official Information'. This was a superficial fudge, intended to be enforced by the Ombudsman with no legal power and no right to documents, only information. It covered only a few of the non-departmental executive bodies and was quite impotent.

This Code has been seen as a device for the Conservative Party to avoid any real commitment to freedom of information, which they saw as a hindrance to ministerial responsibility to Parliament. The Labour Party has proved just as craven.

When 'Your Right to Know' was published in 1997 it seemed almost too good to be true. It would be legally enforceable by citizens; it would cover the entire public sector and some private bodies; it would provide full rights to documents, records and information. In order to withhold it, public bodies would have to be able to prove requested information would cause harm if released to the public; there would be no filter between the public and the Information Commissioner, who would have the power to order departments to disclose information; and, finally, cabinet committees would not be excluded from the jurisdiction of the Act and there would be no right of ministerial or cabinet veto. In all these ways it was superior to the previous Code of Practice.

However, the man who originally published it, Dr. David Clark, Chancellor of the Duchy of Lancaster, was removed from government. The government then became somewhat panicked about what they had proposed, and the responsibility for drafting the legislation for the Freedom of Information Act was passed to the Home Office. As Lord McNally said in the House of Lords at the time: "Putting the Home Office in charge of the FOI was like asking Count Dracula to look after the blood bank."

The draft bill on FOI was published in May 1999 and was met by near universal hostility, in stark contrast to the praise heaped on the White Paper 'Your Right to Know'.

Although in some ways the draft FOI bill wound up as an improvement on the existing Code of Practice, in others it was weaker. Basically it failed abysmally to live up to either the White Paper or the Labour Manifesto in providing any real freedom of information: authorities were not legally required to help applicants, ministers were not obliged to give reasons for their decisions to reject requests for information, and they were not compelled to publish their internal manual and guidance.

FOI has produced a limited amount of useful information, but it is not functioning as we had been led to expect, and we are far from living in an era of open government as promised/heralded by ministers.

"New figures show that half of all requests are now being refused. It is impossible to believe that all these are for information that would compromise national security, impede the functioning of government or trample on an individual's right to privacy. We can, however, imagine that much of it might embarrass or shame those in power."[1]

Other problems with the implementation of the FOI include the late supply of information, the inadequate and incomplete supply of information and the failure of the Commissioner Richard Thomas to rule on appeals quickly enough (rulings have often taken over a year). This last is said to be due to the Government giving him insufficient resources to do his job; it is claimed the Government likes the fact that he is overworked and perhaps, therefore, ineffectual as a watchdog.

It has been suggested that the Commissioner should be directly responsible to – and funded by – Parliament. But even this may not be enough to make the Act work as it should. In September the Commons Speaker Michael Martin vetoed a request for making public the names and salaries of MPs' staff paid for by the taxpayer, despite a ruling by the Commissioner that there were no legitimate grounds for withholding this information. Parliament has sadly failed to prove itself a consistent champion of freedom of information – particularly where its own affairs are concerned.

Subsequently, Conservative ex-minister David MacLean MP proposed a Private Member's bill seeking to exempt MPs' expenses from the Freedom of Information Act. The bill was talked out of Parliament but it is nevertheless indicative of some members' negative approach towards strengthening the Act. Unsurprisingly, too, the proposed bill was supported by many current ministers.

There have been a number of requests from, among others, Lord Falconer's department that the information should be charged for in such a way as to discourage those seeking it. For example, the Department of Constitutional Affairs proposed in December 2006 that the £600 cost limit on each request should include the time of officials and ministers. It is easy to see how ministers might involve themselves for much longer consultation periods in applications that reflected badly on themselves, so that officials could refuse to issue information on cost grounds. Inefficient authorities with wasteful processes will be better able to avoid difficult disclosures than decisive or efficient ones. It is interesting that government appears to wish to reward inefficiency in this way.[2]

The Government is also proposing that a series of requests from the same organisation, such as a newspaper, over a period of sixty working days could be considered as one request, even if they related to different topics. This, too, would greatly widen the scope for government to refuse reasonable requests from journalists on cost grounds.

Where is the Government's justification for all this? A few years ago ministers were "willing to trust the people", or so they said. Now they claim that their priority is to minimise the cost to the taxpayer of the functioning of the Act.

Bearing in mind how the Government has changed its mind about the scope of the Act from the time of its manifesto through to the slow and incomplete implementation of the Act, it is clear that the right of the public to know has not been respected.

This is typical of so much that government does. No wonder the public distrusts it; surely the time to be open and transparent has now come. Who do they think they are fooling?

Proposals for *change*

Fundamental reform of the Freedom of Information Act

We should go back to the original concepts of "Your Right to Know" and also look to the US experience. We must establish a full Freedom of Information Act with strict timetables for the provision of information to be adhered to by all departments at no (or very little) cost to the public. The Commissioner should be adequately funded so that delays in reaching his decisions could be reduced from the current period of around a year to a matter of weeks.

There might be reasonable restrictions on the provision of early policy advice from, say, the Civil Service (since the tabloid press would no doubt sensationalise any extreme ideas), but once the minister has started to fine tune the options, the public should be entitled to know about them. Security would also provide reasonable grounds for withholding information.

The few MPs with whom I have discussed Freedom of Information have had a healthy dislike of it becoming too powerful. They also make the point that blanket requests, often of a frivolous nature, tie down hard working officials for weeks attempting to answer them. There are reasonable grounds for levying a small charge to deter such applications and perhaps limiting the number of applications on a particular subject. (However, I have been disappointed to note that the new Supreme Court is proposing to charge £350 to each member of the public who wishes to receive abstracts from their judgements plus printing costs – a charge that will deter many from requesting such decisions. Most similar organisations charge printing costs only and I can but suspect that the Ministry or Minister of Justice has had a hand in imposing such a punitive charge.)

I believe that a committee of judges or one under the chairmanship of a single senior judge should be set up to find a reasonable path through legitimate objections, but in such a way that our imperfect and cumbersome system is speeded up and greatly improved. The whole thing should be closer to the original ideas set out in the Labour Party's 'Your Right to Know' proposals published in 1997.

Such a strong Act would have the wonderful effect of restricting the power of MPs and ministers to spin inaccurate stories, and do much to open up government to public scrutiny. It is not difficult to anticipate MPs' and Ministers' reaction to these suggestions, but being honest and transparent would be well worth their initial discomfort. It would do wonders for the care with which they undertook their work and the quality of what they produced.

Chapter 13
The House of Lords

Surely we don't have to wait a further ten years for the job to be completed?

It is impossible to resist mentioning the extraordinary incompetence connected with the obvious necessity of reforming the House of Lords. Originally, Prime Minister Tony Blair was in favour of a substantial elected element as part of the solution, but when push came to shove he made an abrupt U-turn and supported a chamber based on fully appointed members (albeit selected by an 'independent' group of worthy citizens). Patronage is indeed a wonderful thing.

This action again illustrates the House of Commons' deep fear of creating something that might constitute a threat to its own authority: it cannot bear the idea of losing control of the make-up of the House of Lords, to which every party hack or donor would no doubt be speedily appointed.

Surely the whole idea of a second chamber is to strengthen the law-making process. It must be right to let a second group of individuals from very varied backgrounds and experience express their opinions on policy and, above all, carry out the invaluable task of scrutinising new legislation proposed by the Commons, with the object of improving it. The suggested reform of Select Committees should bring the reformed House of Lords into a proper, workable, relationship with the House of Commons.

Heaven knows the mess our laws would be in without the House of Lords. It is ironic that, even in its current truncated form, it has behaved admirably – not least in preserving the freedom of our citizens against successive Home Secretaries (no doubt instructed by the current and ex-Prime Ministers and influenced by Mr Bush) who have wished to take them away.

It is almost unbelievable that the Government, under strong pressure from the rank and file Labour Party, decided to embark on reform of the Lords without the foggiest idea of what the end result might be. The to-ing and fro-ing of Prime Minister Blair and other ministers perfectly illustrates their amateurish approach to such matters.

In the same way, the votes in 2007 by the Commons for a fully elected House of Lords, and by the Lords for a fully appointed House, only illustrates the Alice in Wonderland quality in how we are ruled. It seems inconceivable that we can have an appointed House of Lords in the light of the money for peerages row that filled our newspapers for weeks, and the opportunities for patronage that this would put into the hands of the serving Prime Minister.

The appointment of Gordon Brown as Prime Minister has also brought forward the whole question of whether Scottish MPs at Westminster should have the right to vote on English bills which may be in direct opposition to policies voted through the Scottish Parliament. Personally (part Scot myself), I am in favour of Scotland having the largest possible measure of independence. Small states are often very successful and find a spirit which drives them to build a successful economy and society. I agree with Simon Jenkins' clearly expressed views that local democracy and the taking of decisions as close to the people as possible will in the end produce the best government and the most contented electorate.

But having MPs from Scottish constituencies voting on purely English legislation seems likely to cause much unhappiness and disagreement, particularly if the vote is narrow. To avoid this, and bring some logic to the system, the ideas suggested by a shadow cabinet committee chaired by Kenneth Clarke seem to make a lot of sense. Clarke is suggesting that all MPs, including those from Scottish seats, should vote on English legislation at the initial second reading stage of parliamentary scrutiny, but that only English MPs should be permitted to vote during the committee stage of the legislative process, where real changes can be effected. At the third and final reading all MPs could vote, but a parliamentary undertaking would prevent any party using Scottish votes to block amendments made by English MPs.[1] This proposal would at least mean that all MPs were involved in the legislation, but that the views of the locally enfranchised MPs would prevail.

We seem at last to be approaching the final act in this saga and, happily, to have settled on a mostly elected chamber. Judges and churchmen of all religions could be ex officio members (with some other special categories by appointment) and it would be good to allow the present group of hereditary members to continue (perhaps by being deemed to have been elected without actual election) for at least a term. They have served us well and gained a lot of experience.

If, as I fervently hope, something can be done to reform the parliamentary committee system, then the House of Lords could play its proper enhanced role. To avoid some of the class implications I would prefer the use of the name Senate.

Proposals for *change*

- Reform the House of Lords using ideas close to those currently being discussed, and adopt Kenneth Clarke's suggested approach regarding the participation of Scottish MPs.

- Reform the Pay and Rules of the House of Lords in much the same way as the House of Commons.

Chapter 14
Short termism

It is only sixty-eight miles from London to Folkestone. 'Our' bullet train was forty years late.

British MPs are, of course, subject to the necessity of being re-elected every four or five years, which unfortunately encourages an appallingly bad habit – a wish to change everything within a short period of time so that the electorate can experience the supposed benefits of whatever changes are made in time to influence their voting intentions at the next election.

Little is done (Lord Adonis aside!) to formulate policy over a longer and more appropriate time span with all the care, planning and preparation that is required to work over the longer term. The history of government computer projects is a clear case in point. A major survey in September 2005[1] ranked Whitehall worst of seven major governments for computer procurement, measured in 'scrap rate' (failed projects), weakness in contract negotiations and unbalanced supplier market. By 2006, the Texas firm EDS had amassed over a third of the entire UK Government computer market. The Government's performance has been described as poor to say the least.[2]

The recent break up of the Home Office into two separate ministries is another perfect case in point. It all sounded so simple when announced in the press: a separate Ministry of Justice to be responsible for the courts, prisons, sentencing and the probation service, and a Home Office responsible for the police, terrorism, crime prevention and immigration. In practice of course it is vastly more complicated.

The changes involve the combination of the old Home Office responsibilities for prisons, probation and sentencing with the old Department for Constitutional Affairs. The new Ministry of Justice has 76,000 employees and will fund a further 21,000 probation staff. The Home Office will be slimmed down from 75,000 to 25,000 staff.

How much all these changes will wind up costing the taxpayer is apparently hidden in a Cabinet Office paper.[3] All this was rushed through by John Reid and Lord Falconer so that it would be a done deal before Tony Blair stepped down, with no formal consultation and many of the details of its implementation left vague. (Lord Falconer said he would be consulting after the event on any objections or comments raised!) The budget for the new Ministry of Justice is apparently £8bn–£9bn – also a fairly vague but an undoubtedly hefty sum.

The office of Lord Chancellor was abolished and then hastily reinstated. Wow!

This is the largest reform of the Home Office in decades and has wide-reaching repercussions. There are questions about whether the budget for the court system should be ring-fenced or whether it will have to compete for money with other departments. The judiciary wants it protected, reflecting the view that the rule of law and administering justice is socially and economically indispensable.[4] A new Supreme Court was established with little or no prior consultation with the judges affected.

There are concerns not only about retaining the vital independence of the judiciary but also the administration of the courts and the possibility of a conflict of interest for judges between the workings of the new ministry and their apolitical work.[5] There are all kinds of issues about how the two ministries will communicate, how the Home Office will prioritise its budget for policing, for example favouring neighbourhood policing, closer relations with the Muslim community, or crime prevention; how these issues will compete with funding for the 'war on terror' and the extra costs of MI5 and MI6. Where is the current (inadequate) prison building programme among all this? The list is almost endless.

It is beyond rational belief that all this could have been rushed through in weeks without even the publication of an official document on the projected workings of the new ministries and a detailed budget. It is a disaster waiting to happen – like so many others under recent government – and likely to be enormously costly.

It will of course be almost impossible to organise as two efficient ministries working together without years of confusion, maladministration and disarray. No doubt extraordinarily expensive and inexperienced consultants will be given the job of overseeing it. The general public will not be informed of much, if any, of this.

Much the same has been said of the decision to combine the Inland Revenue and the Customs departments.

According to a March 2010 report by the National Audit Office up to £1 billion has been wasted on Whitehall reorganisations. Since 1980, twenty-five new departments have been created, of which eighteen no longer exist. During the same period in the USA, by contrast, two new departments were formed. This says it all!

Recent history shows that a huge amount of parliamentary time has had to be devoted to correcting as far as possible the most obvious failings in the huge volume of legislation being enacted. Many of the laws passed under the present system are subsequently reversed or modified. Many of these laws have short-term effects that prove very different in the longer term. Scant regard is paid to the costs involved of rushing through such measures or to the subsequent costs of policing them, and finally (even in the case of a well-judged change), of ensuring that these amendments are capable of efficient implementation in the time periods allocated.

The tax credit system is another case in point. It had to be modified several times, the internet application arrangements had to be scrapped due to substantial fraud, and the system itself led to overpayments of over £6 billion pounds, most of which will never be recovered.

The demise of the unlamented Child Support Agency is an egregious example of a hopelessly badly managed operation, which cost untold millions and was recently wound down with over £3 billion of unrecovered child support outstanding.

The Health Service computer system is another, eventually costing something like £16 billion and delayed over four years until at least 2015 while hardly having been used at all. Alas, the list is almost endless and likely to lengthen (looming, but perhaps abandoned, at considerable cost, is the National ID card initiative, the potential cost of which has been estimated at anything up to £19 billion).

We need to move to a radically different system that creates and implements these major projects in a controlled way. These projects may indeed take ten or fifteen years to complete but they must be properly researched to ensure there is a need for them and managed in a way to ensure this need will be fully met. Such time spans will necessarily have to be adopted by successive governments. They should be considered as being outside party politics for the long-term benefit of the nation. A new parliamentary committee system would help this process along.

For example, it takes years to design, gain planning permission for and implement a new railway system. The French, among others in Europe, seem to manage these processes far better than we do. Their TGV system was built and has been running for years, while we have only just completed our high speed rail link from Folkestone to London – a distance of about 68 miles! We now face the consequences of massive underinvestment in the railway system and the rushing through of privatisation without proper review and planning.

Our road system, too, has been neglected for years in terms of resources to maintain and expand it. We are also faced with the prospect (and indeed current reality) of widespread gridlock on roads that have received very little investment for decades. Happily, the suggested solution (the imposition of universal road charging) has seemingly been abandoned as a result of an electronic referendum which showed the then Prime Minister how unpopular it was.

Finally, a word about nuclear power: the Government has recently come out strongly in favour of a massive expansion of our nuclear generating capacity to fulfil its European commitments towards increasing the country's production of energy from renewable sources.

Having left this decision so late, I suppose we should be pleased that the Government has eventually succeeded in selling its share in British Energy to the French government-owned company EDF, so that it has a chance of getting the job done. Plus of course the Government pockets £4 billion towards the huge clean up costs of the present generation of reactors.

We have known for more than the past twenty years how long the first generation of nuclear power stations would last. Surely we could have spent some of that time gearing up our renewable power supplies and improving the efficiency of our housing stock in terms of energy usage, so that the scale of nuclear requirements could be much smaller? We are way down the European table in terms of renewable energy production. The headlong rush for gas-powered electric generating stations (as opposed to using gas directly in our homes) was also misconceived in terms of efficiency and cost per therm (and also it seems in terms of security of supply). We are simply incapable of planning efficiently. At least the French (whether one agrees with them or not) have a clear policy which they have implemented with great success, so that 80% of their electricity is nuclear and their global warming credentials are impeccable.

The Germans have an industry based on production and supply of renewable energy sources worth many billions of pounds and are miles ahead of us in most aspects of this. So much for the endless spin of the Prime Minister and others.

The most recent Gordon Brown plan to catapult our renewable energy programme from 0 to 100 in 10 seconds – namely the enormous proposed expansion of off-shore wind power, which will make us by far the largest and most expensive wind generator in the world – seems fundamentally misconceived. It has the potential to become the largest white elephant of them all by some margin. During the cold spell of January 2010 there was virtually no wind at all, an inevitable consequence where high pressure exists. So 20% of the nation's users would be without energy for days on end! At least we should give it careful thought and compare it carefully against other options.

Surely there is a more intelligent way of planning and managing long-term projects in all our ministerial sectors. We are after all the country that gave the world its first railways and much of its early industrial plant.

Finally it seems to me that the credit crunch has taught us something about the way in which governments can increase their borrowings to astronomical totals without affecting their credit ratings, as long as the reason for doing so is likely, in the end, to show them a profit – or not too huge a loss. I have been amazed at how sterling has survived (so far!) with a potential annual deficit of £178 billion or more. Sir Samuel Brittan who I have always greatly admired as an economist, seems fairly sanguine about the fact that the national debt is doubling to £800 billion or more in terms of our ability to service and repay it. I worry that the interest on this is rising at an alarming rate and will burden our children and future generations so that it will be much harder to achieve the higher national growth that low taxes encourage.

It has been suggested that when the banks start repaying the huge loans that they have received from the Government it would be a wonderful opportunity to set up a multi-billion pound infrastructure fund to be used for the long-term investment in railways, roads and so on.[6] The same could be done with the last £25 billion of Quantitative Easing gilts that the Government owns, thus creating a fund of £50 billion.

I am somewhat dubious about the benefits of Quantitative Easing as practised at present. I can understand, if one finds oneself in the unfortunate position of having to raise the odd £200 billion through gilt sales, it is convenient to be able to walk down the passage and find someone ready and willing – indeed instructed – to buy them. I can even understand that in the short term it is beneficial in terms of the interest rates one is likely to pay for the loan. But of course what goes around comes around, and when the moment comes that you have to sell £200 billion of gilts at the same time as an additional amount of, say, £150 billion or so in current needs, then the opposite of a benign market situation becomes apparent.

Using this huge sum predominantly to buy gilts probably has some beneficial effect in providing liquidity for banks to lend to their larger customers but there doesn't seem to be much evidence that it has done a lot for the economy as a whole. I would far rather use some of it for the long term development of the much needed national infrastructure. These investments could be structured in such a way that they were self-supporting. The Government would receive both interest and the long-term return of capital. It should not affect our credit rating if we can also show an ability to reduce the overall national debt over the long term to support it. It would be less expensive and cumbersome than the endless increase in PFIs.

Used in partnership with industry, this fund would have a fantastic effect in building a modern infrastructure for important projects which would transform our country. I am thinking of tramways in major cities, high-speed railway links, perhaps a new major airport in the Thames Estuary (involving the closure of Heathrow and the building of much needed housing) and so on. It would provide a massive antidote in terms of job creation to the very necessary slimming down of the public sector and the lack of investment now appearing as a serious problem in many sections of British industry.[7] It would have a long term effect in stimulating demand for companies of all sizes as well as the benefit from the use made of the facilities forever after.

How could any government resist this as a popular and constructive policy?

Proposals for *change*

• Set up a central planning organisation

Set up an elite group of highly intelligent and experienced men and women of vision under a top manager, which could in turn arrange detailed research into particular areas of long-term development as designated from time to time by government.

If possible we should try to persuade Lord Adonis, a clear star in the Labour Government and a man with a real vision of how, for example, the railways should be developed for the future, and a practical approach to achieving it, to take on the job. Prior to this he was an outstanding Minister of Education.

The research teams should be dedicated to each project using experienced industry operators, planners, technicians and scientists to propose the most beneficial options. The Central Planning Organisation should be responsible to a dedicated senior minister whose job as chairman of its Council would be to agree the priority areas for research with other members of the government. Support should be given to both short and longer-term projects, some spanning many years. It would be helpful if this planning organisation included members of opposition parties in its overall council so that the results would take on a bipartisan following.

• Combined research capability

The Central Planning Organisation should be tied in with access to considerable research funds so that it could undertake – perhaps in partnership with independent charitable, governmental or commercial, organisations – agreed research in all kinds of interesting and possibly productive areas. If such research became successful for a project it should, where possible, negotiate the future development of the project on the basis of a shared royalty benefit.★

• Set up an infrastructure fund

Divert £50 billion into an infrastructure fund from the repayments by the banks of the loans they owe as a result of Government bail

---

★ A good deal of research is sponsored by the Government through universities and other research establishments and occasionally it has a rush of blood to the head and passes an emergency bill to encourage research into special (usually green) projects. I don't want to cut across anything it is doing but perhaps reorganise it into a simpler, larger-scale effort with better-planned projects.

outs (and from gilts purchased as a result of Quantitative Easing), as seed corn for investment alongside private industry in major infrastructure projects which are so badly needed. It might enable Britain in the future to be closer to the forefront in such investment rather than lagging decades behind as we are now. Japan has had high speed trains for forty years!

The Government has recently launched a fund to work with private industry in building up a planned £1billion innovation investment fund. I am sure this is the right thing to do but believe the opportunity for an overall infrastructure fund is the way to ensure proper control and systems and a joined-up approach to the huge job of dragging Britain into the twenty-first century. The Japanese, the French (with railways as well as nuclear power), and others, could not have achieved what they have without proper long-term planning and implementation.

• Involve the public

It should even be possible to encourage members of the public to submit ideas for the improvement of Britain in any aspect, no matter how small, which should, of course, be properly sifted before reaching the Central Planning Organisation. It would be a terrific way of tapping the brains of concerned individuals and could produce some exciting initiatives.

• Adapt parliamentary practices through the reformed committee system

The regeneration and future development of Britain should be one of the foremost topics at the centre of any parliament. Within the committee structure time should be devoted to working closely with the central planning organisation to make sure that whatever laws are needed for the smooth implementation of the major projects that are given the go ahead, are passed on a timely basis. Committees should have resources to improve their own research capabilities considerably.

Postscript

I would like to end by simply reiterating that my intention in writing this book has been to try to provoke discussion and – out of that discussion – action. I have tried not to be partisan in political terms, which has been difficult, as we have had the same Government for over twelve years. There are also, of course, many other areas where we should be initiating debate.

I hope someone agrees with me that we need to do better and maybe there are a few ideas in this book that could help move the debate forward.

My own belief, of course, is that they could have a huge effect in reinvigorating the entire nation.

Further reading

I have read fairly widely during the past couple of years and among the books that have influenced me particularly, I include:

Bartholomew, J. *The Welfare State We're In*. Petersfield: Politicos Publishing, 2004.

Butler, E. *The Rotten State of Britain*. London: Gibson Square, 2009.

Craig, D. and Elliott, M. *The Great European Rip-Off*. London: Random House Books, 2009.

Craig, D. and Elliott, M. *Fleeced*. London: Constable and Robinson, 2009.

Craig, D. *Rip-Off*. London: The Original Book Company, 2005.

Craig, D. *Squandered*. London: Constable & Robinson, 2008.

Craig, D. and Brooks, R. *Plundering the Public Sector*. London: Constable & Robinson, 2006.

Elliott, L. and Atkinson, D. *Fantasy Island*. London, Constable & Robinson, 2007.

Foster, C. *British Government in Crisis*. Oxford: Hart Publishing, 2005.

Jenkins, S. *Thatcher & Sons*. London: Penguin, 2006.

Jenkins, S. *Big Bang Localism*. Policy Exchange and Localis, 2004.

Johann Hari's writing, which can be found at www.johannhari.com.

Martin, D. *Benefit Simplification*. Centre for Policy Studies, 2009.

Morgan, P. *The War between the State and the Family*. The Institute of Economic Affairs, 2007.

Oborne, P. *The Rise of Political Lying*. London: The Free Press, 2005.

Oborne, P. *The Triumph of the Political Class*. London: Simon & Schuster UK, 2007.

Saatchi, M. & Warburton, P. *The War of Independence*. Centre for Policy Studies, 1999.

Smith, D. B. *Living with Leviathan*. London: The Institute of Economic Affairs, 2006.

Social Justice Policy Group reports including: "Breakthrough Britain," 2007 and "Locked up Potential," 2009.

Endnotes

Part 2

Chapter 2

1. Sutton Trust Report, 12.07.
2. Unicef Report.
3. Elliott, L. and Atkinson, D. *Fantasy Island*. London: Constable and Robinson, 2007. pp. 50, 63, 82.
4. Butler, E. *The Rotten State of Britain*. London: Gibson Square, 2009. p. 37.
5. Ibid. pp. 36–38.
6. Elliott and Atkinson. *Fantasy Island*. pp. 50, 63, 82.
7. Smith, D. B. *Living with Leviathan*. London: Institute for Economic Affairs, 2006. p. 58.

Chapter 3

1. Jenkins, S. *Thatcher and Sons*. London: Penguin, 2006. p. 286.
2. Bartholomew, J. *The Welfare State We're In*. Petersfield: Politicos Publishing, 2004.
3. "Quangos: The Unseen Government of the UK". Report by the Taxpayers Alliance, May 2008.
4. Butler, E. *The Rotten State of Britain*. London: Gibson Square, 2009. p. 59.

Chapter 4

1. For example, see Young, M. and others. *Family and Kinship in East London*. London: Penguin Modern Classics, 2007 (First published 1957) and Dench, G. and others. *The New East End: Kinship, Race and Conflict*. Coventry: Profile, 2006.
2. Audit Commission, 14.09.2009.
3. Smith, D. B. *Living with Leviathan*. London: Institute for Economic Affairs, 2006. p.121.

Chapter 5

1. Lambert, R. "Youngsters left on the scrapheap." *Sunday Times*, 16th August, 2009.
2. Palmer, M. "Microsoft pledges help for jobless." *Financial Times*, 9th September, 2009.

Chapter 6

1. Denham, M. "How decentralisation can help tackle our fiscal crisis" in *How To Cut Public Spending (and still win an election)*, Matthew Sinclair and The Taxpayers' Alliance (eds). Biteback Publishing 2010. p.96
2. Jenkins, S. *Big Bang Localism*. London: Policy Exchange, 2004.
3. Jenkins, S. *Thatcher and Sons*. London: Penguin, 2006. pp. 26-27
4. Ibid.

Chapter 7

1. See the Centre for Social Justice (www.centreforsocialjustice. org.uk) for a range of reports on the family, family law and young people in Britain.

Chapter 8

1. See for example "Crime, Courts and Confidence," the report of an independent inquiry into alternatives to prison led by Lord Coulsfield. Esmée Fairbairn Foundation, 2004; and Baroness Corston's "Report on Vulnerable Women in Prisons." Home Office, March 2007.

Chapter 9

1. Butler, E. *The Rotten State of Britain*. London: Gibson Square, 2009. p.147.
2. Wolf, M. "Outside Edge: Big Nanny's plan for us all." *Financial Times*, 13th November, 2009.
3. Ibid.
4. Butler. *The Rotten State of Britain*. p. 150.
5. Templeton, S. "Doctors say working week is killing patients." *The Sunday Times*, 11th October, 2009.
6. Butler, E. "Think tank: We've all been made criminals." *The Sunday Times*, 1st March 2009.

Part 3

Chapter 1

1. Craig, D. and Elliott, M. *Fleeced*. London: Constable and Robinson, 2009. p.13.
2. Bartholomew, J. *The Welfare State We're In*. Petersfield: Politicos Publishing, 2004. p.57.
3. Martin, D. *Benefit Simplification*. London: Centre for Policy Studies, 2009, p.4
4. Martin. *Benefit Simplification*.
5. Bower, T. *Gordon Brown Prime Minister*. London: Harper Perennial, 2007. p. 64.
6. Martin. *Benefit Simplification*. p.10.
7. Bartholomew. *The Welfare State We're In*. p. 85.
8. Ibid. Quoting the Beveridge Report, 1942.
9. Government's own figures for 2007–2008.
10. Horwitz, W. Community Links, 17th September 2009. (www.community-links.org). I have read other estimates as high as £200 billion – the truth is no one really knows, but anecdotal evidence would encourage one to believe in the higher figure.
11. Millennium Cohort Study. Centre for Longitudinal Studies. (www.cls.ioe.ac.uk)
12. Portillo, M. "Idle young should be entitled to nothing." *The Sunday Times*, 30th August 2009.
13. Ibid.
14. Ibid.
15. Timmins, N. "Child welfare ill targeted says OECD." *The Financial Times*, 1st September 2009.
16. Morgan, P. *The War Between the State and the Family*. Institute of Economic Affairs, 2007. I have drawn heavily on this work, it goes into great detail and suggests further references. Bartholomew, J. *The Welfare State We're In* is a book I can highly recommend.
    Duncan Smith, I. *Breakdown Britain*. Centre for Social Justice (www.centreforsocialjustice.org.uk) provides important research and a far reaching analysis of everything to do with welfare, family, young people and poverty.
17. Martin. *Benefit Simplification*.

Chapter 2

1. Darwall, R. "A better way to help the low paid." Centre for Policy Studies, 2006.

Chapter 3

1. Butler, E. *The Rotten State of Britain*. London: Gibson Square, 2009. p 241. A marvellous, well written and informative book, that unfortunately came out after I had written most of this.
2. "Public sector pensions unfairly high say Business Leaders." Institute of Directors (www.iod.com), 10th March, 2009.
3. Office for National Statistics (www.statistics.gov.uk).
4. Craig, D. and Elliott, M. *Fleeced*. London: Constable and Robinson, 2009. p14.
5. Butler, *The Rotten State of Britain*.
6. Field, F. "A plan to abolish pensioner poverty." Letter to the editor, *The Financial Times*, 27th May 2009.
7. Jackson, T. "New pensions model must rise from rubble of the old." *The Financial Times*, 21st February 2010.

Chapter 4

1. *Fair Society, Healthy Lives: Strategic Review of Health Inequalities in England post 2010*. The Marmot Review, 2010.
2. Smith, D. B. *Living with Leviathan*. London: Institute for Economic Affairs, 2006.
3. Saatchi, M. and Warburton, P. "The War of Independence." Centre for Policy Studies, 1999, has been of great help in this section.
4. Statistics from HMRC (www.hmrc.gov.uk).
5. "The effects of taxes and benefits on household income 2007/2008." Office for National Statistics (www.statistics.gov.uk).

Chapter 5

1. Total Place (www.localleadership.gov.uk).
2. Timmins, N. "Big idea to reassess public spending." *The Financial Times*, 2nd September, 2009.
3. Ibid.

Chapter 6

1. Hari, J. "Crime problem? Just lock 'em in the lavatory." 24th July 2008, (www.johannhari.com).
2. Public Accounts Committee, 53rd Report. (www.publications.parliament.uk).
3. Hari, J. (www.johannhari.com).
4. "Locked up Potential." A policy report by the Prison Reform Working Party, chaired by Jonathon Aitken. Centre for Social Justice, March 2009. (www.centreforsocialjustice.org).
5. Butler, E. *The Rotten State of Britain*. London: Gibson Square, 2009. p.207.
6. See information from the Centre for Crime and Justice Studies (crimeandjustice.org.uk) and the Howard League for Penal Reform (www.howardleague.org).
7. "The argument against the use of prison custody for children." Howard League for Penal Reform (www.howardleague.org).
8. Worsley, R. "Young people in custody 2004-2006." HMIP and YJB, 2006 (www.justice.gov.uk).
9. Howard League for Penal Reform.
10. Ibid.
11. Ibid.
12. Ibid.
13. Boxell, J. "'Education with fences' seen as youth jail model." *The Financial Times*, 14th February 2010.
14. "Education of young people supervised by the Youth Justice System: Background Paper." (www.dcsf.gov.uk).
15. "Does Prison Work? Overseas Evidence." Civitas: The Institute for the Study of Civil Society, 2003 (www.civitas.org.uk).
16. Ibid.
17. Leppard, D. "Met chief Sir Paul Stephenson attacks light-touch justice." *The Sunday Times*, 8th November 2009.
18. Knight, G. "How to really hug a hoody." *Prospect*, November 2009.
19. www.johannhari.com.
20. Brooker, C. and Ullmann, B. "Out of sight, out of mind." Policy Exchange, 2008 (www.policyexchange.org.uk).
21. Hari, J. "Crime is going to rise – unless we get liberal." (www.johannhari.com).

22. Brooker and Ullmann, "Out of sight, out of mind."
23. Hari, J. "Crime problem? Just lock 'em in the lavatory." (www.johannhari.com).
24. Ibid.

Chapter 7

1. British Crime Survey 2006/7 (www.homeoffice.gov.uk).
2. Ibid.
3. "Drugs 'blight' most parts of the UK." (www.news.bbc.co.uk).
4. "Gauging the UK's drug use." (www.news.bbc.co.uk).
5. "Tackling Drug Networks and Distribution Networks in the UK." UK Drug Policy Commission. (www.ukdpc.org.uk).
6. Ibid.
7. Drugscope. (www.drugscope.org.uk).
8. Hari, J. "Face the Facts – and end the War on Drugs." (www.johannhari.com).
9. Ibid.
10. Ibid.
11. Ibid.
12. Hari, J. "Crime problem? Just lock 'em in the lavatory." (www.johannhari.com).

Chapter 8

1. "The Government is creating a surveillance state." *Daily Telegraph*, 9th February, 2009.

Chapter 9

1. Foster, C. *British Government in Crisis*. Oxford: Hart's Publishing, 2005. p.128.
2. Ibid.
3. Engel, M. "How second-rate politicians brought Westminster low." *Financial Times*, 15th May, 2009.
4. Ibid.
5. Ibid.
6. Jenkins, S. *Thatcher and Sons*. London: Penguin, 2006.
7. Timmins, N. "Watchdog fears NHS Trusts will lose their autonomy." *Financial Times*, 17th September, 2009.
8. Parker, S., Paun, A., McClory, J. and Blatchford, K. *Shaping Up: A Whitehall for the Future*. Institute for Government, 2010

Executive Committee of the Better Government Initiative. *Good Government: Reforming Parliament and the Executive.* 2010.

9. Craig, D. and Elliott, M. *Fleeced.* London: Constable and Robinson, 2009. Chapter 5 provides current figures.

10. Craig, D. and Brooks, R. *Plundering the Public Sector.* London: Constable and Robinson, 2006. p.2.

11. Ibid.

12. Jenkins, *Thatcher and Sons.* Chapter 17.

13. Ibid.

Chapter 10

1. Bowers, M. and Coates, S. "Whitehall employs dozens of union officials at taxpayers expense." *The Times*, 14th September, 2009.

Chapter 12

1. Verkaik, R. "'Right to know' fails to open the Government's vaults of secrets." *The Independent*, 31st December, 2005.

2. Ibid.

Chapter 13

1. Kirkup, J. "Scottish MPs must be barred from amending laws for England, say Tories." *Daily Telegraph*, 1st July, 2008.

Chapter 14

1. Jenkins, S. *Thatcher and Sons.*

2. Craig, D and Brooks, R. *Plundering the Public Sector.*

3. Burns, J and Hall, B. "Warning of resources for split ministries." *Financial Times*, 9th May, 2007.

4. Ibid.

5. Ibid.

6. Letter to the editor from Bridget Rosewell, *Financial Times*, 7th October, 2009.

7. Wolf, M. *Financial Times*, 24th February 2010.

Index

Note: subsections of autobiographical detail are listed chronologically